CHARLES

Also by Penny Junor

Diana Princess of Wales
Margaret Thatcher
Babyware
Burton

CHARLES

PENNY JUNOR

Sidgwick & Jackson
London

To James

First published in Great Britain in 1987 by
Sidgwick & Jackson Limited

ISBN 0-283-99345-6

Typeset by Hewer Text Composition Services, Edinburgh
Printed by Adlard & Son Ltd, The Garden City Press, Letchworth, Herts SG6 1JS
for Sidgwick & Jackson Limited
1 Tavistock Chambers, Bloomsbury Way, London WC1A 2SG

ACKNOWLEDGEMENTS

My most sincere thanks to everyone who has helped me in the course of researching this book, including the Prince of Wales himself. I won't mention any other individuals by name because they are too numerous, and many spoke to me in confidence, but I am deeply grateful to them all nonetheless as I am sure each one is well aware. They gave up valuable time to talk about the Prince, and some gave up more in order to read and check the manuscript before it was published. I do appreciate the trust they have placed in me, and the time and trouble they have gone to on my behalf.

I am also grateful to my editor, Susan Hill, to Esther Jagger, and to Anne-Marie Ehrlich who found the pictures, to Joan Frankis who transcribed some of my taped interviews, and to my agent Dasha Shenkman, who is a reassuring voice in times of need.

I would also like to say a special thank you to Dee Nolan, now editor of the *Sunday Express* Colour Magazine, who in a previous incarnation first put me on to the subject of Prince Charles.

As usual my family have been fantastic.

BOOKS CONSULTED

I am very grateful to the authors and publishers of the following books for kind permission to quote from their works.

Charles Prince of Wales, Anthony Holden; Pan Books, 1979
Mountbatten, Philip Ziegler; Fontana/Collins, 1985
Edward VIII, Frances Donaldson; Weidenfeld and Nicolson, 1986
The Mary Rose, Margaret Rule; Conway Maritime Press, 1982
Kurt Hahn, compiled by D. A. Byatt MA; Gordonstoun School, 1976
Is That It?, Bob Geldof; Sidgwick and Jackson, 1986
Mr Speaker, George Thomas; Century Publishing, 1985
The Men Who Would Be King, Nicholas Shakespeare; Sidgwick and Jackson, 1984
Majesty, Robert Lacey; Hutchinson, 1977
Settling Down, James Whitaker; Quartet, 1981
Gordonstoun, Henry L. Brereton; Gordonstoun School, 1982
H.R.H. The Man Who Will Be King, Tim Heald and Mayo Mohs; Sphere Books, 1980
Royal Feud, Michael Thornton; Michael Joseph, 1985
King George III, John Brooke; Constable, 1972
Jung And The Story Of Our Time, Laurens van der Post; Hogarth Press, 1976

LIST OF ILLUSTRATIONS

INTRODUCTION

Shortly before I completed this book I had a telephone call from a reporter writing for one of Fleet Street's gossip columns. He understood that I had had an interview with the Prince. Did I ask him whether he talked to flowers?

Anyone who is looking for that sort of detail within these pages should slip it quietly back on to the shelf without more ado. I am not uncritical of the Prince – I may yet face sentence in the Tower for what I have said about him – but he is judged here on the serious attempts he is making to help his fellow men, to save the environment from being ravaged and the world from being destroyed.

Never have I met anyone who has done so much – largely unrecognized and unrewarded – and yet who feels he has contributed so little. He is one of the saddest people I have ever encountered. His entire life has been sacrificed to duty. He has been criticized, he has been hounded, he has been ridiculed, and still he battles on, carrying his bruised and fragile ego into another minefield of controversy. He lives well and has a number of good friends, yet he is lonely as only one other person on earth is lonely: the Queen. He is plagued by the belief that he has no role, which saps his confidence. The role for which he has spent nearly forty years being trained is not yet vacant, and even when it is it will be a sad day. It is nothing short of a miracle, after all that he has been through, that Prince Charles is so warm and unassuming a man – also sane, whether he talks to his plants or not.

'You may think I don't know anything about disadvantage,' he said to a group of unemployed black youths in the riot-torn streets of Birmingham. 'All I can tell you is . . . there's relative disadvantage.'

CHAPTER ONE

After the faintly jaded grandeur of Buckingham Palace, arriving at Kensington Palace to see the Prince of Wales is like going into a very comfortable home. A friendly young butler greets you at the door, knows your name and offers coffee. The decor is bright and pretty, the carpet in colours of lime green and pink with the Prince of Wales feathers interwoven. Obviously good oil paintings, mostly portraits, cover the walls and the furniture is a mixture of antique and modern, with vases of fresh flowers everywhere.

I met the Prince in his study on the first floor. My first impression, as he extended a hand in greeting, was of a man far slighter in build than I had expected, fragile almost. He was clearly anxious about the wisdom of agreeing to admit someone who wanted to write about his life. He sat behind his desk, touching his signet ring, fingering his tie, playing with his fountain pen and pulling out a large, crisply laundered handkerchief from time to time to blow his nose. Although the meeting had taken months to set up I was not asked to provide in advance the questions I would ask, and no restrictions whatsoever were imposed. He was obviously waiting for the one about flowers. As time progressed and he realized that I had not come to ask if he really talked to his tulips, he began to relax and the warmth and humour that so many of his friends had spoken of came filtering through.

He spoke with great sincerity about his concerns and anxieties for people, about his attitude to politics and disillusionment with politicians, about his admiration for black people and the need to harness their talents – they are part of our country, he says, they have a role to play, and we must not make the mistakes America has made with its black community. His speech was well measured but considerably faster and livelier than in public. Every answer displayed knowledge as well as considerable thought, and was peppered with examples to support his point or demonstrate his argument.

Yes, he agreed, he had changed in the last six or seven years. He had become more philosophical: he had entered what the Swiss psychologist Carl Jung would probably have described as the 'middle period'. He talked about the important part that intuition played in his life, even in the writing of his speeches; and how so many of the things he said were ridiculed at first, but eventually people came round to thinking he was not so mad after all.

I applauded the work he had done for young people in the inner cities, the scheme I had seen in operation, the no-hopers given a new sense of purpose and some reason to get up in the morning. He was pleased, but he is not a willing recipient of praise. It was not him, he says – he has done nothing. It is other splendid people who have done the work, he insists. But, alas, it was hardly a start, he felt: there was such a long way to go and in the end so much came down to lack of money. The Prince is clearly deeply distressed by the problems that he sees around him, the living conditions, the drug abuse, the racial tensions, the unemployment, the disintegration of the family and the despoliation of the environment. Some friends fear that he feels it all too deeply and too personally for his own good, that he will make himself ill.

His own lifestyle, his own secure circumstances, are poles apart from those of millions of people in Britain who live with next to nothing. As a result he not only feels intense compassion for them, but most of his thirty-eight years have been spent trying to justify his existence to them. The royal treadmill is not a life for which he is ideally suited, he admits. He is not an extrovert, and meeting large crowds of people or speaking in public do not come easily, but he had no choice in the matter. A painting of the Queen hanging above his head is a poignant reminder that he is not the only one whose life has been dictated by an accident of birth – nor is he the last.

His study is a portrait of disorder. The desk is covered with papers, books, envelopes with scribbles on the back of them, and a large diary. He opens it up to find a free hour or two, and sighs deeply. It is filled months in advance with people to see, places to go, receptions, ceremonies, presentations, openings. A private secretary clears his throat discreetly to remind His Royal Highness that he has already over-run my appointment by three-quarters of an hour, and he really must get on to the next.

Books and general clutter are piled everywhere in a homely

fashion, and paintings – including a still-life of his own – are on the floor, propped up against the wall. I asked if I might see some more of his work, and his face lit up with enthusiasm. Would I *really* like to? They were not frightfully good, he insisted, but he did get such tremendous pleasure out of it. He reached behind him and hauled over from the floor a brown canvas fishing bag, which contained his painting equipment – sketchbooks, pencils, pens and a small tin box of watercolours – and turned the pages of two books slowly, explaining the sketches, while I looked over his shoulder in genuine amazement. For all his modesty, the heir to the throne is a very gifted artist.

Despite the comforts of Kensington Palace, Prince Charles hates London, he says. He feels claustrophobic and hemmed in. Security is so tight: he is restricted in where he goes, what he does and whom he sees. Highgrove is another matter. It is one of the places he loves best. Set deep in the Gloucestershire landscape, this comparatively modest country house, with the garden he created and sheep and cattle grazing roundabout, is an escape. He finds the peace and quiet so therapeutic that he has even been known to bring the royal helicopter down on a working day so that he can spend a couple of hours between engagements digging the garden and taking stock.

The Prince of Wales is a curious combination. For a man who delights in the toughest of sports – his fragility is of frame, not physique; he is actually strong and very fit – he is surprisingly sensitive, in all senses of the word. He has lived his entire life under scrutiny, he walks through a political minefield and has caused explosions time and again, yet he is undoubtedly naïve. More curious still, this leader of men, a potent force for good and for change, is himself quite easily led.

Apart from the strong familial features which mark him as a Windsor any day, he is quite unremarkable to look at. His shoulders slope too much, his hips are too wide, his legs too short – he is in every way an average man. Yet he has a magnetism about him which sets him apart, and such a talent for listening that even the toughest kids in the toughest tower blocks talk to him, and cheer him when he leaves.

His charm is extraordinary. When he turns his attention on you, and smiles, it is as though for that moment there is nothing more important in his life. He is straightforward, direct and sincere, but there is a twinkle quietly simmering behind his eyes, and a very acute, schoolboyish sense of humour, which appears to keep him sane through the endless days of protocol, handshaking and tedium. He conducts a zany correspondence with ex-Goon Spike Milligan, who addresses the envelopes: 'Trainee King, Buckingham Palace, up the road from Admiralty Arch', and once, when he went to the comedian's house for dinner, he thoroughly enjoyed himself reading the 19th-century self-styled poet McGonagal out loud all evening, while they shared an excellent bottle of 1947 wine.

The charm, like the diffidence he exudes, is not the whole picture, although 90 per cent of the time he is hugely caring and concerned for everyone, even the most junior of his staff. Anyone who underestimates the Prince of Wales, however, or oversteps the bounds of familiarity, does so at their peril. He can be selfish and spoilt, both symptoms of the fierce frustration he feels from time to time. Friends fall in and out of favour; so do confidants and servants. Inefficiency and bureaucracy make him angry, as does the popular press sometimes; and when he loses his temper, for whatever reason, he lashes out at those closest to him, mostly his staff. 'I always used to write and tell him if I thought he'd been rude to someone,' said one, 'and he'd get angry because he knew I was right.' His staff have to turn the other cheek, however, even when the attack is personal and unjustified. Whatever their rank, they are servants, and know better than to answer back to the Prince of Wales.

That is the side the public never sees. His self-discipline is far too strong for that. His entire being is subjugated to duty, to serving the people of Britain and the Commonwealth, and to justifying the position of privilege to which he was born. The motto on his crest, 'Ich Dien' (I serve), is no trite sentiment. He became heir to the throne at the age of four, and from that day he has been set apart from his peers.

Today he is still in limbo – searching, as he has searched all his adult years, for a role to play. At the age of thirty-eight, at the prime of life, when his contemporaries are settled in their careers, securing senior positions, running their own businesses, amassing money and security for the future, Prince Charles has nothing. He cannot go into business, he cannot go into politics. There are even restrictions on his charitable work. He is waiting – waiting to inherit the crown, waiting to do the job for which he has been prepared, which may come to him tomorrow, or may never come in his lifetime. If it does come, everything he has at the moment will vanish; even Highgrove. The house and surrounding farm belong to the Duchy of Cornwall, and when he becomes King he ceases to be Duke of Cornwall.

It is true, of course, that he will move into bigger and better houses the day he becomes King, but promotion for Prince Charles is unlike promotion for any other. It will come only if the Queen abdicates or dies. But Prince Charles believes that in an hereditary monarchy abdication is not a desirable option; he also feels that the Queen does the job far better than he could. The alternative is succession upon the sovereign's death, and while he might well long to be able to do the job, and implement his own ideas, to admit it – even to himself – is tantamount to wishing his mother dead.

His ideas, therefore, he keeps very much to himself, although Prince Charles is first and foremost a traditionalist, so the likelihood of fundamental change is remote. His personal feeling about the job is not at issue. The constitution of Great Britain requires a monarch to preside as Head of Church and State, and as eldest son of the Queen that job will fall to him. The fact that he believes in the system is a bonus, and a measure of the skill with which he has been educated.

However, nobody is more aware than he himself that, in a day and age when there is great poverty and deprivation in our inner cities, soaring crime rates, mass unemployment and grave despondency amongst the young, not everyone agrees. An increasing number of voices, some quite vociferous within the House of Commons, resent the money spent on supporting what many people regard as an anachronism. The Royal Family is, after all, immensely rich, and although as Prince of Wales he receives nothing from the Civil List, which the rest are entitled to, he clearly enjoys a very privileged lifestyle. As he said at our meeting:

> But the Royal Family must have money. If they have to look to the State for everything, they become nothing more than puppets, and prisoners in their own countries. That's what's happened to the Japanese Royal Family. They can't even go on holiday without asking Parliament. That would be an intolerable situation; but I think it might be a good idea if the Royal Family stopped receiving money from the Civil List and lived instead on the income from the Crown Estates. After all, last year they made profits of over £4 million. That seems sensible to me, although I suspect I might get some opposition.

It was a radical suggestion to use money from those estates still in Crown hands – namely Sandringham and Balmoral – and a very real pointer to the sort of monarch Prince Charles will be. As he once said, 'What my forbears did was excellent, but what I want to do is my thing. You can't have the mark of yesterday's royals on our back for all time.'

Dispensing with all the trappings of royalty, however, and riding around on bicycles, as the Royal Family do in Sweden, is nonsense, he says. If you are going to have a monarchy, you might as well do it properly. If you do away with the trappings, you destroy the mystique, and then you discover, as Frederick the Great of Prussia observed, that 'a crown is just like a hat that lets the rain in'. It is partly because his position is so exalted that he can achieve as much as he does.

He would also hate it. Prince Charles enjoys his luxury. He was born to it, and is every bit the archetypal hunting, shooting and fishing aristocrat. Much as he might enjoy the occasional evening with his less privileged friends, eating spaghetti on their laps, that is not his style. He likes a degree of formality. He has always dressed for dinner at home with his parents, has always been waited on by butlers and footmen, has always had a valet to take care of his wardrobe, always had cars, helicopters and aeroplanes on tap to take him where and when he wants to go, and this is the way he enjoys living.

Where he differs from the archetype is in his very real concern for people less fortunate than himself. Most of the upper classes have no idea how the other half lives, and are not interested in finding out. Charles, by contrast, believes that everyone in employment has a duty towards those who are unemployed. He has no socialist ideals about making everyone equal. He espouses true democracy: the idea that everyone has a role to play within society, and that equality of opportunity is a basic human right. Everyone should have a chance to realize their potential.

This is the belief by which he conducts his own life. He is constantly putting himself to the test, and this is what he hopes to achieve for others in the various charitable schemes in which he involves himself. He does not want to give handouts to people; he wants people to use the money he raises on their behalf to do something to help themselves.

He may live in an ivory tower, he may be swathed in cotton wool and protected from the outside world by layers of courtiers, but Prince Charles has probably met more drug addicts in

Britain, listened to more disillusioned youths, talked to more disabled people and visited more strife-torn inner cities than most leading politicians. He is kept remarkably well informed by a wide circle of experts. This is not something that automatically occurs with every Prince of Wales; but it is something that this Prince of Wales wants, and organizes. He quite unashamedly cultivates people who can feed him information and be useful in a variety of ways.

His problem is that nothing does occur automatically for the Prince of Wales. There are no specifications for the job, and previous incumbents have not provided much guidance. Unlike some of them Prince Charles is not a playboy, and despite the image that the press at one time foisted upon him, never has been. He is a highly moral, deeply religious man who feels a constant need to prove himself worthy of the position that fate has imposed upon him.

His saving grace is a sense of humour; but that, like the rest of him, is slightly anachronistic. Given half a chance, even now, he will lapse into the dialogue of the Goons, the radio series popular in the 1950s. He is a practical joker – custard-pie sort of humour – a magician who is a member of the Magic Circle, and a good mimic. He is a great supporter of the Royal Family's tradition of playing party games, such as charades, at Christmas time. He will laugh at himself as much, if not more, than he laughs at others, and at the right time in the right place freely jokes about his position. When asked in the Navy once to take command during damage control exercises which were going dreadfully wrong, First Lieutenant HRH The Prince of Wales was heard to say, 'Well, if you're going to have a cock-up, you might as well have a right royal one.'

The Navy was Prince Charles's initiation in life. It was not for him the happiest of times, but it was there that he learned most about his fellow men; he worked as part of a team, did what they did, ate what they ate, explored the seamier parts of foreign ports with them, and lived and slept in the same confined, uncomfortable surroundings for months at a time. The only luxury he had was a cabin to himself, but even this luxury was comparative, and he found life on the ocean wave claustrophobic and depressing. It also made him quite seasick at times. Flying was another matter. He loved it, and still relishes the opportunity to fly aircraft of the Royal Flight whenever possible. But flying is dangerous, particularly helicopters, and supersonic fighters more so, and thus his military career at the controls was a short one.

At the age of twenty-eight he left the secure structure of life in the services, and began to feel his way into the job of heir to the throne and a fully-fledged member of the 'family firm'. The press were more interested in observing how he felt his way with women, and seemed eager to marry him off to each and every girl he glanced at. Their constant attention made life very difficult for him, and normal relationships became almost impossible. The pressure to marry grew more intense with every year that passed, and by the time he had turned thirty and still showed no signs of finding the right partner his family began to agitate too. He did, after all, have an obligation to provide an heir to ensure the succession.

He was thirty-three when he fell in love, one of the greatest love stories of the century. Since then, and with the arrival of children, he has undergone a radical rethink. His values, his interests, his concerns and his fears have all been brought sharply into focus. Now, with his fortieth birthday looming, like many men of the same age he is more confused than ever about where he is going and what his life is all about.

As with everything else, this sense of futility and loss of youth is harder for a Prince of Wales to cope with than for most people. Many men make new beginnings, change jobs, habits – even wives. He can do none of these things. He is locked into a way of life; booked up months in advance. Ducking out of just one engagement means disappointing perhaps thousands, and causes chaos to complicated arrangements that he knows people will have taken trouble over. There is no chance of changing pace; nor indeed of changing much on the personal front. Prince Charles has become public property, and the public is interested in nothing quite so much as his private life. It has to be beyond reproach, and such is his sense of duty and responsibility that it is.

He tolerates it with good grace, but bitterly resents having his private life intruded upon. He feels it is grossly unfair. Most other public figures are there because they choose to be. They have set themselves up in some way, and the reverse of the coin to public recognition is a certain amount of interest in the way such people live. He, however, had no choice in the matter. He was born to it, and feels that what he does in his own home is his own affair.

For much of his life this was more or less respected. Since his marriage, however, things have changed. Interest in the Royal Family, and the Princess of Wales in particular, has become obsessive, almost hysterical. Much of the gossip has concerned the state of his marriage, which seemed at the time of the royal wedding in 1981 to be the ultimate fairytale. Alas, fairytales are seldom true, and there have been difficulties for them both, not least of all because of the considerable difference in their ages. The Princess of Wales is lively and fun and quick-witted, all qualities which appealed to the Prince and which appeal to anyone who meets her, but she has little of his depth, and his philosophical and psychological wanderings take him on to a different plane.

Marriage came as something of a shock to him. Like most men who have lived alone for more than thirty years, he was somewhat selfish and set in his ways. Learning to accommodate to someone else's idea of how life should be lived, particularly when most of those ideas were diametrically different from his own, has been difficult.

A further problem, and the most insuperable of all, is that Diana has become a superstar. Through no fault of her own she has frequently been in danger of casting a shadow over her husband. When they appear together, she is the one whose photograph appears in the morning's papers; very often she is the one whom the public, tactlessly, make clear they want to see and talk to. When the Prince makes a speech which he considers important, in which he is trying to put across a serious message, the newspapers ignore it and describe the outfit the Princess was wearing or some change in her hairstyle. Proud though he undoubtedly is of his wife, adore her though he does, this constant upstaging has taken its toll on the relationship. As a result they now work on their own most of the time, and only appear together on foreign tours or social occasions like film premieres, pop concerts or occasions when Charles has nothing to say.

Whatever the strains on the marriage, his children are an unalloyed pleasure to him. At the weekends he regularly takes Prince William out walking over the farm near Highgrove. He is bright, exhausting and extremely wilful, but his father is no soft touch. It was freezing cold one day and four-year-old William had brought no gloves. As his hands became colder he began to grumble, and finally he started to cry. 'I told you to bring some gloves,' said Charles, 'and you wouldn't listen, so shut up.' Prince Harry is still at the enchanting age, and like every two-year-old has his father running round in circles for him.

Charles loves children, and they respond to him. He has much the same effect on the young people whom he meets on the streets: an instant rapport, which frequently surprises his entourage and leaves the young people he has met even more surprised. He is neither fatuous nor patronizing, but has an unerring ability to get straight to the heart of their interest or problem, and say something worthwhile, or – more importantly – learn something worthwhile. He is by nature a listener rather than a talker, although a great deal of his professional duties, of course, involve the latter.

Off duty, he likes nothing more than his own company and a chance to get to grips with nature. He gardens, he fishes, he goes for long, lonely walks across the countryside, and he paints. The flip side is the sportsman: the man's man, passionate about polo, one of the toughest and most dangerous games on earth. Men are killed and maimed playing polo – the Prince himself has a deep scar on his left cheek as a result of a mishap on the polo field – and yet he plays as often as he can manage throughout the season. Whenever the opportunity arises abroad he will borrow a pony – which is an additional hazard – and take to the field with a bunch of strangers.

The passion is partly inherited from his father and his great-uncle Lord Mountbatten, partly the pleasure of the skill and teamwork required, and partly a perpetual need to test himself. The game demands tremendous fitness. 'I am one of those people who must take exercise not only to be able to give of my best but just to survive – I mean, I can't function without it,' he says. 'If I can have a game of polo I feel five hundred times better in my mental outlook. But without some form of exercise I'm afraid to say I get terribly jaded and – well, not depressed but below par.' If polo is not on offer, he goes running, or cycling to strengthen his thigh muscles for riding.

Hunting is another passion, and in some respects equally dangerous. Many men and women have been killed or confined to wheelchairs as a result of accidents on the hunting field, and the Prince has come unseated often enough too. He does it because it encompasses most of the elements he enjoys best. He is working in tandem with an animal that he loves, riding free in the country-side, unencumbered by detectives or courtiers, and at one with nature. He particularly enjoys riding near the front of the field where he can watch the hounds at work, which fascinates him.

If pushed to defend fox hunting, he would use the conservation argument: in order to encourage foxes to live and breed in the countryside, farmers leave tracts of land unploughed, which as well as providing a habitat for the foxes allows all manner of other wildlife and plants to flourish. The charge of cruelty leaves him unmoved. The killing of animals for sport is so much a part of the way of life for the landed upper classes in Britain that they accept it without question, much to the dismay of his friend Spike Milligan, who is a veteran anti-blood sports campaigner.

Charles has broken away from the family mould in many ways, and made many brave innovations, but not in the matter of blood sports. For three or four years he gave up pheasant shooting, not so much because he disliked the mass slaughter, where thousands of birds are bagged in the space of a few hours, but because he became bored by the sport and the ease with which the prey is caught. He likes challenge. Deer stalking is one of the greatest challenges, and requires infinitely greater skill, cunning and patience than blasting over-fed, half-tame birds from the sky.

Not only must he be fit for all these activities, he also has to keep a close eye on his weight. He is not a vegetarian, and has no intention of becoming one; he simply prefers light meals, and vegetarian dishes are usually less rich than meat, less calorific and healthier. Besides, he enjoys meat and fish far too much to forego their pleasures entirely. It would also be quite impractical with the number of banquets he has to eat away from home. What he has done is cut down, and eat more salads and vegetables from the garden at Highgrove. This appeals to the Princess too, who also watches her weight.

One thing Charles has never been noted for is sartorial elegance or a sense of fashion. In his time he has tipped the top of the Worst Dressed Men list, and although Diana has tried to create a minor revolution in his wardrobe she has had only limited success. He is stubbornly conservative, fond of double-breasted suits with turn-ups, and round-toed shoes. Catching sight of a young man in a pair of winkle-pickers not long ago he said, 'What I've always wanted to know about those shoes is, how do you get your feet into them?'

He quite simply prefers comfort to style. His vanity does not extend to following the dictates of fashion. He is aware of his physical shortcomings, and dresses in the way which will least accentuate them. Jeans emphatically have no place in his wardrobe, and never did, not even when he was younger. They are not part of any image he has ever wanted to project. On duty he will wear one of the several dozen uniforms he possesses, or a suit, and off duty, even out on the farm or digging in the garden, he will wear tailored trousers: the uniform of the country landowner.

Conjecture at what he might have done with his life had he not been the Prince of Wales is practically impossible. He himself says he would like to have been a farmer. He certainly does take a great interest in his own farm, and is eager to try out new methods of agriculture, new ideas about conservation, and new schemes to market the produce. In some ways he is quite an astute businessman, and not at all shy about exploiting his name and his coat of arms to sell his wares. He might have made a successful entrepreneur. He is certainly good on ideas, and on motivating other people to put them into practice, and needs constant stimulation and challenge to prevent him from becoming bored.

The field in which he has been able to exercise both these requirements in recent years is youth unemployment, and here the Prince of Wales has led the way with tremendous effect. He has not just put his name to other people's schemes, and taken on patronages. He has initiated projects, found the people to run them, provided the funds to get the ideas off the ground, and reaped the rewards. Some schemes have sent young people round the world, working as part of an international team in areas of need. Others have taken them off the dole and given them a year's paid work, combing community service, teamwork and physical challenge. Yet others have given unemployed young people the chance to set up in business on their own by providing not just a grant to get them started, but professional guidance to help them over early problems.

Despite his unwillingness to take the credit, these projects have been remarkably successful and have given him enormous pleasure. He finds the ordinary man in the street far more interesting than the stuffed-shirts he meets at official functions. He cares about them and tries to improve their lot. When violence erupts he does not swallow the accepted wisdoms. He goes to the trouble spots to find out for himself, to ask people – not just the safe ones, the roughest ones too – what they think, what they are angry about, what life is like for them. Then he gathers together architects, builders, youth employment officers – anyone whose services he thinks he can manipulate to good effect – and tells them what he thinks should be done.

Prince Charles entertains widely, but as the many top businessmen, media executives and corporation bosses flattered by an invitation from His Royal Highness have soon realized, there is no such thing as a free lunch, not even at Kensington Palace. The Prince dispenses with formalities early on in the meal, and gets straight down to what he would like his guest to do or provide.

This is what he feels justifies his existence. The royal tours, the factory openings, the ceremonies are necessary tasks that he tolerates, but they are vapid and leave him feeling he has achieved nothing. If he can act as a catalyst – listen to the needs of people he meets, and find ways and means of helping them to improve their lot – he can be persuaded that he is doing something worthwhile with his life.

He needs to be persuaded. The Prince of Wales has a pitifully low opinion of himself and a debilitating lack of confidence in his own worth. Like many children of powerful and successful parents, he found that growing up in their shadow was not easy. He is devoted to his mother – almost worships her – and feels inadequate by comparison. His father has done nothing to correct the feeling. Prince Philip is bluff, outspoken, hearty, tough and something of a bully, and he has no patience with his eldest son's soul searching. Sensitivity is not one of the qualities he expects in a man, and although he undoubtedly has great affection for Prince Charles he has spent a lifetime criticizing him and quietly undermining his self-esteem.

In his late teens Lord Mountbatten, known to Prince Charles as Uncle Dickie, or Honorary Grandfather, stepped into the breach and gave him some much-needed help and direction which saw him into manhood. The Prince adored Mountbatten and came to rely upon him heavily as mentor, friend and confidant. The relationship gave both men a great deal of pleasure, and when the former First Sea Lord was blown up in 1979 by an IRA bomb the Prince was lost.

Two men filled the vacuum. John Higgs, Secretary of the Duchy of Cornwall, who was knighted on his deathbed in 1986, was one. The other was the South African writer, explorer and mystic, Sir Laurens van der Post. John Higgs introduced Prince Charles to business and turned the long-neglected Duchy, one of the largest and most run-down estates in Britain, into a thriving concern which in 1985 made a profit of over £1 million. The two men worked well together, saw eye-to-eye on most issues, and found one another's company stimulating. John put body and soul into the job, and sadly his health gave under the strain. He died quite suddenly after a short illness, leaving the Prince of Wales once again bereft. His friendship with Sir Laurens van der Post goes back many years. Charles was always intrigued by the writer's knowledge of Africa and his wisdom about people, and always enjoyed the chance to listen to him talk, but in recent years the nature of the friendship has altered: the old man has become something of a guru, and exerts considerable influence over the heir to the throne.

There is one other person who has his ear: Queen Elizabeth the Queen Mother. Prince Charles is utterly devoted to his grandmother. It was she who virtually brought him up when as a small boy his parents had to leave him, sometimes for months on end, while they went on foreign tours. The relationship is very close, and the Queen Mother has a lot of common sense to offer; also a lot of fun. There are other friends, but Sir Laurens and the Queen Mother provide the mainstay in his life, build up his confidence and hear his troubles. Both are now old, and unless someone else can fill their position in the Prince's life their loss might have very serious consequences.

Contrary to the public image, the Royal Family is not serious and stuffy. They all have a keen sense of fun, and share a rather earthy sense of humour. The Queen is a wickedly good mimic and prone to fits of the giggles, like all her children, and off duty is warm, easy-going and quite unpretentious. When she was going down the Mall in an official car one afternoon, her driver was flagged down by a very young and green policeman who had evidently not noticed the royal crest on the grille. He stubbornly stood by the driver's door, jotting down details in his notebook, while the driver desperately motioned at him to look in the back. The Queen, meanwhile, wanting to spare the policeman embarrassment, had slid down beneath the seat, so from where he stood it looked as though there was no one in the back of the car at all. He persevered with his cautioning, and the driver persevered with his gestures, until finally the policeman put his hands to the glass and peered more closely. Suddenly he spotted the sovereign and her lady in waiting squatting awkwardly on the floor, and instantly vanished into thin air, as though his dearest wish had come true and the ground had swallowed him up.

Prince Charles has a great deal of his mother in him, and quite frequently behaves with the same endearing humility; but, like the Queen, he bridles if anyone tries to take advantage of it, or fails to display due courtesy or formality. Even his close friends call him 'sir', and although he is keen to play the role of the common man when getting to grips with the inner cities, for example, he is not at all amused if he is treated as such.

Much as he likes to be on his own, and indeed needs solitude from time to time, at other times the Prince is thoroughly gregarious and amongst the right people can be the life and soul of the party. He is at his best with friends, but close friends are few, and have a tendency to drift in and out of favour. This has been particularly noticeable since his marriage. Diana had a great many friends of her own with whom she has remained close, and in the early days at least many of his fell by the wayside. Now they have decided it is often easier to see their own friends separately.

Despite the small number of close friends, he has a vast array of acquaintances collected over the years from all walks of life; he sees them and writes to them occasionally, and sends Christmas cards. This is as much as he can cope with. His position does indisputably set him apart, and he cannot conduct friendships in the way that other people do. Detectives have to follow wherever he goes, security checks have to be carried out to ensure that the area or the house he is going to visit is safe, and his hectic schedule means he seldom has time to entertain informally.

This is true for all members of the Royal Family, and one of the reasons why they are so closely knit. A certain amount of professional jealousy may exist between them, but they do all understand, in a way which outsiders simply cannot, both the pressures and problems and the funny side of the way they live.

They can also relax 100 per cent by themselves, with no fear that anything they say or do is going to be leaked to the gossip columns. As Prince Charles has found to his cost repeatedly, outsiders, with very few exceptions, can never be wholly trusted. The temptation to exploit his friendship for their own advancement has proved too much for some, and others have simply breached confidence. When he is let down Prince Charles has felt betrayed and saddened. He is, after all, entirely vulnerable. He cannot function without a small army of courtiers: secretaries, under-secretaries, equerries, valets and press secretaries; not to mention all the people involved in running his houses, his horses, the Duchy, his farm and all the different schemes and projects and hobby horses he has going at any one time. He relies upon them all, and on the whole they have been completely loyal and dedicated, although the relationships have not always been easy. The Prince of Wales is a demanding and at times unreasonable man to work for, but their affection for him, coupled with an understanding of his problems, has for the most part outweighed any difficulties.

In the early days the Prince was surrounded by establishment figures, with fixed ideas on what royalty should and should not do and say. It is only in the last year that the Prince has finally rid himself of professional courtiers, men whose families for generations have been in the service of royalty, and appointed a private secretary and other office staff from the world outside.

He is finally his own boss, and has the freedom and ability to express himself as he wants. He has carved a very significant role for himself. All that is missing, perhaps, is the confidence to believe he is doing a good job, and to follow his own instincts, instead of relying on the support and approval of others. His ideas are sound, his heart is in the right place, and he has a remarkable gift for communicating with the man in the street and understanding his needs. Furthermore he cares about those needs, and has the clout amongst businessmen and politicians to make mountains move.

His position may not be easy. It is certainly not enviable, but with sufficient confidence and strength of character he could achieve miracles. His speeches could be reported in every newspaper, on every television news broadcast, and journalists would soon stop focusing on the size of his turn-ups. The nation is in desperate need of someone to take a lead in curing its ills, without using it to jockey for political gain.

The Prince of Wales is outside politics. It is constitutionally improper for him to be involved and he has no desire to change that. The area he has chosen for himself is purely human, and that is where his talents lie. The tragedy is that he is not convinced of his own worth, and not sufficiently boosted by those around him.

CHAPTER TWO

Even as a small boy, Prince Charles had an aura which set him apart from other children. It was something to do with his eyes, people say, the way he stood calmly, meeting the gaze of everyone he encountered, appearing to take everything in with a maturity beyond his years.

He mixed well with other children, he laughed a lot and enjoyed the games they played, and in every other respect the young Prince – not yet Prince of Wales – was a perfectly normal little boy. Yet even at the age of four or five there was a quality about him, a stillness and sensitivity, which made him rather special. Even if he had been the boy next door, those who knew him then insist, he would still have had this rather haunting presence.

For as long as he can remember Prince Charles has been exceptional. Much as his parents might have wanted a normal childhood for their eldest son, and much as they might have striven to achieve it, he has never come close to being the boy next door. He has been in a kind of goldfish bowl since the day of his birth, when fifteen hundred people stood for most of the day and well into the night outside the gates of Buckingham Palace in a fever of excitement waiting for news. Within hours the message that a prince had been born was flashed to the furthest corners of the world, and signalled the start of lavish celebrations in dozens of countries on several continents. As his mother soon wrote to a friend, 'It's wonderful to think, isn't it, that his arrival could give a bit of happiness to so many people, besides ourselves, at this time?'

Champagne corks popped, and delighted well-wishers burst into song, chants and hoorays at such volume that his mother, exhausted after her day in labour, had to ask them to tone it down. The next morning church bells pealed all over London, the British fleet was dressed overall, twenty-one gun salutes rang out, music was composed, poetry written, and over four thousand telegrams decended upon Buckingham Palace, and enough clothes and nappies to dress an orphanage, let alone one 7lb 6oz little boy. The warmth of his welcome into the world was staggering, and public fascination and adoration have done nothing but increase over the years, making it ever more difficult for him to be a normal human being.

The Prince has lived in palaces attended by courtiers and soldiers, and never, not even as a baby, did he have his mother entirely to himself for any length of time. He has had to endure periods of separation from both parents all his life. He has had police protection for as long as he can remember; and wherever he has gone, he has been on trial. Everyone wants to know what the heir to the throne is really like. Half the population is eager to find out if he is as lovely as his mother and grandmother. The other half wants to know just who the hell he thinks he is; and no one has been more aware of this than Prince Charles.

The Prince was born at 9.14 p.m. on Sunday, 14 November 1948, in a specially prepared delivery room which had once been a nursery on the first floor of the Palace. The event was a great fillip to a Britain still suffering the austerity of post-war shortages. His mother, Princess Elizabeth, known since her marriage as the Duchess of Edinburgh, was attended by a team of medical men and women, including Sir William Gilliatt, President of the Royal College of Obstetricians and Gynaecologists; Sir John Peel; Sir John Weir; Dr Vernon Hall, the anaesthetist; and Sister Helen Rowe, the midwife.

She was under anaesthetic when her first son came into the world, and did not come round until her parents, King George VI and Queen Elizabeth, and the proud father, the Duke of Edinburgh, had already had a preview. The first thing the Princess saw, in fact, upon regaining consciousness, was not her baby, but her husband standing by her bedside with an enormous bunch of flowers. No couple could have been happier.

The Duke had not been present at the birth – a forceps delivery. After hours of nervously pacing corridors during the day, he had taken his friend and equerry, Michael Parker, off to the other end of the building for a game of squash. It was before fathers were allowed, let alone encouraged, to be present at the birth of their child, and he was on the squash court when the King's private secretary, Sir Alan Lascelles, came running in with the news.

There was disagreement about whom the child resembled. As the then Queen's sister, Countess Granville, told a convention of girl guides, 'The Queen says that she thinks the baby is like his mother, but the Duke is quite certain that the baby is very like himself.' Queen Mary, on the other hand, thought he looked like the Prince Consort, and she spent an afternoon with Lady Airlie, her lady-in-waiting, looking through old photograph albums of Queen Victoria and Prince Albert to prove her point. His mother thought he bore some resemblance to his father, but was intrigued by his hands. As she wrote to her former music teacher, Miss Mabel Lander, 'He has an interesting pair of hands for a baby. They are rather large, but fine with long fingers – quite unlike mine and certainly unlike his father's. It will be interesting to see what they will become.' Princess Elizabeth was twenty-two, and heir presumptive to her father, King George VI. Thus the new prince was second in line to the throne, so there was little doubt about what he would become.

It had not always been so. Sovereignty had been thrust upon George VI quite unexpectedly in 1936 by the abdication of his elder brother, known as David, who had been King Edward VIII for a matter of months. It was a shattering blow to Parliament, to the nation and to the monarchy; and a personal blow of immense proportions to the hapless Duke and Duchess of York, who were left with no option but to forsake the quiet family life they enjoyed and take over as King and Queen.

Edward VIII, who subsequently became the Duke of Windsor, abdicated because he wanted to marry a twice-divorced American woman by the name of Wallis Simpson. Such a consort for a king was unthinkable, and Edward was left with the choice of abandoning his desire to marry her or abandoning his office. He chose the latter; and spent the rest of his life in voluntary exile in France, an outcast whom the Royal Family felt had disgraced them.

No one feels more bitter about Edward's dereliction of duty and his betrayal of the British people than Queen Elizabeth the Queen Mother, the then Duchess of York. Her husband, with his stammer and crippling shyness, was most ill-suited for the task of restoring a nation's confidence in the monarchy. He did a magnificent job, nevertheless. The monarchy's popularity and security today are a tribute to the remarkable way in which he rallied to the need, and laid the foundations of a respected and popular institution upon which his daughter has built, and which his grandson will one day inherit. But his health suffered as a result. He died, debilitated by arteriosclerosis and cancer, when only in his mid-fifties. His widow blamed the selfishness of his elder brother, who lived on in good health until his mid-seventies. When Prince Charles was born the King was already ill, and his mother's vision of leading a relatively normal family life for the next decade or two was soon to be shattered.

The Edinburghs, just six days away from their first wedding anniversary, were living in Buckingham Palace while their own home, Clarence House, a short walk across the Mall, was being made ready. It had not been used as a home for some years, and the House of Commons had voted £50,000 towards the cost of doing it up. Set behind high walls, the house had originally belonged to the Duke of Clarence before his accession to the throne in 1830 as King William IV. In more recent times it had housed the Duke of Connaught; and during the Second World War the British Red Cross had used it as their London headquarters. Major renovation was called for, and it was not until the following July that the family were able to move in.

By this time the eight-month-old Prince had two nannies to look after him, Helen Lightbody and Mabel Anderson, both spinsters from north of the border. Because of her seniority Miss Lightbody, who had previously worked for the Duchess of Gloucester, was given the courtesy title of 'Mrs'; Miss Anderson had come to the job by answering an advertisement in a nursing magazine. Both remained with the family for many years as loyal, trusted and much loved members of the household.

Princess Elizabeth was excused most of her royal duties for the first year of Charles's life, but much as she adored her baby she did not spend very much time with him. As was customary among the upper classes it was the nannies who took responsibility for his day-to-day care. In the tradition of well-trained nannies they in turn had two nurserymaids to do the more menial tasks associated with the job; and even the nurserymaids had a nursery footman to handle the heavy work. It was the nannies who fed, bathed, changed his nappies, dressed him in the mornings and got up for him when he woke in the night. They took him for walks in the park in his large old pram, with the family terrier in tow plus the statutory detective. They took him to have tea with his great-grandmother, Queen Mary, at Marlborough House – one of his earliest memories – where he played with her famous collection: priceless pieces of jade, crystal and silver lovingly gathered from all over the world, which normally spent their days in the safety of splendid display cabinets. They had been out of bounds to children and grandchildren, but a first great-grandson was another matter.

His mother saw him regularly for half an hour after breakfast, looked in on him briefly at lunchtime, and spent another half hour with him at the end of the day before he went to bed. He and his entourage lived on the third floor of Clarence House, while she and her husband and the remainder of the household inhabited the rest. Although less formal than her own upbringing, which in turn was infinitely less formal than that of previous generations, it was very different from the way in which Prince Charles has chosen to bring up his own children. Kensington Palace is their home, and despite the nannies, come bedtime Prince William is as likely to be found hiding in his Daddy's study as anywhere else. He has the run of the house and the indulgence of his parents.

The formality of the household went further. When the family moved into Clarence House the Princess and her husband, in accordance with upper-class tradition, took separate bedrooms, with connecting doors, and have continued this arrangement ever since. Hence when a stranger by the name of Michael Fagin climbed over the wall of Buckingham Palace in the middle of the night some thirty-five years later, found his way to the Queen's bedroom, sat on the edge of her bed and asked whether she had a cigarette she could give him, he found the sovereign alone.

The young Prince was christened Charles Philip Arthur George by the Archbishop of Canterbury, Dr Geoffrey Fisher, a month after his birth, on 15 December. It was the first time the public had heard the choice of names, although speculation had been rife. His parents had chosen the name Charles, according to the Palace, for 'personal and private reasons'; and because the King was not fit enough to travel to Windsor, where most royal christenings take place, the golden Lily Font was specially transported to London, and the Edinburghs' first-born was formally admitted to the Protestant Church of England in the Music Room at Buckingham Palace. No one but close friends, trusted servants and family were present; and only six of his eight godparents. King Haakon of Norway and the Duke of Edinburgh's uncle, Prince George of Greece, were too elderly to travel. The others were the King and Queen; Princess Margaret; David Bowes-Lyon, the Queen's brother; the Duke of Edinburgh's grandmother, the Dowager Marchioness of Milford Haven; and his cousin, Earl Mountbatten's elder daughter, Lady Brabourne.

While everyone's thoughts had been turned to the baby's christian names in the weeks leading up to the birth, the not insignificant matter of a surname had been quietly forgotten. Suddenly, with less than a week to go before the birth, King George VI's private secretary, Sir Alan Lascelles, realized that unless the King did something quickly his grandchild would be no more noble than an earl – hardly a fitting title for an heir to the throne. He or she would not be styled His or Her Royal Highness, because the Duke of Edinburgh had forsaken his own title of Prince on his engagement to Elizabeth.

He had previously been called Prince Philip of Greece, although he was in fact not Greek at all. He was Danish, but his father, who had been born on the island of Corfu, became known as Prince Peter of Greece, and his son followed suit. In 1947, however, when Philip became a naturalized Briton prior to his marriage, he decided to adopt his mother's surname. His mother was Princess Alice of Battenberg, daughter of the German Prince Louis of Battenberg and sister of Lord Louis Mountbatten, Prince Charles's great mentor. Prince Louis was a passionate Anglophile who had been serving in the Royal Navy when the First World War broke out, and, wanting to remain in the Navy, thought it wise to change his name to something less Germanic. He anglicized it to Mountbatten, and this is the name that Philip adopted in 1947. When he married Princess Elizabeth the King made him Baron of Greenwich, Earl of Merioneth and Duke of Edinburgh.

However under an edict issued by the King's father, George V, in 1917, when he created the House of Windsor to replace the German family name of Saxe-Coburg-Gotha, the title of Prince would go only to the children of the sovereign and of his sons. Thus Princess Elizabeth's children, although direct heirs to the throne, would not have the rank of Prince or Princess, but would take the surname Mountbatten and at best be called Earl or Lady.

So George VI issued Letters Patent under the Great Seal, by which any children born to the Duke and Duchess of Edinburgh would have the title Prince or Princess, and the style of His or Her Royal Highness. The title of Prince of Wales was conferred on Charles by the Queen much later, in 1958. Just a year before, the Queen had made the Duke of Edinburgh a prince in recognition of ten years' service to the country, and he officially took the style of Royal Highness, which many people, including King George VI, been erroneously called him for years.

The Princess had spent the first ten days after the birth in bed, as was normal in those days, particularly after a general anaesthetic, and she was breast feeding her son. However when he was just a week old she developed measles, which can leave children blind if they catch it at so young an age, so she had to be kept away from him. It was the first of a childhood of separations for Charles.

There were long periods away from his father, too. Philip was a serving naval officer, conveniently based at the Admiralty in London when Prince Charles was born. After a short spell there he took a staff course at the Royal Naval College in Greenwich, to further his ambition of one day commanding his own ship. He would stay in Greenwich during the week and return home at weekends; but within the year he was further afield, with a posting as first lieutenant and second-in-command aboard HMS *Chequers*, leader of the first Mediterranean destroyer flotilla.

The first major separation from his mother occurred soon after Prince Charles's first birthday. The King was ill: he had been suffering cramps in his legs and loss of sensation in his feet for the best part of a year. Doctors finally diagnosed early arteriosclerosis – hardening of the arteries resulting in poor circulation – and insisted he cancel his engagements and rest. Their cure seemed to work, and by the autumn George VI was sufficiently well for Princess Elizabeth to leave the country and join her husband for a brief holiday in Malta. Their small son spent the Christmas of 1949 in the care of his grandparents, the King and Queen, at Sandringham.

The next occasion on which he saw his father for any length of time was the following summer, when the Duke of Edinburgh flew home for the arrival of their second child, Princess Anne, born at Clarence House on 15 August 1950. That very day he heard the news that he had been promoted to lieutenant commander; soon he was back in the Mediterranean, commanding his own frigate, HMS *Magpie*. A few months later Princess Elizabeth was gone again too, to spend Christmas with her husband aboard *Magpie*, and for the second year running Prince Charles spent the festive season with his grandparents at Sandringham.

Alas, his father's command lasted for less than a year. In July 1951 he took indefinite leave from the Navy and never returned. He was needed to help with the 'family firm' – to take pressure off the King, who had become ill once more. George VI's health had grown progressively worse; he had had influenza, which had dragged on and on. His doctors finally diagnosed cancer – although the King was never aware of this – and, passing it off as a bronchial tube blockage, they decided to remove one lung. Everyone prepared for the worst; the danger of coronary thrombosis was very real, but the King came through the operation and recovered so well that the Edinburghs were able to go off on a tour of Canada and the United States at the beginning of October.

Prince Charles and his sister did not see either of their parents for thirty-five days. They were still away when his third birthday came round in November, and once again it was his grandparents, and his aunt Margaret, who deputized. They had a tea party for the birthday boy at Buckingham Palace and it was there that the King posed for photographers with his grandson – the first time the public had seen him since his operation – and a picture taken on that occasion sits in the Queen's private sitting room to this day.

The visits to Sandringham were no hardship; Charles was in excellent and loving hands – out of which has come the strongest of relationships today – and, given that the nannies went too, the disruption was minimal. He suffered a loss, nevertheless – a bereavement every time he had to stand on a dockside or an airport tarmac and wave goodbye to his parents.

That Christmas the whole family was at last together, but the joy was short-lived. In January the Duke and Duchess of Edinburgh embarked yet again on a tour in place of the King, who was still too ill to travel. It was a tour of the Commonwealth, which would be their longest and most taxing yet; but they had not been gone a week when the news they had been dreading arrived. George VI was dead.

He and the Queen had been looking after their grandchildren at Sandringham. On 5 February, after a particularly good day hare shooting, the King had dinner with his wife, worked on his boxes until midnight, went to sleep and never woke up. He was fifty-six, and his death shocked and saddened the entire nation. Prince Charles, as a three-year-old, was simply puzzled that his grandfather had gone away without saying goodbye.

What his grandfather's death meant, however, was that life would never be the same again for Charles. His small world was turned upside down, his mother taken even further from him, and the degree of normality that the family had been able to enjoy while the King was alive was suddenly and rudely snatched away. His mother was Queen of England, Scotland, Wales, Northern Ireland and the Commonwealth, Head of Church and State. Prince Charles was first in line.

CHAPTER THREE

None of the changes brought about by the death of King George VI was more apparent to the young heir than the physical upheaval of moving house. Having just settled comfortably into Clarence House, the family had to give it up and move back into the vast and impersonal wastelands of Buckingham Palace, where the sovereign has traditionally lived in recent times. This was precisely what had happened to his mother as a ten-year-old child. Cosy family life at 145 Piccadilly had been rudely interrupted when King Edward VIII abdicated and she too was uprooted and moved to Buckingham Palace.

The Palace has been in the Royal Family since 1762, when George III bought it from the Dukes of Buckingham, and as well as housing the sovereign it accommodates 'the firm', all the royal offices and the general machinery of monarchy. Palatial though it may be, it is not homely, and although the furnishings and fittings have improved over the years it still resembles a museum more than a comfortable place to live.

The move took place after Easter, and Queen Elizabeth, now the Queen Mother, took up residence in Clarence House with Princess Margaret. Prince Charles had therefore not entirely lost the security of his old home surroundings. At the Palace, his life continued much as it had before. His grandfather's death had been explained to him, but he had been spared the old King's funeral and the grief of the adults in his life. He was blissfully unaware that overnight he had inherited a string of titles and honours which made him Duke of Rothesay, Earl of Carrick, Baron Renfrew, Lord of the Isles, Great Steward of Scotland and Duke of Cornwall.

When George VI became King so suddenly in 1936 Queen Elizabeth insisted her daughters should curtsey to him every morning to reinforce the dignity of his position. The new Queen, however, was adamant that her own small children should do no such thing; she wanted them to be protected for as long as possible from the facts of life, and was remarkably successful in doing this. Prince Charles once said, 'I didn't suddenly wake up in my pram one day and say "Yippee". I think it just dawns on you, slowly, that people are interested . . . and slowly you get the idea that you have a certain duty and responsibility. It's better that way, rather than someone suddenly telling you "You must do this" and "You must do that", because of who you are. It's one of those things you grow up in.'

Even if he did not realize who he was, the Queen's coronation the following summer certainly made Prince Charles aware that his mother was someone rather special. It was a magnificent spectacle, with the full pomp and ceremony and pure magic that are the hallmark of British state occasions. She was crowned on the morning of 2 June 1953. The mile-long route down the Mall, under Admiralty Arch and along Whitehall to Westminster Abbey, was packed with cheering crowds standing twelve deep; thirty thousand people or more had camped out in the rain overnight to be sure of the best possible position to see the procession of horse-drawn carriages make its way from Buckingham Palace. The Queen and her husband travelled in an extravagantly gilded and curlicued coach built in 1761 for George III, and were attended by scarlet and gold-coated Yeomen of the Guard and postillions.

The Queen herself was dressed in a white satin gown, specially designed with the emblems of England, Scotland, Ireland, Wales and, at her special request, those of the Commonwealth countries too. Over that lay a rich crimson train.

'Sirs,' called out the Archbishop of Canterbury as she reached the top of the aisle, 'I here present unto you Queen Elizabeth, your undoubted Queen.' There were loud shouts of 'God Save Queen Elizabeth', and as the stately music of Handel's 'Zadok the Priest' filled the highest vaults of the Abbey, the Queen's maids of honour carefully removed her jewellery and robes, leaving her symbolically dressed in a simple sleeveless overdress of plain white linen in preparation for her consecration.

'Be thy hands anointed with holy oil,' proclaimed the Archbishop, 'be thy breast anointed with holy oil, be thy head anointed with holy oil, as Kings, Priests and Prophets were anointed.' Seated in King Edward's chair she was solemnly presented with the tokens of kingship: the orb, the sceptre with the cross, the rod of mercy and the royal ring. Then came the crowning, and the Prince of Wales, standing on a footstool beside his grandmother so that he could see over the balcony in the royal box, watched in wonder as the Archbishop held St Edward's crown aloft and slowly and gracefully brought it down to rest on his mother's head.

A sudden roar of 'God Save the Queen' came from all sides of the Abbey as the congregation burst into voice. The bells rang out, trumpets blared and the noise of gunfire from many loyal salutes could be heard all over the capital. The senior peers, led by the Duke of Edinburgh, then came forward, while the choir sang, to kneel before their sovereign and pay homage. The Queen took communion, the choir sang some more, and the ceremony that has taken place in much the same form since William the Conqueror appropriated the throne in 1066 was over. The major difference was the existence of television. This was the first piece of royal pageantry ever to be televised, albeit in black and white, and many people in Britain bought sets specially for the occasion. It was the beginning of a new era in more ways than one.

Prince Charles travelled back to Buckingham Palace in the same manner as he had come, discreetly by car rather than in a royal coach, but he was allowed on to the balcony for the first time in his life to wave to the crowds cheering below. Dressed in a smart white satin suit specially made for the occasion, he stood alongside his parents, grandmother and the rest of the family, wrapped in wonder as a display of Royal Air Force planes flew overhead. The only member of the family missing from the occasion was Queen Mary, who had died two months earlier at the grand age of eighty-six and been buried alongside her husband in St George's Chapel, Windsor.

The following November Prince Charles was five. His grandmother, with whom he spent the day at Windsor, gave him a set of gardening tools and perhaps sowed the seeds for the hobby which nowadays gives him the greatest pleasure of all. It was also she who introduced him to one of his other passions in life, fly fishing – but that came later. His parents were at Sandringham on his birthday, preparing for yet another foreign trip which would mean the longest separation so far. They were resuming the Commonwealth tour that they had had to abandon when the King died, and would be away for six whole months.

By this time Prince Charles had begun his education, so although the parting was difficult, and he missed his parents, there was plenty going on at home to keep his mind occupied. A governess had been taken on, Miss Catherine Peebles. A Scotswoman in her mid-forties, she had no formal qualifications whatsoever, but she had been in charge of the Duchess of Kent's two younger children, Princess Alexandra and Prince Michael, and her style appealed to the Queen.

Prince Charles had also begun a number of extra-curricular activities. He had weekly dancing classes given by the celebrated Miss Betty Vacani who with her aunt, the now late Marguerite Vacani, has spent more than fifty years teaching the offspring of the rich, famous and royal to point their toes, hop and skip in time to music. Twenty-five years later, by a strange coincidence, the Princess of Wales, then Lady Diana Spencer, spent a brief spell teaching at Miss Vacani's school in the Brompton Road. By that time royal children such as Prince Frederick, Prince Michael of Kent's son, came to her; but in Prince Charles's day Miss Vacani took the class at Buckingham Palace, and a select group of friends joined in. She remembers Prince Charles as the sweetest little boy she ever taught. He was sweet and sensitive to a fault. Miss Peebles, or Mispy as she came to be known, said of those early days, 'If you raised your voice to him, he would draw back into his shell and for a time you would be able to do nothing with him.'

There were also regular gymnastics lessons, which took place at a nearby London gymnasium; and piano lessons at the Palace under the practised tuition of Miss Hilda Bor. He was learning to ride by this time too, on a Welsh pony called William which was kept at Windsor; although he was never as keen as his sister, he was proving himself quite able. His great-grandfather would have approved. 'The English people like riding,' had been George V's advice to his eldest son, later Edward VIII, 'and it would make you very unpopular if you couldn't do so. If you can't ride, you know, I am afraid people will call you a duffer.'

In 1953 his proficiency reflected more his parents' love of riding than any fear that he might grow up to be called a duffer. The Queen had been riding since the age of two and a half, and had been given her first pony at the age of three. She is at her happiest in the company of horses, and has frequently said that were she not Queen of England she would like to live in the country surrounded by dogs and horses. The Duke of Edinburgh now drives four-in-hand, but at that time he was a passionate polo player, like his uncle, Lord Mountbatten. It was a horsy family through and through.

It was not just the horses however. Prince Charles's entire education reflected his parents' own personal wishes rather than the accepted convention. In the past royal children had been taught exclusively by private tutors, away from the company of other children or normalizing outside influences. Even the Queen and her sister had had a governess, Miss Marion Crawford, who later fell from grace by writing about her time in royal employment, albeit in the most harmless of ways. She was with the family for about fifteen years. 'For goodness' sake,' said King George V upon being introduced, 'teach Margaret and Lilibet to write a decent hand, that's all I ask you. None of my children could write properly. They all do it exactly the same way. I like a hand with some character in it.'

The only brief that Miss Peebles had from the Queen and the Duke of Edinburgh on the way she handled her charge, was 'no forcing'. She began the day with a story from the Bible, then there was some painting, and some rudimentary geography with the help of a large globe on which the Prince could chart his parents' progress around the world. Most afternoons they would venture out to explore the cultural sights of London, or go off for a nature walk through one of the surrounding parks.

It was not long, however, before the press realized that the heir to the throne was out and about most days, and photographers began to accompany him, much to the annoyance of the Queen. She had deliberately avoided giving out details about Charles and Anne, because she felt that too much exposure would be bad for them. In April 1955, therefore, she sent her first missive to Fleet Street editors asking them not to bother her children. Several more were to follow over the years. For a while, at least, they observed her wishes.

This daily routine, with a progressively greater emphasis on the educational part, continued for nearly two years, when the Queen decided the time had come to investigate proper schools. The royal parents wanted their children to receive a normal education. As the Duke explained at the time, 'The Queen and I want Charles to go to school with other boys of his generation and learn to live with other children, and to absorb from childhood the discipline imposed by education with others.' Thus, on the recommendation of a friend, Prince Charles was enrolled as a pupil at a small select school in Knightsbridge called Hill House.

He was nearly eight years old, and in all that time he had never really been exposed to other children. He had had parties at Buckingham Palace occasionally, when the children of his parents' friends and staff had come, and he had been to those children's parties from time to time; but he had no friends of his own age, and had never socialized with strangers. His companions had been his sister, nearly two years his junior, his nannies and Mispy. It was a daunting prospect, and so he was broken in gradually, going to school initially in the afternoons only, and working up to a full day in the spring term of 1957.

The episode was made more traumatic by changes at home. In a short space of time Prince Charles lost two of the people who had been closest to him. Helen Lightbody, the nanny who had been closer to him than his own mother, retired and went to live in a grace-and-favour flat in Kennington; and Mispy now turned her attention to Princess Anne. At the same time he moved out of the security of the nursery wing, where he had spent his whole life so far, and into a suite of his own.

Not for the last time, however, he kept his feelings to himself and put on a brave face for the outside world. He donned the uniform blazer and cap and went to school – the first heir to the throne ever to do so. He ran the gauntlet of public curiosity, coped with the strangeness of his new environment, surrounded by 120 other children, and emerged from the first term with a glowing report in everything but arithmetic. His best subjects, even then, were history and art – the two which he loves to this day.

Hill House was intended as a gentle introduction to his ultimate destination of boarding school. Some voices said he should be sent to a state school, but this was more than the Queen and the Duke of Edinburgh were prepared to do. In addition, state schools are day schools, and if the persistence of the press during his months at Hill House was anything to go by, life would be intolerable. A boarding school where he could be protected from intrusion was the only answer.

Thus in September 1957 Princes Charles went to Cheam, probably the oldest preparatory school in Britain. They chose Cheam in part because it was where the Duke of Edinburgh had been educated as a small boy. He said later, by way of explanation,

> There are a vast number whose financial limitations are such that they cannot afford to educate their children any way they like. We were certainly not limited that way, but there were many other considerations that entered into it. It would have been very difficult to select out of the blue because people would say of any selection, 'Why have they done that? There must be some reason.' They wouldn't admit that this was done for the children's benefit or because we had any particular theory of education. They would have said, 'Oh well it must be to discourage this or discourage that.' People are always looking for strange reasons.
>
> When Charles first went to school one of the problems we were confronted with was 'How do you select a prep school?' In the end he went to Cheam, where I had been. But this is something better understood in this country than almost anything else – that people very frequently do what their fathers have done. People said, 'Oh, he's gone because his father went,' and there was no further argument.

Despite the name, which had once reflected its location in the Surrey suburb of Cheam, the school was situated on the Berkshire Downs near Headley, about sixty miles from London. The royal instructions to the headmasters, Peter Beck and Mark Wheeler, were that there should be no alteration in the way the school was run, and that Prince Charles should be treated just like any other boy. Apart from the fact that fellow pupils called him by his christian name while calling everyone else by their surnames, and the presence of a detective living in the grounds, this was achieved.

Nevertheless boarding school was a considerable shock to Charles. It is a shock to most little boys who have never been away from home before, but the more so for Prince Charles whose life to this point, despite six months at Hill House, had been extraordinarily sheltered and unreal. He had never had to sleep in the same room with other boys before nor look after his own clothes, clean his shoes, make his own bed – the most uncomfortable he had ever slept in – or wait on others at table. The greatest handicap of all, however, was that he did not even have much experience at making friends.

He had dreaded the thought of going, and for the first few weeks was utterly miserable. He was lonely and alone. The boys were suspicious of making advances towards him, in case they were thought to be sucking up, and he was wary of boys that did, knowing all too well that his name rather than his personality was probably the reason for their overtures. It was a problem that dogged the Prince throughout his education, and which to some extent remains with him to this day. For the most part he has managed to avoid the wrong people, but by no means always.

Despite the initial misery Charles coped well, desperate that he should not let down his father, who had high hopes for his son and was a hard task-master. When he was around, the Duke enjoyed the time he spent with his children, and to some extent his son hero-worshipped him. 'He was a marvellous father,' said Mabel Anderson. 'When the children were younger he always set aside time to read to them, or help them put together those little model toys.' Not so long after the model toys were put away the Duke introduced Charles to field sports, and by the age of ten he was accompanying his father on pheasant and coot shoots around Sandringham. By twelve he had learnt to drive a Land Rover round the estate.

Philip was and is an outdoor enthusiast, a sportsman, a man's man. He has little time for intellectuals, and having achieved little of an academic nature during his own schooldays saw no real virtue in it for his son. Thus in some respects Prince Charles grew up to be a disappointment to his father. He was quiet and introspective and disliked most forms of sport; and although he became captain of the football team at Cheam it may be no coincidence that during that time the team failed to win a single match. Too gentle for the sport, he had an endearing habit of apologizing if he got in anyone's way or knocked them to the ground in a tackle. He was altogether too sensitive, and has remained so, and over the years it is this as much as anything else that has driven a wedge between the two men.

For the time being Charles was simply eager to please and to do what was expected of him, and had soon earned the friendship and approval of his peers at Cheam, mostly by demonstrating that at heart he was just like one of them. In turn he was caned just like everyone else when practical jokes – a family tradition – and other misdemeanours backfired. He took up the trumpet, but found it a difficult instrument. History and art were still his best subjects, and in his first year he won a commendation in the Under Ten modelling competition; and he made his first appearance on the stage at Cheam in Shakespeare's *Richard III*.

His routine may have been the same as the others', but there was no escaping the fact that he was different from everyone else, and never so acutely as the day on which the Queen created him Prince of Wales. The school had been forewarned, and Charles heard his mother's speech announcing her intention over the radio in Peter Beck's study. It was the final day of the British Empire and Commonwealth Games in Cardiff, 26 July 1958, and before a crowd of thirty-six thousand the Queen said:

> I want to take this opportunity of speaking to all Welsh people, not only in this arena, but wherever they may be. The British Empire and Commonwealth Games in the capital, together with all the activities of the Festival of Wales, have made this a memorable year in the Principality. I have therefore decided to mark it further by an act which will, I hope, give as much pleasure to all Welshmen as it does to me. I intend to create my son, Charles, Prince of Wales today.

There was a roar of approval from the stadium, and shouts of 'God Bless the Prince of Wales'. Then the Queen's voice continued: 'When he is grown up, I will present him to you at Caernarvon.' His schoolmates, aghast at first, soon clapped and cheered, but it was not the easiest moment for a nine-year-old trying hard to be accepted as one of the boys.

In his last year he became head of school. Having finally conquered the difficulties, overcome his homesickness and settled happily into life at Cheam, it was time to enter the fray all over again. The next stop was Gordonstoun, a boys' public school set on the north-east coast of Scotland in an isolated and windswept corner of Morayshire. The establishment and its regime, unique among British public schools, left a deep impression on Prince Charles – one which has been reflected time and again in his later life.

CHAPTER FOUR

Gordonstoun's uniqueness arose partly from the educational philosophy upon which it was based, and partly from the inspirational, somewhat eccentric personality of its founder, Dr Kurt Hahn. He was a German whose unconventional ideas about education had been prompted by his country's defeat in the First World War. Educated in Berlin and at Christ Church, Oxford, he had been in England when war broke out but had returned to Germany as reader of English newspapers to the German Foreign Office, and later private secretary to Prince Max of Baden, the last imperial Chancellor. During their time together the two men formed the same conclusion about their fellow countrymen: they were weak, not because of the German character but because of the German system, particularly education. They both believed that the right action by the right man at the right time could alter the course of history.

When Prince Max retired from public office in 1918 he put part of his castle at Salem at Dr Hahn's disposal, and the two men founded a school there. It was designed to train citizens who would not shrink from leadership and who could, if called upon, make independent decisions, put the right moral action before expediency and the common cause before personal ambition.

Salem was the culmination of ideas that had been percolating in Dr Hahn's head for several years. As a young man he had suffered a long period of illness, and while convalescing had read Plato's *Republic*. Inspired by the ideals he discovered there, he had conceived the idea of starting an entirely new sort of school, broadly based on the Platonic view that 'any nation is a slovenly guardian of its own interests if it does not do all it can to make the individual citizen discover his own powers; and further, that the individual becomes a cripple from his or her own point of view if he is not qualified by education to serve the community.' The system he founded became famous, particularly for the success achieved by its athletics teams when competing against English public schools at White City; but in 1933 it came to an abrupt end, and he was forced to leave Salem and flee to Britain.

The trouble began with an incident known as the Potempa murder in 1932, when five of the Nazi party's strong-arm bullies from the Sturmabteilung were tried and imprisoned for trampling a Communist to death in front of his mother. They were sent a telegram of appreciation and praise by Hitler, who called them his comrades. Hahn then wrote an open letter to all old Salem boys condemning the murderers and calling for them to do the same. A few months later Hitler became Chancellor and Hahn was imprisoned. After the intervention of several people including the British Prime Minister, Ramsay MacDonald, he was later released. Hahn came straight to Britain and the following year founded Gordonstoun.

It was a school in the mould of Salem, with the same guiding principles. He wanted to make the tough compassionate and the timid enterprising, to 'find a substitute for war' as a means of achieving this. In Plato's *Republic* Socrates asserts that his citizens, if they are to be guardians of the state, must be 'spirited, swift and strong' and yet, at the same time, gentle and swayed by 'beauty and truth'. 'Our youth should dwell in the land of health, amid fair sights and sounds; and beauty, the effluence of fair works, will meet the sense like a breeze, and insensibly draw the soul even in childhood into harmony with the beauty of reason.'

The fundamental divergence from Plato's philosophy, however, was in religion. Gordonstoun was a Christian school, whereas Plato's *Republic* was a pagan slave state. Hahn, who was himself Jewish, simply took the best from Plato, just as he took what he saw as the best ideas from the best in English education. He introduced the institution of colour bearers, a unique system whereby boys who earned promotion were awarded colours, not for sport as in other schools, but for being good, honest, all-round individuals: 'swift and bold' yet 'gentle' and lovers of truth. Furthermore, they were elected colour bearers by the other boys, like Eton's 'Pop', a similarly self-elected hierarchy, which gives the school a limited form of self-government. The headmaster can only appoint official helpers from the elected colour bearers.

Hahn turned the traditional 'fagging' system that existed in most boys' public schools at the time into service not just for an older boy, but for the community as a whole. This was one of the most fundamental principles on which the school was run. Another was the trust system. Hahn believed that every boy should be trusted to discipline himself, and rather like the unwritten laws of Pericles, 'whose only punishment is dishonour', failure to do the morning run or have a cold shower might not go detected by the staff but created a deep sense of guilt.

If people have heard nothing more of Gordonstoun, they have always heard about the cold showers and the morning run, and although the regime is softer now it did for many years have the reputation of being a rough, tough spartan place. That reputation was not undeserved. If the boys were not out running half-naked in midwinter they were sailing in the icy North Sea, climbing down cliff ladders and scrambling over blazing roof-tops.

Hahn passionately believed that physical health was more important than anything else, and just as much of the school day was devoted to physical exercise as to academic work. But it was exercise with a difference, not the usual round of hockey, rugby or football. Hahn was convinced that competition brought out the very worst in children. Instead, boys should compete against themselves: they should throw discus, run or jump, for example, and instead of trying to beat other boys and becoming either resentful or boastful depending upon the outcome they should simply try to improve their own best performance, and thus discover strengths in themselves that they might never have known existed. Hence the school motto '*Plus est en vous*' (There is more in you).

All of this created an unorthodox curriculum, and made the school a somewhat controversial choice for Prince Charles. There were many people, including the Queen Mother, who thought Eton would be more suitable, and were against the idea of sending him off to the north of Scotland, but once again the matter was determined by family tradition. Not only had the Duke of Edinburgh been one of the first pupils at Gordonstoun, and thoroughly enjoyed his time there, but the Duke's sister had married Berthold, Prince Max of Baden's son, and he had frequently been to visit her at Salem. In addition, the regime appealed to Lord Mountbatten, whose voice was not uninfluential in such matters. In fact his grandson, Norton Knatchbull, had recently started at Gordonstoun, and would provide a familiar and reassuring face amongst the sea of strangers for Charles.

There was one further consideration which tipped the balance. The press, which had been so intrusive in Prince Charles's education up to this point, would surely be less likely to bother him five hundred miles or more from Fleet Street than they would if he were just a short drive up the M4 at Eton. This was in general true, but the press still tried, particularly in the early days. The boys at Gordonstoun, however, had been thoroughly drilled about how to handle journalists and did so with great aplomb. One boy met a reporter in the drive who tried to engage him in conversation.

'Hello, sonny,' he said. 'Nice day.'

'No comment,' said the boy and went on his way.

Another was approached on the school train. 'I'm from the *Sun*,' said the journalist.

'Well then, you've come a long way,' retorted the boy.

Others realized there was a bit of capital to be made. One boy was stopped by a reporter from the *Mirror*, who offered to give him £5 if he directed him to the Prince. The boy pocketed the five-pound note, then took the trusting hack on a long and circuitous tour of the grounds. Finally they came up behind a figure huddled in a duffle coat.

'There he is!' said the boy.

The reporter sped up to the boy, tapped him on the shoulder and was confronted by a face as black as coal.

Furious, he rounded on his 'guide', who was convulsed with laughter. 'Give me back my fiver!' he roared. 'You said you would take me to the Prince.'

'Yes,' said the boy. 'But you didn't say which Prince.'

The Gordonstoun estate has an intriguing history going back to medieval times. It used to be in the parish of Ogstoun, and the Ogstouns 'of that ilk' were the first occupiers. Simon de Hogeston, who died in 1240, was the first recorded owner, but there are indications that it had been in his family for some time beforehand.

The house, however, which Hahn bought for his school in 1945, is largely the work of the 1st Marquess of Huntly, George Gordon the 6th Earl, a friend of King James VI of Scotland and I of England, and one of the great builders of his age. He bought the estate, known then as Bog o' Plewlands because of the marshy surrounds, in 1616 from the son of his murdered friend Robert Innes the Informer. He built on to the existing house, and much of his work still stands today, although altered and extended by later Gordons. In 1638 his cousin, Sir Robert Gordon, 1st Baron of Gordonstoun, bought the estate and renamed it Gordonstoun.

The next significant building work was carried out by the 3rd Baronet, known as Sir Robert the Wizard, who constructed a stable block that was not the traditional square shape but circular, and became known as the Round Square. According to legend – which Henry Brereton, warden of the school, would faithfully relate to the pupils – the reason for its odd shape arose from the fact that Sir Robert had struck a bargain with the Devil while a student in Padua. The Devil agreed to teach him 'the hidden secrets of the universe that the King of Heaven has denied to men' in return for his soul, which he would collect one year hence. A year to the day later, when the Devil arrived, Sir Robert outwitted him and the Devil gave him another twenty-five years.

As the years passed Sir Robert brooded on the awful fate that approached. He finally hit on the idea of constructing a circle of magical proportions, a mathematical sanctuary in which the Devil would never be able to catch him. The dreadful day dawned, and feeling in need of company to see him through the evening Sir Robert invited the parson from the Old Manse at Duffus. At midnight the window burst open, a gust of wind penetrated the room, and then beneath the flapping tapestry appeared a cloven hoof.

'Now, Robert, the hour has struck – your time has come.'

'Oh no, you old Devil,' replied the laird. 'You know very well I put that clock on by sixty minutes and I still have an hour of freedom.'

The voice laughed. 'You win, but for the last time. In one hour I claim your immortal soul.' There was deathly silence, the wind and rain that had raged all evening ceased, and, quivering in terror, the parson begged his friend to go to the only place holy enough to grant safe sanctuary, the kirkyard of Birnie.

So Sir Robert abandoned the Round Square and set off for Birnie, which lay beyond Elgin. He never arrived. The minister encountered him running over the heath in the darkness. A few moments later a dark figure on horseback appeared.

'Has a man passed this way?' asked a voice.

Sensing a vague but profound emanation of evil, the minister said, 'No. Not a soul has passed this way.'

The rider went on his way and a dreadful silence filled the air. Seconds later there was one long piercing shriek. The sound of trotting hooves returned and the rider reappeared with a limp human body hanging from the saddle in front of him. A bloodhound ran alongside with its fangs buried in the neck of the corpse. . . . The year was 1704.

The Round Square now houses the library, several classrooms, teachers' accommodation and a few sleeping quarters, and it is said that the ghost of Sir Robert can be seen to this day. The Wizard's son was just eight years old when his father met his grisly death, and went on to live for seventy-six years at Gordonstoun, feared and hated by his tenants. But it was he, Ill Sir Robert Gordon, who built the basic house, the Do'ecotes, the little water tower and the Michael Kirk into which the school moved in 1934, and where apart from the war years, when it moved to Montgomeryshire, it has been ever since.

When Hahn took over the house it was in a state of neglect and dilapidation. The last incumbent had been Sir William Gordon Cumming, whose fortunes had plummeted after a famous scandal in the 1890s. At the age of forty-two he was an officer in the Scots Guards, a handsome bachelor, popular in aristocratic society and a close friend of the Prince of Wales (later King Edward VII). But while staying in a Lincolnshire house party for the St Leger racing week at Doncaster he was accused by his hosts of cheating at a game of baccarat at which the Prince was present. Sir William was asked to sign a promise never to play cards again, and although he protested his innocence he agreed, in order to protect the Prince from embarrassing scandal. However, the story got out. As a result Sir William brought an action for slander, which he lost, and although many people believed him innocent he was forced to resign his army commission and spent the last forty years of his life ostracized from society.

Dr Hahn had his difficulties, and although the mould was there there was no comparison between setting up Gordonstoun and his experience at Salem. Once a rich man in Germany, he was now an impoverished refugee. Yet the house and estate needed vast sums spent on them, and there was no patron owner as he had had in Prince Max at Salem. In addition, there were no facilities for a school on the site. His pioneering spirit was not daunted, but it was a long time before Gordonstoun could compete with the established public schools of England and Scotland. A few parents had heard of the Salem system and sent their sons to Gordonstoun for that reason; among these were the parents of Prince Philip of Greece, who had just finished his time at Cheam. The remaining pupils were boys who had been rejected by other schools or expelled, and whose parents were relieved to have found somewhere that would take them.

By the time Prince Charles arrived at the school twenty-eight years later things had changed dramatically. Some of the pioneering zeal had been lost; the memory of Nazi oppression had faded. Hahn, now seventy-six, had retired; and the present headmaster, Robert Chew, who had been at the school since its inception, was a tired and worried man who was himself to retire the year Charles left, and died two years later. It was true that the school had become more competitive, but it was still unorthodox and never likely to have depleted the lists of Eton or Winchester. Its reputation for excessive exercise and physical hardship made a number of parents shy away. In addition, there was no requirement for boys to pass the common entrance examination, a prerequisite of other schools; the clear implication was that if brains were not a priority in the selection of pupils the school was unlikely to boast high academic results at the other end.

To allay suggestions that they had chosen Gordonstoun because Prince Charles would not have passed common entrance, the Queen insisted that he should take the examination; the result was a perfectly acceptable paper.

Having been brought up in the spartan regime of Gordonstoun himself, and thrived on it, the Duke of Edinburgh was certain it would make a man of his son too. He was slightly disappointed in Charles so far. The boy had not thrown himself into the rough and tumble of the rugger scrum, for instance, as he himself had done. He was of a different mettle and showed every sign of being introverted – no doubt because he had been pampered by women for most of his life. Pitting his wits against the elements in Morayshire would soon take care of that, his father thought.

Charles went to his new school in May 1962, and once again the timing was less than perfect. He was not arriving like a normal boy at the beginning of the school year. He was the odd one out before he had even hung up his coat; and not surprisingly, perhaps, he found the entire experience horrendous.

It is a measure of his generous nature that Prince Charles can look back now on those years at Gordonstoun and admit that they did him good. He has even kept up a friendship with the man who admits he was partly responsible for making his celebrated pupil so unhappy: his housemaster, Bob Whitby. And for all the misery, the intrinsic values that the Prince of Wales holds dear today, the principles upon which he has not only lived his own life, but extended into the lives of those who benefit from his charities, are not far removed from the values and principles of Kurt Hahn. The process of absorbing them, however, was a trial. He was thirteen when he arrived at the school, a shy, awkward boy who despite his years at Cheam still found adults far easier to talk to than boys of his own age.

The headmaster had decided that he should go into Windmill Lodge, one of the outhouses a distance from the main school building, next to the old windmill Do'ecote. It was an obvious choice, as Norton Knatchbull was in the house, and they thought he would provide a friendly face; but the two boys scarcely knew one another at that stage, and his cousin, a year ahead, was little consolation. Charles found himself isolated and alone. As at Cheam, no one came forward to make friends with him for fear of being accused of sucking up.

Bob Whitby had been given specific instructions by both the Queen and the Duke of Edinburgh that Prince Charles, or plain Charles as he was to be called by everyone, was to be treated in exactly the same way as everyone else. He was to make no exceptions, and Mr Whitby carried out his instructions to the letter. Thus Charles was thrown headlong into the austere routine, including the notorious morning run and cold showers, but without the companionship that other boys enjoyed. They slept in large dormitories with no carpets, no creature comforts and a minimum of heat. Windmill Lodge had one bath among fifty-nine boys, and six showers. The only trace of home was a selection of cherished photographs on top of the locker beside his bed: his grandmother, his parents, and his sister and new little brother, Andrew.

Any thoughts of home were banished each morning by the ringing of a bell, and a voice that would bellow up the stairs: 'Seven o'clock, time to get up!' There was an agonizing pause while the boys waited for the second half of the order: 'Morning run', or on rare occasions if it was deluging with rain, 'No morning run.'

Then they climbed out of their pyjamas and into running

shorts and shoes – nothing else – and set off on a short circuit of not much more than a hundred yards, while a master, wrapped up in a duffle coat, scarf and gloves, ticked the bare-legged, bare-chested boys' names off on a register as they ran past. Back indoors they went to stand naked in front of one of a row of basins in the washroom and splash hot water all over themselves with a loofah, followed by a dive under a cold shower; then breakfast.

Every boy from the bottom of the school to the most senior wore the uniform of short trousers with a single back pocket into which everything was crammed, long socks, shirt and V-necked sweater. The entire outfit changed colour according to the season, the time of day and the seniority of the wearer. The trousers, however, never changed, much to the embarrassment of the older boys. They were short to the day the boy left, and a source of much derision to the locals in Elgin. Everyone had a duffle coat invariably wrapped around them, rather than fastened, and clasped to by arms folded against the force of the wind. In winter they would wear coats plus a purple and white striped scarf for moving between classrooms, which were scattered about in different buildings, and every boy had an army-style canvas bag for carrying his books in.

Apart from the wind, which blew incessantly, Gordonstoun enjoyed surprisingly clement weather for its position so far north, which accounted for the siting of two air force stations nearby. The trade-off was the noise. Jets taking off from RNA Lossiemouth, whose runway was almost an extension of the school drive, screamed overhead day and night.

The jets were not the only nocturnal disturbance. One of the features unique to Gordonstoun was the rescue services that the school operated: the fire service, mountain rescue, beach rescue and coastguard watchers. These were genuine, operational services with professional vehicles and equipment, manned by staff and boys, and they formed part of the official rescue services for the area. If there was a fire, for example, no matter what time of day or night, the call would go through to Gordonstoun, the siren would sound, and members of that particular service would be expected to leave whatever they were doing, be it work, play or sleep, run to the services centre and prepare for action. Many are the times that the boys' unit has been the first to arrive at the scene of a blaze, and dealt with it.

Prince Charles joined the coastguard watchers service, which involved keeping watch in four-hour shifts, and many a night – sometimes two or three nights in succession – was spent in the lonely hut on the cliff top with just one other boy for company. His detective, however, was never far away with his Land Rover, which provided a most welcome chauffeuring service.

Kurt Hahn once explained how this particular service came into being.

> The Morayshire coast is dangerous and the strip on which Gordonstoun is situated is, for miles, hidden from the lookouts both in Lossiemouth and Burghead. I had learnt that in the eighth century a monk, Gernadius, came over from Ireland to live in one of the Covesea caves, within our grounds. On stormy nights he used to walk about through all the hours of darkness, waving a lantern to warn the fishermen of rocks and shoals. I thought I could enthuse the boys for coast watching by telling them this story of the saint. But I had a bad reception. I saw in their eyes that glint of mistrust, indicating that they had suspected me of wanting to improve their souls.
>
> By accident, the Board of Trade heard of my good intentions. The two leading Captains of HM Coastguards came down and told me that our stretch of coast would have been watched all these years if the Treasury had not intervened: 'But if you will build us a coastguard hut, and your boys are ready to man it at need, we will put a telephone in at our expense, and lend you all the lifesaving gear.' (Pistol, rockets, breeches buoy.) I asked them to tell the whole school exactly what they had told me: they did so, and encountered no suspicion. As soon as the boys heard that the Board of Trade were willing to fork out cash, they felt the need of the service required of them.

That was in the 1930s, when the school was in its infancy, and in those days the watchers were called into action two or three times a term. By the 1960s, when Prince Charles joined their ranks, the call-outs were even fewer; the little timber hut on the top of the cliff had been replaced by a splendid three-storey octagonal tower, with an observation room and open gallery at the top, living room in the centre, and sleeping accommodation below that. In stormy weather the boys kept a twenty-four-hour vigil, none the less, as they still do today.

Charles had two detectives during his time at Gordonstoun. The first, Donald Green, had caused almost as much of a stir when he arrived that summer term as the Prince himself. The early James Bond films were all the rage, and Mr Green, who faintly resembled Sean Connery, drove around in a customized Land Rover, with a hand gun nestling beneath his jacket and a gun rack on the roof. He was the envy of every boy in the school. Much to their disappointment, however, SPECTRE never seemed to pose quite the threat in the farflung reaches of Morayshire that it had to 007, and Mr Green did little more than drive the Prince about the countryside.

The boys ate in their own houses, and after a cooked breakfast, with plenty of thickly sliced brown bread, they went down to the main school for morning prayers and the start of the day's work. There were five forty-minute conventional lessons before lunch; every day one of these periods would be a training break during which all the boys had to go out into a big field and work to keep themselves fit. This was Hahn's theory working in practice, that boys should better their own standards. There was no gymnasium and no formalized gymnastics. The boys just went out and ran, jumped, negotiated the assault course, or threw discus or javelin.

Next came lunch, with hot, stodgy food and nursery puddings. A well-known statistic circulating amongst the boys at the time was that the school spent 1s 9d (about 8p) on food per boy per day, and any hopes that having the Prince of Wales in their midst might improve the quality of the food were unfulfilled. After lunch came a rest period, when boys read books or listened to music. Following that was a choice of outdoor activities: games – cricket, tennis or athletics in summer and rugby football or hockey in winter; seamanship; or practical work on the Gordonstoun estate. Then there were two more hours of work before supper at 6.20, prep, which was done in the houses, and bed, with lights out at 9.30.

Charles struggled manfully with sport, but never enjoyed it and was never much good. He was the wrong build and the wrong temperament, and quite frequently on the rugger pitch found himself being tackled harder than anyone else, just so that people could say they had felled the future king. What he did enjoy, however, was seamanship, and there was plenty of scope at Gordonstoun for keen sailors, from one-man canoes to sailing expeditions on the school cutter. It was while out on one of these expeditions that the famous cherry brandy incident took place.

The school yacht *Pinta* came into Stornoway on the Isle of Lewis, and Prince Charles, accompanied by Mr Green as usual, and four other boys went ashore for lunch in the local hotel, the Crown. It was not long before the entire community knew of their royal visitor and had made their way, every last man, woman and child, to take a look. They caught up with him at the Crown, and amid the crush Charles lost the rest of the party, who had headed for the dining room, and found himself in the bar. He had never been into a bar in his life, and was no doubt quite unaware about the law on selling alcohol to minors. 'And being terrified,' he later explained, 'not knowing what to do, I said the first drink that came into my head, which happened to be cherry brandy, because I'd drunk it before when it was cold out shooting. Hardly had I taken a sip when the whole world exploded round my ears.'

His misfortune was that standing at the bar beside him was a freelance journalist, who soon had the sensational story lodged on the front page of every newspaper in Fleet Street. The Queen and the Duke of Edinburgh were quite amused by the tale, although Mr Green was disciplined for ever having allowed such a thing to happen. Charles was devastated, and returned to school to have liberal doses of salt rubbed into his wounds.

Bob Whitby confesses that he too thought the offence quite tame, and had it happened to any other boy would probably have let him off with a stern talking to. Because it was the Prince of Wales, however, and because the world was waiting to see how the school handled the matter, he was forced to punish him severely. Charles lost the grades that he had spent his first year in the school acquiring, and was demoted to the rank of a new boy. Such was his reserve and control over his emotions that Mr Whitby had no idea at the time just how much it had hurt Charles, and it was not until many years later that the Prince confessed he felt he had been very harshly treated.

Bob Whitby was hard on the boys in his house, particularly the younger ones. He had been a housemaster for seven years by that time, and although he and his wife grew to be very fond of the boys under their roof he admits he shouted at them a good deal, and it was not until they were older that he started showing any kind of friendship towards them.

It was he who put paid to the young Prince's musical aspirations. Charles had had piano lessons as a child at Buckingham Palace, and attempted to play the trumpet at Cheam, but had never really progressed very far musically. On arrival at Gordonstoun he seized the opportunity to learn the bagpipes. He had dreams of playing in the school pipe band one day, but the housemaster's patience and eardrums rebelled. The noise, as Charles practised night after night, was so appalling that Whitby told him in no uncertain terms to stop. 'To hell with the bagpipes,' he said, 'you're not going to play that thing around my house any more. Take up something else, and for God's sake practise it somewhere well away from here.'

The result was that Charles took up the cello, and in the end became a very proficient player and derived immense pleasure from it, but not without sweating blood in the process. He set himself very high standards in his cello playing, just as he did in everything else he attempted, and would lose his temper and become quite furious with frustration if he made a mistake or did not reach the standard he expected from himself.

Art was another subject he loved, yet where he frequently felt frustrated at his inability to achieve on paper what he could see in his mind. In the end he virtually abandoned drawing and painting in favour of pottery, which he found more satisfying. Moulding the clay with his hands, and throwing bowls and mugs on the potter's wheel, was hugely therapeutic, and however misshapen the results, he experienced a great sense of achievement at having created something. Charles got on particularly well with the art master, Bob Waddell, a kindly man and amusing conversationalist who had a small bachelor flat in the Round Square filled with canvases, books, antiques, knick-knacks and works of art which he had collected like a magpie over the years. He was an inveterate collector, often going off to auctions at Sotheby's and returning with some new treasure which fascinated Charles. He always wanted to know what he had paid for it. Thus Bob Waddell's art room, smelling of oil paints, turpentine and damp clay, provided a haven for Charles. Here life was altogether less aggressive; he felt he was among friends and could relax and be himself.

In his first two years at the school this was a lifeline. He was deeply unhappy throughout that time, although he kept his emotions so tightly to himself that only in looking back do his contemporaries recognize the symptoms for what they were. They never saw Charles upset or thrown by anything that anyone did or said, much of which was cruel in the way that only poisonous schoolboys can be, like putting toothpaste up his nostrils to stop him snoring in the dormitory at night. At the time Charles simply seemed cripplingly shy, and physically and socially awkward.

Bob Waddell knew how miserable he was and gave what comfort he could. Bob Whitby also knew, but he had been given clear instructions from the Duke of Edinburgh as to how he should handle the Prince, and believed Charles would come through it. Besides, he had seen other boys unhappy for two years before settling down and so he was not unduly anxious. Had it continued into Charles's third year in the school, he says he would have begun to worry.

Charles finally made friends, and in Bob Whitby's words he began to 'take off'. His principal friends were not from the handful of aristocrats in the school, and not the most distinguished or popular figures of his year. They were two quite ordinary boys: Philip Bagnall, who came from East Africa and spoke Swahili, and Dick Illingworth. Both were in different houses from Prince Charles, which made their friendship somewhat unusual since boys tended to make friends within their own houses, and the three were regarded as slight misfits in their different ways. Nevertheless they were good friends and spent a lot of their time together. Two others who were less close were Lord Robert Mercer-Nairne, from a Perthshire landowning family, and Geordie Gordon, nephew of the Marquess of Huntly, whose ancestor, the 1st Marquess of Huntly, had built the seventeenth-century house which now formed the basis of Gordonstoun.

If Charles went out at weekends he would sometimes take one of his friends with him. He was invited to Sunday lunch or a day's shooting occasionally by Captain Iain Tennant, Lord Lieutenant of Morayshire and a school governor; and whenever the Queen Mother was at Birkhall, her house on the Balmoral estate, she would take him home for the day. She was enthusiastic about taking her grandson out, but not always quite so punctual about bringing him back. On one occasion he was so late that he missed chapel, which was compulsory on a Sunday night. Bob Whitby remembers spotting the lonely figures of Charles and a friend standing in the dark outside his garage one Sunday night. 'I don't want to know,' he said. 'As far as I'm concerned you're in chapel.' This unaccustomed tenderness was because the Queen Mother had rung in person to apologize. 'I'm very sorry to have got them back late,' she said, 'but you know what grannies can be like.'

Yet again it was his grandmother standing *in loco parentis*. Charles seldom saw his parents during termtime, but he did keep in touch. Where most boys rang home, however – usually reversing the charges – Prince Charles wrote long, chatty, informative letters. He has kept up the practice to this day, always preferring to write to his friends rather than use the telephone – and good, witty letters they are too.

His sense of humour and delight in practical jokes became very low-key during those first two years in the school when he was so unhappy, but once he found his feet his confidence returned and with it his showmanship. He would mimic the masters and had caught the intonation of his housemaster to a tee. 'So much so,' says Bob Whitby, 'that he could put quite a fright up the other boys if they were doing something wrong. The one thing that struck me about his sense of humour was that it was always kind. It might bite a bit here and there,' he says, 'but he never set out to hurt or upset anyone. He really enjoyed making people laugh and he was the first to laugh at himself if someone succeeded in getting his own back.'

It was the time of the Goons, the popular radio show staring that now legendary team of comics Peter Sellers, Harry Secombe, Michael Bentine and Spike Milligan, and Prince Charles thought they were the funniest thing he had ever heard. He became quite obsessed by them, listening to every programme and acquiring tapes of them all, and could imitate to perfection every ridiculous rabbit and squirrel voice that they uttered. The Goons were his party piece, which he produced with or without encouragement, both then and for several years afterwards. The four comedians were his heroes, and meeting them, which he first did in his teens, was one of the high spots of his life. Spike Milligan remembers this first meeting at a party at Kensington Palace with the Queen and Princess Margaret. Charles was about fourteen, and much to Milligan's amazement every time Charles spoke to him it was with a perfect Goon voice.

Whenever Charles put on a comic voice like this, or acted in front of an audience – no matter what size – the awkwardness he showed in real life dropped away and he spoke with a new-found confidence and presence. For the first few years at Gordonstoun, however, he had to confine his thespian activities to the dormitory or the common room, because there had been no drama at the school for some time. However the arrival of Eric Anderson provided Charles with a new interest in life.

Anderson, now Head Master at Eton, had come to the school principally to teach English – an early step in a meteoric teaching career – but found himself with the task not only of reviving the literary life of Gordonstoun but also of producing school plays. The first one he decided to do was *Henry V*, in which Charles played the part of Exeter. With no established drama society to cast from, Eric Anderson simply put a notice on the board asking anyone interested in volunteering for the school play to put their name down; and amongst the surnames was one christian name: Charles. In the subsequent auditions he was quite noticeably the best, and quite obviously the one who should have played the king. Yet Anderson gave the part to someone else.

It was a perfect example of the sort of inverted snobbery that has dogged the Prince of Wales all his life. Mr Anderson's thinking went like this, and he admits that had it been any other boy he would have given him the part without hesitating. He was afraid that everyone would think he was giving Prince Charles the part just because it was him. He was also afraid of what would happen if he chose Charles and he failed to live up to the promise he had shown at his audition. That would be doing the boy no service at all. 'And being a cautious Scot,' he says, 'I gave him the Duke of Exeter. And he did it to the manner born.' The play, staged in the unheated Round Square, was a great success. People who had sat huddled in rugs with flasks of hot soup and whisky for the interval left saying, 'Marvellous production, but what a pity your best actor was playing the Duke of Exeter.'

Eric Anderson needed no further prompting. The next production he was planning was *Macbeth*, and he had no doubts at all about who should have the lead; but there was a problem. In January 1966 Prince Charles was due to take a term off to go to Australia to broaden his education and give him some experience of school in a Commonwealth country. If they were to use their best actor, therefore, the school play would have to be put on before Christmas, which meant finding somewhere else to stage it. The Round Square was not much fun in summer, but in midwinter it was out of the question.

The answer was the Services Centre, where the fire engines were garaged. There was an upper floor they could use, reached via steps which came up in the middle of the room, so it had to be theatre in the traverse, with the audience in two banks on either side of the staircase. It added a nice historical touch. King James I had once been to see a production of the play at Oxford University and he and his court had occupied one side of the stage while the rest of the audience sat opposite.

There was no such segregation when Queen Elizabeth II came to see this production. She was there more as a mother than as the sovereign, but delighted as he was that she was attending Eric Anderson was afraid the actors would all be so nervous that they would forget their lines. He was particularly worried about Charles. He need not have been. Mrs Anderson was helping backstage with the boys' costumes and make-up when the Queen and the Duke of Edinburgh arrived. As the royal entourage made their way up the stairs the audience rose to their feet and the school orchestra began playing 'God Save the Queen'.

'Oh dear,' said Prince Charles, 'I do feel for my mother. She'll be so nervous.'

He played the part better, Mr Anderson swears, than he has ever seen any other actor, amateur or professional, play it. He has seen better productions over the years, but never a better Macbeth. Charles instinctively understood the character. Macbeth was not simply a butcher, as some actors have portrayed him, but a tragic figure: a tower of strength in war, but in private a sensitive, poetic man with all the more feminine virtues, which by a twist of personality he is persuaded by his wife to drown. Eric Anderson discussed this interpretation of Macbeth with Charles at the beginning of rehearsals; he saw it at once, and produced to perfection the great sense of waste that is in the play.

Charles revelled in the poetry of Shakespeare. He had learnt his lines well before anyone else, he was always on time for rehearsals, and won the approval of the rest of the cast – plus a bit of teasing – by arranging for some deerskins to be sent over from Balmoral to decorate the set. When the costumes arrived and Macbeth's crown fell smartly over his ears, there was scarcely a voice that didn't ask why he didn't bring a better one from home.

Macbeth is traditionally an unlucky play. Actors are so superstitious about it that they never mention its name for fear of tempting fate, and Anderson's production was not without its problems. It was the night of the dress rehearsal. The director had just called 'Act I, Scene I, three witches please,' when the lights went out.

'Sorry,' said the man in charge of lights. 'Blown a fuse, won't be a moment.' More than a moment passed, and the actors began to feel uneasy in the pitch blackness. 'Sorry,' said the electrician again, sounding baffled. 'This isn't working. Something else must be wrong.'

At that point someone chanced to look out of a window, and discovered that the entire district was in darkness. A tree had fallen over the main power lines and half the county was without lights.

CHAPTER FIVE

Gordonstoun may have provided the mould that made the Prince of Wales into the man he is today, but it was the six months in Australia that cemented it. 'I took out a boy,' says Sir David Checketts, who travelled with the Prince, 'and I came back with a man.' Charles returned to Gordonstoun the following autumn transformed: confident, self-possessed and matured beyond measure, as everyone who knew him bears witness, but once again he had been through baptism by fire to achieve it.

This interruption in his schooling was imposed on him for several reasons, but principally because the Queen felt that as her son was heir to the throne not just of Great Britain, but also of the Commonwealth, she had a duty to entrust at least part of his education to one of its member countries. Since she had promised the Australian people, during her post-coronation tour of the Antipodes, that she would one day send her son to visit them, this seemed an ideal opportunity to kill two birds with one stone. The Australian Prime Minister, Sir Robert Menzies, was therefore consulted as to which school would be most suitable, and Prince Charles was duly despatched at the end of January 1966 to a remote settlement on the other side of the world.

He was seventeen, shy, awkward and deeply apprehensive about what lay ahead. It was the first time he had been abroad without a member of his family, and he did not much care for the sound of the place he was going to. His destination was Timbertop, an annexe to the prestigious Melbourne public school, Geelong Church of England Grammar School, where boys were sent for a year of character building and self-reliance in the Australian bush. It was nearly two hundred miles inland, on the slopes of the Timbertop mountains, and creature comforts were few and far between. Geelong itself, which is frequently called the

Eton of Australia, was not unlike Gordonstoun. A previous headmaster, Dr Darling had been a disciple of Kurt Hahn, and although there was not much scope for the Hahn regime in urban life a year spent in the outback amply made up for it. This appealed to the Duke of Edinburgh, who still thought that his eldest son could do with some toughening up.

The Prince was accompanied on this venture by Detective Inspector Derek Sharp, who had replaced Donald Green shortly after the cherry brandy episode, and Squadron Leader David Checketts, Prince Philip's equerry. Equerries are men who have been taken from active service in one of the armed forces and assigned to a member of the Royal Family for two or three years. Historically they were in charge of his or her horses (*écurie* is French for a stable); nowadays they organize the logistics of that person's life, reconnoitre visits, handle transport, work out timetables, deal with the press and generally oil the wheels.

In 1966 David Checketts was on the verge of leaving. At thirty-five he had been with the Duke of Edinburgh for five years and was keen to get back to the Royal Air Force. Prince Philip appealed to him to stay on for a few months longer, purely on a temporary basis, to keep an eye on Prince Charles at Timbertop. He and the Queen wanted Charles to have a home base in the country, and Checketts fitted the bill. Not only was he a family man, he already knew the country and some of the people there quite well; and from his years with Prince Philip he was skilled and experienced at the job. So he packed up his wife and young children and set up home in a house called Devon Farm, about 120 miles from Timbertop, where on weekends out Charles became one of the family.

His first weeks in Australia were difficult. Charles was the first Prince of Wales to have visited the country for forty-five years, and the enthusiasm of his reception was daunting. The press were everywhere, and threatening to be just as persistent as they were at home. David Checketts struck a deal: he allowed reporters and photographers complete access to the Prince on his first day at Timbertop, on condition that they left him well alone for the rest of the term. It did the trick. But the press was not the major hurdle that faced Prince Charles on foreign soil. More terrifying were the 135-odd boys, all fourteen- to fifteen-year-olds.

Australian teenagers were a tough bunch to be thrown

amongst. They had all of the schoolboy cruelty of their British counterparts, but none of their in-built deference to royalty. It would have been hard for any boy from England, but being Prince of Wales and arriving in such a blaze of publicity made his lot infinitely worse. Far from wanting to be able to say they were friends of the heir to the throne, which had so often been the case at home, their attitude was just who the hell does this boy think he is? And Australians are not famed for mincing their words.

Charles was in a difficult position in any case. He was not there as a pupil, although he had work set by Gordonstoun as part of his A level preparation. He was there as an assistant master, and he taught the boys English and constitutional history as well as accompanying them on their expeditions and forays into the wild. Stuart Macgregor, a boy of the same age who had recently left Geelong, had been brought in as an assistant master too, but he was really there to act as a companion – and one which at first Charles sorely needed.

He soon realized that the only way to survive amongst the mob was to stand up for himself and to fight back. This was not the place to be shy, and as time passed and the going became no easier he finally learnt how to deal with people – not prince to commoner, but man to man – how to mix with them, meet them on their own terms and handle confrontations. This is something that most ordinary children learn to do in kindergarten, but which because of his cloistered start in life, and because of the difficulties inherent in being Prince of Wales in Britain, he had never wholly mastered. The more he held his own, the more he began to earn their respect, until returning from a walk in the rain one night with a rolled umbrella under his arm he was greeted by a chorus of 'Pommy bastard!' That was when he knew he had made it.

From that time onwards he was popular with everyone in the school, and certain for the first and possibly the last time in his life that he was liked for himself, not for who he was. It was also the first time that he had been truly happy. The physical work was punishing and he missed home, but he saw life through new eyes and revelled in the community spirit, the freedom to wander at will with no one watching, and the challenge that every day presented. He wrote long, enthusiastic letters to his family and to friends at Gordonstoun, including his housemaster, Bob Whitby.

He also sent the school magazine an account of life at Timbertop, which he called 'Timbertop: or beating about the bush'.

> Almost everyone, masters and boys, enjoys themselves up here. One never seems to stop running here and there for one minute of the day, from 7.30 a.m. breakfast – and no morning run, though there's worse to follow – until the lights go out at 9.15 p.m., having had tea at the unearthly hour of 5.30. If you have done a cross-country at 4.45 p.m. and arrived back at 5.05 p.m., it's difficult to persuade your stomach to accept food.

The boys lived in timber huts and had to look after themselves and the school's smallholding in every respect. They had to feed the pigs, shear the sheep, clean the lavatories, empty the dustbins and stoke the boilers; if they forgot to chop any wood there was no hot water – it was as simple as that. It was a crash course in living back to nature, and for Australians, 80 per cent of whom live in cities, the experience was as much of a culture shock as it was for Prince Charles. 'The first week I was here,' he wrote, 'I was made to go out and chop up logs on a hillside in boiling hot weather. I could hardly see my hands for blisters.' His first attempt at sheep shearing was no easier. 'I made rather a mess of it, and left a somewhat shredded sheep.' But there was no doubt that he was quite the best fisherman in the place.

They were given projects like chopping down trees, planting more, conducting a butterfly or kangaroo census for the government conservation body, or delivering logs to war widows. Most afternoons they did a cross-country run; and at weekends they would go off on expeditions into the bush in parties of four, with a map, a compass, tents and two or more days' worth of supplies strapped to their backs. They cooked, slept and ate out in the open, and chose their sites with care, as Prince Charles recounted in the *Gordonstoun Record*.

> You virtually have to inspect every inch of the ground you hope to put your tent on in case there are any ants or other ghastly creatures. There is one species of ant called Bull Ants which are three quarters of an inch long, and they bite like mad! Some boys manage to walk fantastic distances over a weekend of four days or less, and do 130 or even 200 miles. The furthest I've been is 60–70 miles in three days, climbing about five peaks on the way. At the camp site the cooking is done on an open fire in a trench.

> You have to be very careful in hot weather that you don't start a bush fire, and at the beginning of this term there was a total ban in force, so that you ate all the tinned food cold.

On the rare occasions when he was not spending the weekend on foot he would go home to the Checketts' at Devon Farm, and delight in his reunion with creature comforts. He enjoyed being part of the family and was a very easy member of it, particularly with the children. They would go off on picnics together, or on fishing trips, shopping, or visiting friends and local landowners, where he might get the occasional game of polo.

The original plan had been for Charles to spend just one term at Timbertop. But when he discovered that he might get a chance to go to Papua New Guinea in the holidays, which he desperately wanted to do, he sought permission from his parents to stay on for a second term. Every year the headmaster took a party of thirty boys there to meet boys from the missionary schools on the island, with which Geelong had ties. It is a primitive country where the lingua franca is pidgin English, and where until not so very long ago the natives had been headhunters and cannibals. It was the first time Charles had encountered such a primitive society, and although his presence attracted a certain amount of publicity he found the experience fascinating. He said:

> We arrived at the entrance to the village and the drums stopped and the whole village was assembled there and for some unknown reason they suddenly started to sing 'God Save the Queen', and it was the most moving, touching thing I have ever experienced, I think, to see these people, miles from Britain, singing the National Anthem. And the tears practically rolled down my cheeks. It was the most wonderful occasion and I shall always remember that.

His interest in anthropology, which he subsequently read at Cambridge, was well and truly whetted by this trip. He was also very moved by the freshness and sincerity that he found among the Christians whom he encountered at an Anglican mission in Dogura. 'Everyone was so eager to take part in the services, and the singing was almost deafening. One felt that it might almost be the original Church. Where Christianity is new, it must be much easier to enter into the whole spirit of it whole-heartedly.'

Christianity was, of course, something that Prince Charles had grown up with. He had been to church regularly throughout his childhood, and the previous year he had been confirmed by the Archbishop of Canterbury, Michael Ramsey, in St George's Chapel, Windsor. One day, as heir to the throne, he would be Head of the Church of England; a belief in God and an acceptance of the teachings of the Church were fundamental to his existence. He did, nevertheless, have a genuine faith – one which has remained strong to the present day.

He had found particular solace in the church at Gordonstoun. Built in 1705, the tiny chapel called the Michael Kirk was set some distance from the main school buildings down a tree-lined avenue known as the Silent Walk, because no one was allowed to talk while walking down it. The Michael Kirk was a place apart, a place of peace and beauty in the wild and rugged countryside, and the one place where boys could escape the frantic physical activity going on in the rest of the school.

One other incident occurred during the Prince's six months away which had a significant effect on him and completed the transformation in his confidence. Charles discovered that he could talk to people: he discovered that the crowds that pressed against the barriers and jostled for the best view of him everywhere he went were not as terrifying as he had always thought. It happened at a small airport on the Gold Coast of Australia. Charles had been staying with Sid and Joyce Williams in Cairns, Northern Queensland, and on the way back to Melbourne in a little twin-engine transit plane they touched down at Coomangata to refuel. The stop took no longer than an hour, but the people of Coomangata had rolled out the red carpet. A little reception had been organized on the tarmac, a table surrounded by an awning was set up with drinks, and the mayor and his wife and all the local dignitaries were on parade to make their royal visitor welcome. Charles greeted them all warmly and stood chatting for a while, but soon ran short of conversation.

'I can't stand here doing this all day,' said Charles.

'Well, go and talk to the holidaymakers,' suggested David Checketts. Standing almost immediately behind this makeshift reception were hundreds of people dressed in shorts and bikinis, all waving and shouting out to the Prince.

'All right,' he said. He walked over to a group and took the plunge. . . . 'Where do you come from?' he asked.

'New South Wales.'

'Are you here with your wife? . . . Which one is she? . . . And are these your children? . . . Do you come here every year? . . .'

He suddenly discovered that by asking a simple question he had set up a dialogue, and ever since that day has found walking up to crowds of people – the thing that he had always dreaded – far easier than he had ever thought possible.

CHAPTER SIX

Charles returned to Gordonstoun for the autumn term in September 1966 a very much happier man. He had conquered his shyness, gained composure, and turned from an awkward, naïve teenager into a strong and confident young adult.

He returned in glory. In his absence Bob Whitby had decided to appoint him head of Windmill Lodge. 'I knew people would accuse me of favouritism,' says Mr Whitby, 'but too bad. I chose him because he was the outstanding candidate, although I don't think he ever believed that. But I was vindicated; he was one of the best heads of house I ever had.'

One of the incidents which earned him such praise was when two fifteen-year-old boys in the house found themselves in trouble with the police for robbing the village garage-cum-shop armed with a gun. The boys had stolen a set of keys from the school, then a rifle, and to speed them on their way had stolen Prince Charles's bicycle.

The crime was soon traced back to the boys, and the headmaster wanted to expel them. But such is the system at Gordonstoun that the most senior boys have a say in what goes on in the school, and as head of Windmill Lodge the Prince of Wales gave his opinion. Having spoken to the boys, whose fathers had by this time paid back the money they had stolen, he felt sorry for them, and felt they should have a chance to demonstrate that they had learned their lesson. So he went to Robert Chew and pleaded on their behalf. His pleas fell on deaf ears, however, for he had failed to appreciate the gravity of the crime, and the boys were expelled, but the headmaster was nevertheless impressed by the maturity with which Prince Charles argued his case and handled the whole business.

This was typical. Whenever boys came to him with a tale of

woe, or of some injustice committed by another boy, however clear-cut it might have appeared, however glaring the evidence, he would always insist upon hearing both sides of the story before making any kind of judgement. It was a wisdom that he had learned from his great-uncle, Lord Mountbatten, and Prince Charles is the same today. He is always prepared to listen to every side of the argument, even to people whose views he finds fundamentally disagreeable. Some would say he does it to a fault, but no one can accuse him of having a closed mind.

He was now in his A level year, continuing the work that he had begun in Australia. He had passed five O Levels before going, in English language, English literature, history, Latin and French, and finally added a sixth after retaking maths. He had chosen to go on and do French and history for A Level, which he passed with a C and a B – not exceptional grades, but perfectly respectable. Some of his teachers felt that, had he not had the interruption caused by two terms at Timbertop, he would certainly have done considerably better.

History was a special pleasure to him, and he is still an avid student. As well as the normal history classes which adhered to the A level course, taken by Bob Whitby and Robin Birley, he was given special lessons in constitutional history by Henry Brereton, the grand old man of Gordonstoun. A master since its inception, a friend of Kurt Hahn's and former headmaster, he was now warden, and knew the place and its history inside out.

Robert Chew not only saw it as his duty to arrange for the Prince of Wales to learn about the constitution, he also realized that he must do something about his public speaking. For whatever else Prince Charles went on to do with his life, one thing was certain: he would be called upon to make a great many speeches, and so far, apart from the acting, the school had done nothing to prepare him for the task. This had been particularly apparent in Australia, when on leaving for home he had written a short speech but given it to David Checketts to read out for him.

> It would be difficult to leave without saying how much I have enjoyed and appreciated my stay in Australia and how touched I have been by the kindness of so many people in making these six months such a worthwhile experience. The most wonderful part was the opportunity to travel and see at least some of the country (I hope I shall be able to come back and see the rest) and also the chance

> to meet so many people, which completes the link with a country I am very sad to be leaving. And yet I shall now be able to visualize Australia in the most vivid terms, after such a marvellous visit.

Eric Anderson, who had directed Charles in the school plays, was allotted the job of equipping him to deliver his own speeches. As with most young teachers, this was not something he knew a great deal about, but he set up a class for a dozen or so boys at the top of the school and it was in front of this select audience that the Prince of Wales delivered his first speech: two and a half minutes on the subject of polo. It was not a dazzling performance. Charles was desperately nervous and read the entire speech from his notes, but Eric Anderson was impressed nevertheless by his preparation. Prince Charles has become considerably more accomplished since then, and he has grown almost to enjoy public speaking, but he still suffers from agonizing nerves beforehand.

Charles frequently used to go with the rest of the family to watch his father play polo at Smith's Lawn in Windsor Great Park during the season, but it was not until he was sixteen that he had any desire to learn the game himself. He was encouraged to take it up not only by his father, who was a fiercely keen and able player, and wanted his son to enjoy it too, but also by Lord Mountbatten, who in his time had been a very good player and had written the definitive book on the subject. Mountbatten was becoming an increasing influence over Prince Charles, particularly since his retirement in 1965.

Louis, Earl Mountbatten of Burma, was a dynamic, tyrannical figure, full of energy and drive and wisdom, who aroused strong passions in everyone who came into contact with him. He was a national hero, he had been Supreme Commander in South East Asia during the Second World War, the last Viceroy and first Governor General of India, First Sea Lord, and finally Chief of the Defence Staff. He had spent twenty-three years at the top, he had travelled all over the world, he had stories and memories of escapades and people and was a colourful raconteur. Charles had been devoted to him ever since he was a small boy. He had spent holidays with him, at Sandringham and Balmoral and in Malta, and Uncle Dickie, as he was known by the whole family, was never out of touch for long.

Obsessed with the concept of the Royal Family, Mountbatten saw it as his role in life to keep it going as a healthy popular institution. He was one of Queen Victoria's great-grandchildren, like George VI, and as young men the two cousins had studied at Dartmouth Naval College together. Indeed, on the night when the former Edward VIII packed his bags and left for the continent, it was to Mountbatten that the new king turned.

'Dickie, this is absolutely terrible,' he said, close to tears. 'I'm only a naval officer, it's the only thing I know about.'

'That is a very curious coincidence,' replied Mountbatten, 'for my father once told me that, when the Duke of Clarence died, your father came to him and said almost the same thing that you have said to me now, and my father answered: "George, you're wrong. There is no more fitting preparation for a king than to have been trained in the Navy."'

The two families were close. Mountbatten's two daughters, Patricia and Pamela, and George VI's daughters, Princess Elizabeth and Princess Margaret, were playmates as children, so his place within the present Royal Family would have been ensured in any event. Yet there are closer ties. Prince Philip was Mountbatten's sister's child, and with no son of his own he took it upon himself to guide his nephew's future, to such an extent that Prince Philip has occasionally objected to the common assumption that the Mountbattens brought him up. 'I don't think anybody thinks I had a father,' he once remarked. 'Most people think that Dickie's my father anyway.' Prince Philip's real father lived in the South of France and had shown no real interest in his son's education, while his mother suffered from poor health; so it was Mountbatten who had steered Philip into the Navy rather than the Air Force, which he would have preferred, and, fiercely ambitious for the family, he was never more delighted than when his protégé married Princess Elizabeth. He then spent the next thirteen years agitating for the children of the marriage to bear their father's name in addition to that of Windsor, which they inherited from their mother, and when the name Mountbatten finally became hyphenated to Windsor in 1960 he was a happy man.

He continued to advise and guide Prince Philip over the years. His suggestions were not universally welcome, and not universally adopted, but he continued undeterred. When the Duke of Windsor once wrote to Mountbatten to complain that his nephew had visited Paris without getting in touch with him, which he considered to be extremely bad manners, Mountbatten wrote to Prince Philip and promised to raise the subject again when they met at Sandringham, but he had no illusions that it would do any good. Yet occasionally his nephew did listen. The day after Sir Winston Churchill's death, for example, Prince Philip planned to shoot. Mountbatten said he thought it was ill advised, but his nephew was determined. 'Well, I won't anyway,' said Mountbatten, and the shoot was called off.

He was quite free with his advice to the Queen too, often urging her towards a course of action. Fond though she was of him, she was aware that his understanding of what could or should be done in a constitutional monarchy was not foolproof, and however convincing he sounded, however sure of himself, it was not safe to follow his advice blindly. On the question of Prince Charles's future, however, his thoughts were positively sought. In December 1965, soon after Mountbatten's retirement, the Queen summoned a conference at Windsor Castle to discuss where the Prince of Wales should go when he finished at Gordonstoun. The people gathered round her dining table included the Prime Minister, Harold Wilson; the Archbishop of Canterbury, Michael Ramsey; the chairman of the Committee of University Vice-Chancellors, Sir Charles Wilson; and Earl Mountbatten. After dinner Harold Wilson suggested they should hear what Mountbatten had to say. 'Ma'am, Dickie has not spoken yet,' he said. 'Can we have his opinion?' It was his opinion, in the end, that came to be adopted.

'Trinity College like his grandfather, Dartmouth like his father and grandfather, and then to sea in the Royal Navy ending up with a command of his own.'

Mountbatten now had time to turn his attention and considerable wisdom to preparing Prince Charles for the way ahead. The two had a great affinity for one another, also vast affection, and because of the generation gap there were none of the tensions that existed between father and son. Charles referred to him as his 'Honorary Grandfather' and relished the time spent in his company. He was a frequent visitor to Broadlands, Mountbatten's home in Hampshire, where the two would spend long hours talking. Mountbatten was an enthusiastic shot and Charles a willing pupil. They were both keen fishermen and lovers of the countryside: and Charles found that he could talk to Mountbatten more freely than to anyone else.

In his second term back from Australia, Prince Charles was made head of school, or guardian as it is called at Gordonstoun;

he moved out of Windmill Lodge and into a room in Bob Waddell's flat in the Round Square. After the usual pop music that came from most boys' rooms at full bore the art master was pleasantly surprised to hear serious music – symphonies and concertos – filtering from beneath his lodger's door. Not only was he listening to music, he had started to sing in the school choir; some of his most memorable performances were in Benjamin Britten's *St Nicholas*, Elgar's *Dream of Gerontius*, and Bach's B Minor Mass. Charles loved singing and went on to join the Bach Choir at Cambridge, and even kept it up after he had left. On a lighter note, he made his final appearance on the Gordonstoun stage as the Pirate King in the Gilbert and Sullivan opera *The Pirates of Penzance*. But he never had the chance to play comedy, which he badly wanted to do. That had to wait until Cambridge.

Charles had done well at Gordonstoun, and although he had been miserable for a long time there, latterly he had enjoyed much of what it provided. He had appreciated the beauty of the surrounding countryside, the skiing trips in the Cairngorms and the fishing in the local lochs and rivers. He had enjoyed his pottery, his acting and his music, and he had made lasting friends with a number of teachers and a handful of boys. Nevertheless he was delighted to see the back of the place. He was now eighteen and ready for a bit of freedom. The six months at Timbertop had provided a taste of it, and that, followed by an extended journey home via the West Indies and America, had given him an even greater sense of frustration at being bound by school discipline.

Looking back, though, he admitted he was glad to have gone to the school.

> It was the character of the general education there – Kurt Hahn's principles; an education which tried to balance the physical and mental with the emphasis on self-reliance to develop a rounded human being. I did not enjoy school as much as I might have, but that was because I am happier at home than anywhere else. But Gordonstoun developed my will-power and self-control, helped me to discipline myself, and I think that discipline, not in the sense of making you bath in cold water, but in the Latin sense – giving shape and form and tidiness to your life – is the most important thing your education can do.

He was a convert. He had in fact met Kurt Hahn during his time at the school, which had greatly enhanced his conversion. He had been particularly keen to meet the school's founder, not only to find out for himself what this man who had him out running half naked before breakfast was really like, but also because he was curious to meet the man who had been his father's headmaster, and who had inspired Prince Philip and dozens of other people to speak about him with almost religious fervour. The two met for tea one afternoon at Dr Hahn's sister-in-law's house, Burnside Lodge. Hahn was nearly eighty by then, and growing ever more eccentric. The stories about him were legion. There was the curious hat he always wore, and his habit of absent-mindedly chewing his handkerchief, his lapel or anything that came to hand; or of running with a hockey stick, shouting, 'Always say to yourself when you are up against a more formidable opponent than yourself Homer's memorable words, "You have suffered worse than this and triumphed at last."' And it was well known that he would frequently invite three people for breakfast, sit them in separate rooms – none knowing the others were there – sit down and begin the meal with one, then make some excuse, move on to the next room, sit and eat for a while and converse, make an excuse again, and move on to the third for his third plate of bacon and eggs, and so it went on. He saw Prince Charles, however, quite on his own, and Charles, who was then fifteen, came away impressed.

Hahn's influence ran deep, and the Prince of Wales's preoccupation with the young today can be traced almost directly back to him. He felt great anxiety about the state of the young. As Dr Lancelot Fleming, a lifelong friend, said of him on his death in 1974, he saw the young exposed to a series of decays: 'The decay of fitness, the decay of self-discipline, the decay of enterprise and adventure, the decay of skill and care that goes to make the craftsman, and, most shattering of all, the decay of compassion.' He attributed these decays to defective education, concerned 'too exclusively with the transmission of knowledge . . . than with the development of character which is basic and fundamental'. The sacred purpose of education was to 'arrest these decays, to restore, to defend, to develop human strength in the young'.

His method was not to preach at the young, which he described as a 'hook without a worm', nor to coerce their opinions, which he said is of the Devil; but to impel them into experiences which would draw out their innate strength and to show them that they were needed. 'He who drills and labours and encounters dangers and difficulties all to be ready to save his brother in peril,' said Dr Hahn, 'he experiences God's purpose in his inner life.'

A more pithy line frequently on his lips was: 'Human nature is very prevalent.' He believed in the good in man, and in particular in the capacity of the young to produce their best when confronted by the challenge of responsibility for others. 'If you do not believe in a boy,' he would say, 'then you have no right to educate him.'

It was this belief in the good in man and the means by which it could be drawn out that Prince Charles took away with him from Gordonstoun. In all his charitable works, which in recent years have principally been with the young, he has never handed over money as an answer to people's problems. He has always made sure there was a worm on the hook, and as a result there are dozens of disadvantaged young people about who have been impelled into experiences they would never have thought possible in their wildest dreams, and who have discovered the truth of the Gordonstoun motto: '*Plus est en vous*'; you've got more in you than you think.

CHAPTER SEVEN

One of the guests who had sat in consultation around the Queen's dinner table that December evening in 1965 to decide the Prince of Wales's future, had been Dr Robin Woods, the Dean of Windsor. Lord Mountbatten had suggested that the next step should be Trinity College, Cambridge, where Charles's grandfather, George VI, had been educated, but it was Dr Woods who was charged with the task of sounding out Trinity to see if it was indeed the most suitable college for Charles.

Trinity had a new Master that year in the splendid and famous figure of Lord 'Rab' Butler, 'the best Prime Minister Britain never had'. After twenty-five years at the top, with posts including Chancellor of the Exchequer, Leader of the House of Commons, Home Secretary and deputy Prime Minister, he had twice missed the top job by a whisker, and had finally retired from the political fray to spend his days immersed in his second great love, scholarship, at his old university. Rab was wise, erudite and immensely well read; he was a distinguished elder statesman, a liberal Conservative and well known to the Queen. She could not hope for a better man to whom to entrust her son.

The Prince was very keen to go to Cambridge, partly because of the history and beauty of the place, with the River Cam winding past the ancient buildings and picturesque quadrangles, partly because it was something of a family tradition, and partly because he already had friends there. There was Edward Woods, the Dean's son, and Sibella Dorman, whose father, Sir Maurice Dorman, was Governor General of Malta. And so, amid much muttering that Charles should not have been allowed into Cambridge on two A Levels when ordinary people needed three, he became the first Prince of Wales to attend university as a normal student and to follow the normal honours degree course. Previous members of the Royal Family who had been to

Cambridge had lived out of town in mansions with their own staffs, and the college tutors came to them.

Rab Butler pooh-poohed the criticism as quite unjustified. 'The boy has great gifts, great gifts,' he said in an interview with Ann Leslie of the *Daily Mail*. 'I think he's really very clever, even more so than his parents.' Butler might have made a good Prime Minister, but he would have been a terrible diplomat. He went on:

> Quite frankly, you know, the Queen and the Duke are not university people – they're horsy people, commonsense people. The Queen is one of the most intelligent women in England and brilliant in summing up people, but I don't think she's awfully interested in books. You never see any lying about her room when you go there, just newspapers and things like that. Whereas Prince Charles has a tremendous affinity for books – they really mean something to him.

His remarks may not have gone down well at Buckingham Palace, but they were spot on; and during the Prince of Wales's time at Trinity Rab Butler made sure that the promise he saw in Charles was nurtured and channelled in the right direction. He became the young Prince's new friend, adviser and confidant.

'He'd often come up to my study in the evening,' said Butler, 'and we'd sit here and discuss politics very frankly and I'd tell him who was a bloody fool and who wasn't, and I'd explain things about the Constitution to him and tell him all about the part he'd have to play. Oh yes, we enjoyed ourselves enormously and got on very well. He's a tremendously cheerful chap, you know.'

It was once again a case of Prince Charles finding friendship in an older man, and Butler's influence on Prince Charles at the time was strong. He did make friends with his contemporaries at the university, but not as quickly as most other people. Once again he was dogged by the difficulties of inverse snobbery. Those people who came forward were offering friendship for the very worst reasons, while the nicer people held back for fear of being accused of ingratiating themselves; and for a while, therefore, he was quite lonely.

Nevertheless Charles enjoyed his years at Cambridge, and looks back on them with great affection and nostalgia. University was his first real taste of freedom. He had been an object of intense curiosity when he arrived, and crowds had gathered to greet him, but he soon became just another student and was able, more or less, to behave like one. He had a detective, of course, known to the general population as Oddjob after the character in the James Bond films, but the detective kept a low profile and Prince Charles was able to ride about the town on his bicycle, attend lectures and tutorials, bury himself in the library, eat and drink in the pubs and cafés around, and join the various clubs and societies that interested him. He took no side, expected no favours, and none was given in return.

There were 650 students attached to Trinity, and like everyone else living in college he had private rooms, although they were admittedly rather more spacious than most people's, equipped and decorated by a team of handimen despatched from Sandringham, and with a few perks such as his own telephone and little kitchen. The result was that Prince Charles could make coffee and cook with slightly more sophistication than most students, whose repertoire was limited by having no more than a kettle and a gas fire. Oddjob had a room next door, but both shared a bathroom with other students on the same staircase. Privacy was something which Prince Charles cherished, and which he had sorely missed at Gordonstoun. Much as he enjoyed company, he needed to be alone at times, as he still does today, and sharing sleeping quarters was never an enjoyable experience.

In that first year at Cambridge Charles read archaeology and anthropology. Although history might have seemed the obvious subject for him to study, he had decided against it, largely as a result of the interest in primitive peoples sparked off in Papua New Guinea. Lord Butler had encouraged it – keen for the Prince to have some fun before he knuckled down to the finer points of the British constitution, and his senior tutor at Trinity, Dr Denis Marrian, had suggested that if he wanted to switch to history after the first year he could do so. Thus archaeology and anthropology it was, and the Prince had a fascinating first year. He had a particularly inspiring archaeology tutor in Dr Glyn Daniel, who in the first spring vacation organized a marvellous trip to the Dordogne region of France; the area is renowned for its cuisine and its caves, both of which they explored to the full. On returning home via Jersey, where they stopped to take part in a dig, Prince Charles declared that it had been not only a megalithic tour but a megalithic eating experience too.

Also in the party were Charles's director of studies, Dr John Cole, his detective and David Checketts, who was now officially acting as equerry to the Prince. On their return from Australia David Checketts had been persuaded by the Duke of Edinburgh to stay on to look after the Prince of Wales. Hitherto any business that needed attending to on his behalf had been handled by Prince Philip's office, but now that he was beginning to play a part in public life, albeit a small one, he was attracting correspondence and needed a permanent aide of his own. David Checketts was the ideal man for the job: he not only had experience from his years with the Duke, but he and the Prince had become good friends during their time in Australia.

In his last year at Gordonstoun Charles had turned eighteen, a significant milestone in his life. It was the age at which he would have been able to reign as King in his own right, without a regent, had any misadventure befallen the Queen; and the age at which he became qualified to act as the senior Councillor of State in place of the sovereign when she travelled abroad. As such he could have conducted a meeting of the Privy Council, given the royal assent to parliamentary bills, made peace or declared war.

He had done none of that, but he had started to adopt a higher profile and was already growing well aware of the duty and responsibility that rested on him. In the autumn of 1966 tragedy struck the Welsh mining village of Aberfan when more than a hundred people, mostly children, were killed by a mountain of slag that engulfed the village school. On his own initiative Prince Charles, as Prince of Wales, composed a message of condolence. He attended his first State Opening of Parliament of 1967, he flew to Melbourne to represent the Queen at the funeral of the Australian Prime Minister, Harold Holt. Closer to home, he was at Sir Winston Churchill's funeral, and during his first summer at Cambridge he had played host with his mother at his first Buckingham Palace garden party.

These interruptions were a small foretaste of the life to come, but for the most part Prince Charles was left to live and study in peace. He played polo at Cambridge, winning a half blue in a match at the end of his first year. He sang in the college Madrigal Society; he played the cello in the Trinity orchestra; he learnt to fly an aeroplane and made his first solo flight; he wrote a piece about life at Trinity for the twenty-first birthday edition of the student newspaper *Varsity*; he joined the Dryden Society, Trinity's drama club; and he finally achieved his ambition to play comedy on stage with the famous university revue group, the Footlights.

Not surprisingly, his various appearances on stage were a box office sensation. People queued for hours to watch the heir to the throne stand on the receiving end of a custard pie, to see him sit in a dustbin, stand beneath an umbrella saying, 'I lead a sheltered life', or setting off in pursuit of a pretty girl with the immortal line, 'I like giving myself heirs.' This typical brand of risqué student humour, which Charles himself described as 'an awful sort of *Beyond the Fringe*-type show full of the most awful sort of groan jokes', attracted as much publicity as a world premiere in the West End of London. The critics approved, the Goon-like voices went down well, and because he set himself up bravely as an object of fun, and demonstrated that he was no prude, Prince Charles's standing amongst his peers rose no end. In one sketch he played the part of a BBC weather forecaster. 'It is 06.00 hours,' he announced. 'Virility will at first be poor. Promiscuity will be widespread. The naval review at Portsmouth will be warm and sunny – so there will be no cold navels. Listeners are advised to avoid falling barometers and on funday and boozeday there will be bold and rowdy conditions.'

Prince Charles was and still is, however, an extremely moral and religious man, and fundamentally conservative. His personal conduct was always restrained and above reproach. He never even flirted with rebellion. He drank, but never too much; he had girlfriends, but always treated them well; he swore, but never offensively; he told jokes, but never obscene ones; he broke university rules, but never serious ones; and such was the sense of duty already deeply entrenched in him that throughout his years at Cambridge he never behaved in any way that could be a discredit to his family.

Charles chose his friends carefully and warily, sticking in the main to the ex-public school fraternity, with whom he had most in common. Some were well connected, others the offspring of professional families, and there was one, whom Prince Charles was always quick to cite in defence of the charge that he only ever mixed with the public school brigade, who was the son of a Welsh non-conformist minister. He and Hwyel Jones shared the same floor at Trinity, but not the same politics. This was the first time that Prince Charles had had the opportunity of meeting a staunch left-winger – most of whose friends and relations had been either railwaymen or miners – and he was intrigued to discover what a boy from the Welsh valleys, who had read Marx at fourteen and appeared to be destined for politics, thought and why. The two would sit up drinking coffee way into the night, and as ever Charles would do most of the listening.

He was also, as ever, turned by eloquent argument. He sympathized with much of what he heard, and even went to Lord Butler to sound him out about joining the University Labour Club. Rab quickly reminded the Prince about the dangers of aligning himself to any political party, and it was a lesson that he has never forgotten. His interest in politics has remained peripheral. He has had sympathies with the Labour Party, while enjoying the lifestyle and fundamental beliefs of the Conservatives, and it was only in recent years with the emergence of the Social Democrat Party, and Dr David Owen, whom he admires perhaps most among current politicians, that he has come close to finding any political home for himself.

At the end of his first year at Cambridge Charles sat the Part I Tripos examinations, and was awarded an upper second: a good, solid result, won entirely on merit and hard work, which no one could sneer at or put down to favouritism. It meant a great deal to the Prince of Wales to know that for once he had taken his chances and been treated like anybody else. He had been through so much of his life feeling that paths were opened for him and honours bestowed because of who he was and not because of what he was. He felt he was at Cambridge under false pretences – and he felt it more acutely than any of the student bodies who had protested so vehemently about his place the year before. The feeling of being unduly favoured is still with him today. It is one of the most crippling obstacles to his emotional confidence, and one of the hardest to conquer.

It is not that he is unique in being treated differently from the rest of us. Famous people are all treated differently. Doors that are closed to everyone else open for them, crowds gather round to stare at them, gifts are showered on them, queues vanish for them, life is made much easier. But famous people are usually famous because of something they have done in their life. Prince Charles is famous for no better reason than that he is the Prince of Wales. He has done nothing to earn it; it is an accident of birth. He cannot feel he has deserved special treatment, he cannot feel proud of his achievements, because the adulation is there whatever he does or does not do. He has found this the most difficult of all the challenges presented to him, and his need to try to find a way of earning that adulation explains why he went in for so many dangerous activities throughout his youth: to prove to himself, if no one else, that there was more to him than his name.

Another major problem is that during his formative years he led a confusing kind of schizophrenic existence. He was exposed to trials and tribulations that no normal child ever begins to experience. Whenever he began to settle down in any one place or any one role, he was uprooted and thrust into another. One minute he was expected to behave and be treated like any normal human being, and the next he would be whisked away to perform some ceremonial duty, with the aloofness that his position as heir to the throne required of him. They were worlds apart.

Within days of winning his upper second at Cambridge, for example, he was dressed up in the most extravagant robes and plumed hat to be invested with the Order of the Garter, the oldest surviving order of European chivalry, at Windsor Castle. His photograph was on every newspaper in Britain as he walked in procession alongside figures like Earl Mountbatten, Viscount Alexander of Tunis and Viscount Montgomery of Alamein, proudly bearing the motto 'Honi soit qui mal y pense' (Evil be to him who evil thinks), which has been borne by members of the Royal Family since King Edward III first uttered the homily more than six hundred years ago. Two weeks later Prince Charles was sunning himself, sailing and water-skiing off the coast of Malta, like any tourist.

He and Princess Anne, accompanied by his detective and David Checketts, had flown out to the island to spend a week with the Dormans at the Governor's Palace. It was an ideal holiday spot. The Royal Family had spent a lot of time in Malta over the years, first when the Duke of Edinburgh had been based there, subsequently with the Mountbattens, and they were very fond of the island. David Checketts also knew it well, having lived there for the first two years of his married life. The Governor's house was comfortable and secluded with gardens and a swimming pool, and in addition Charles and Sibella were good friends.

Prince Charles had a number of girlfriends while he was at Cambridge, but the relationships were mostly platonic. Not a natural womanizer, he was far more likely to present a girl with some hideous practical joke – like the envelope he gave to one which exploded with rubber bands when she opened it – than a single red rose. Like most public schoolboys who have been cloistered in an all-male preserve for five years of their adolescence he was awkward with the opposite sex, unsure of himself, and had never had much opportunity to overcome his diffidence. His peers could practise and make fools of themselves in anonymity. He could never be anonymous.

Unlike many a public schoolboy, however, Charles respected women as people, not merely as objects for indulging sexual fantasies. His was a matriarchal family, after all. His father was a strong man, and aggressively masculine, but it was his mother and grandmother who ultimately held the power; and Charles had spent his early years almost exclusively in the company of women. The result was that he always enjoyed their company and never underestimated their intelligence.

That is not to say that their looks or their attractions passed him by. In his second year at Cambridge he helped pick the new rag queen. This is an age-old tradition in many English universities and rag week, when students raise money for charity by doing outlandish pranks, is one long party and one of the high spots of the academic calendar. The rag queen reigns for a year, and once rag week is over, she has the task of opening fetes and exhibitions, kicking off at rugby matches and generally acting as the glamour girl of the university. Sitting alongside Charles at Peterhouse, which was hosting the judging that year, were the previous incumbent, Priscilla Chadwick, and the senior college tutor. The girls paraded before them in the mini-skirts that were in fashion then, and Charles was not at all shy about casting his vote for the prettiest. The winner was five feet ten and blonde, and seemed to be more than half leg – not unlike the girl he finally chose for himself – and everyone made a great deal of capital out of the Prince of Wales crowning his queen.

Priscilla was a theology student at Girton, a friend of Sibella's and one of a nucleus of about fifteen people who formed the group with whom Prince Charles mixed. The Professor of Divinity at that time was Donald MacKinnon, the man on whom the main character in Tom Stoppard's play *Jumpers* was based and who led lively discussions on religion and spiritual philosophy. Another man at Trinity responsible for cementing Prince Charles's own personal beliefs was the Reverend Harry Williams, a Fellow of the college who had written several lively and provocative books including *Objections to Christian Belief* and *The God I Want*. Charles had read both, and like several of his friends was thoroughly inspired by both the man and his writing. Williams left Cambridge in 1969 to join the Community of the Resurrection in Yorkshire, but Prince Charles has kept in touch, as he has with so many of the people who have crossed his path and left their mark.

Prince Charles also left Cambridge that year – to spend the summer term at the University of Wales in Aberystwyth, an experience he was facing with a certain amount of dread. It was designed to give him some knowledge of the principality and an understanding of its people, culture and language in preparation for his investiture as Prince of Wales at Caernarvon Castle in July.

His welcome as an Englishman in Wales was not guaranteed to be warm. The Welsh had felt bitter about the English, and English princes in particular, for centuries, and with some justification; the ruined castle at Caernarvon was a constant reminder of the wrongs they had suffered at the hands of their neighbours. By no means every Welshman felt hostile, but Welsh nationalism had gained considerable momentum in recent years. The main nationalist party, Plaid Cymru, had won an election in Carmarthen not long before and now had a Member of Parliament, Gwynfor Evans, installed at Westminster; and the Welsh language was being introduced into schools and broadcasting. Gradually life was changing, but there were other groups, like the Welsh Language Society and the Free Wales Army, for whom the change was neither radical enough nor quick enough. They were said to be training freedom fighters in the mountains, and certainly caches of gelignite and machine guns were found shortly before the Prince's arrival at the university.

It had been announced two years previously that the investiture would take place on 1 July, thus fulfilling the Queen's promise made back in 1958, when she had created Charles Prince of Wales, that she would present her son to the Welsh at Caernarvon when he was grown up. It was also announced that the occasion would be a lavish one for which £200,000 of taxpayers' money had been allotted. This, particularly at a time of considerable financial hardship in the country, gave rise to objections and criticism from several quarters; and the entire concept gave the extremists the opportunity they wanted. Even the more moderate supporters of nationalism now had a focus for their grievances. They called it 'a piece of English trickery', and meticulously went about the countryside defacing English language road signs and scrawling revolutionary Welsh slogans on walls and bridges.

Once again, Prince Charles was the fall-guy. He arrived in Aberystwyth like a lamb to the slaughter, nervous about the reception he would find but quite unprepared for such blatant and naked hostility. It was the first time he had encountered such anger, and his guide, host and adviser in all things Welsh, the Secretary of State for Wales, George Thomas (now Lord Tonypandy), who was in charge of the investiture, was in no hurry to shield him from it. The wily Welshman realized that if the term at Aberystwyth was to serve any useful purpose Charles should not be molly-coddled. He needed to learn the facts of life – and although George Thomas knew he was throwing him in at the deep end there were no better people to learn from than young and articulate anti-royalists. If the Prince of Wales was ever going to survive, he had to win them over.

Mr Thomas had not been in favour of sending Prince Charles to Aberystwyth. He thought it patronizing to Wales and unnecessarily provocative, but once the decision had been taken he had given it his full support, despite almost weekly threats to his own life. Once, when he was due to stand outside Cardiff City Hall in support of the Lord Mayor taking the salute at a procession, he received an anonymous letter which said that he would be able to walk to the City Hall but would have to be carried away. His eighty-eight-year-old mother was constantly woken in the middle of the night by threatening telephone calls; and when he drove into Caernarvon in the run-up to the investiture two burly men leaned in through his open car window and spat the word '*Bradwyr*' (traitor) at him.

Shortly before Charles's term at Aberystwyth was due to begin it seemed that the whole exercise might be in jeopardy. In great secrecy George Thomas had been sent a handwritten letter by the principal of Aberystwyth College, Dr Tom Parry, expressing grave fears about the current atmosphere in the town and indicating that he could not accept responsibility for the safety of the Prince. Thomas showed the letter to the Prime Minister, Harold Wilson, who said he would have to advise the Queen, and asked the Secretary of State for his opinion. He said he thought the Prince should go. If he could not go to Aberystwyth, there would clearly be no investiture, and he felt it would be terrible if there was any part of the United Kingdom which had to be declared closed to a member of the Royal Family.

In the event the Chief Constable of Caernarvonshire was confident he could deal with the situation and ensure the Prince's safety, and so the plans went ahead, but no one was more aware of the danger the Prince was in throughout his time in Wales than George Thomas. And no one was more impressed by the courage he displayed during that time. On one occasion they had struggled through a crowd of protesters to the safety of the Welsh Office, and looking down at them through the window of the Secretary of State's office the Prince announced that he was going out to talk to them.

'I would advise against it, sir,' said Thomas.

'I know you would,' said Prince Charles, 'but I'm going.'

'In that case, sir, I'm coming with you.'

He repeatedly took risks. Instead of ignoring students who were penned in behind security barriers, angrily shouting abuse and waving placards, Prince Charles would go over to talk to them, to try and find out what they really thought. Sometimes he was disappointed – they simply swore at him and he had to give up his efforts. But time and again the effect was disarming; and the genuine humility, humour and sheer vulnerability of the man, which came across when he talked one-to-one, won him support from the most unlikely people.

His greatest feat of all, however, came at the end of May, when after only six weeks of studying the language he stood up in front of five thousand people at the Welsh League of Youth Eisteddfod at Aberystwyth and made a speech, in Welsh, that he had prepared entirely on his own. His reception was tumultuous and won approval from even the most hardened nationalists. Gwynfor Evans MP, president of Plaid Cymru, admitted, 'His performance was amazing. I have never heard anyone who has taken to Welsh so recently master the language so well.' Charles had undermined his fiercest opponents by tackling them with their own weapons.

It had been the ultimate test, and he was not among friends. The League had already declared its intention not to attend the investiture, on the grounds that it was 'not going to help a political stunt'. Before he could even begin his speech about a hundred extremists had climbed on chairs and begun jeering, scuffles and fights had broken out in the audience, and dozens of people had

had to be dragged away by the police. Prince Charles was undaunted. He spoke calmly and confidently for seven minutes, and won roars of applause for a side-swipe at the satirical song 'Carlo', a derogatory name they used for him. It had been topping the Welsh charts since his arrival, and the first verse went as follows.

> I have a friend who lives in Buckingham Palace,
> And Carlo Windsor is his name.
> The last time I went round to his house
> His mother answered the door and said:
> 'Carlo, Carlo, Carlo is playing polo today,
> Carlo is playing polo with his Daddy.'
> So come all ye serfs of Wales
> And join in the chorus:
> At last you have a Prince in this land of song.

Asked in an interview shortly afterwards what he had gained from his experience at Aberystwyth, and whether he sympathized with the protesters, he said he disagreed with the violence. 'I am very suspicious of mobs and mob influence . . . because I think the effect they can have on the individual is so dangerous. You can lose yourself in a crowd and you become literally like a sheep. You just go wherever they go: you would never believe what you could say or do.' But he understood their feelings. There was, he had realized, a difference between the Welsh and the English character.

> I think the extraordinary thing about Welshmen is that they have this radical tradition – they are radically traditional and traditionally radical, and this is a curious paradox.
>
> And I think there is a certain amount to be said for Wales having been neglected by a central government – it is on the fringes, and this has led to a certain depressed feeling, I think, and perhaps a slight inferiority complex, I am not sure.
>
> At the same time, in Wales, as a result of the union with England, the upper strata of society moved off to England, and, as it were, relinquished their responsibilities towards the ordinary person.
>
> As a result the people of Wales have established their own culture, their own folk culture, their own music, eisteddfods and folk dancing. Everything like that is

> unique to Wales. This is an essential part of the Welsh character. England has not got anything like this. And if something is unique and special, I think it's well worth preserving.

But he did not dodge the question of violence. In another speech in those days leading up to the investiture – this time while receiving the freedom of Cardiff on behalf of the Regiment of Wales, of which he had just become colonel-in-chief – he said,

> A greater interest in the language and ideals of Welsh culture is being taken by increasing numbers of people, but at the same time tensions tend to build up between Welsh speakers and non-Welsh speakers, who feel themselves, quite rightly, as much a part of Wales as any other Welshman.
>
> It would be more than tragic if these tensions were allowed to build up to too great a degree outside as well as inside Wales.
>
> Tolerance and patience are what are needed, the simple effort to try to understand the other person's point of view and his idealism, and not to condemn it outright.

Edward Millward, lecturer in Welsh language and literature – also vice-president of Plaid Cymru – who had taught the Prince of Wales during his time at Aberystwyth, had done a good job and provided him with a valuable understanding of nationalist aims, ideas and policies, without giving an inch of ground. Charles promised that in future, in the course of visiting various countries, he would 'talk about Wales and spread ideas about Wales that will make people want to visit the country, take an interest in it and perhaps invest in it, but also take an interest in England, to help with various aspects of England and the United Kingdom'.

He had gone a long way to wooing the Welsh; his popularity had grown fast, but the violence was not at an end yet. There were fifteen bomb attacks before the investiture was over, the last one on the morning of 1 July itself, which was to have repercussions for years to come.

CHAPTER EIGHT

The resentment felt by the Welsh towards English Princes of Wales had its origins back in the thirteenth century. For hundreds of years before that there had been native princes in Wales. They had often fought against each other, and sometimes a king had emerged to unite them, such as Hywel the Good and Gruffydd ap Llewelyn; but the common enemy had been the English, whom they had driven out with repeated success. Then in 1267 they made a treaty with the English king, Henry II, called the Treaty of Montgomery, by which Henry granted the Welsh leader, Llewelyn ap Gruffydd, the title of Prince of Wales.

The two could never agree how the terms of the treaty should be carried out, however. Llewelyn did not pay homage easily, and in March 1282 he went to war against Edward I. In December Llewelyn the Last, as he is fondly remembered, was captured and beheaded; the head was crowned with ivy and placed on a tower in London. He was the last Welshman ever to bear the title of Prince of Wales. Edward abolished Wales as an independent state and proclaimed five Welsh counties which would all come under the King's dominion. A year later he tried Llewelyn's brother, David, in Shrewsbury, and found him guilty of breach of fealty, because he held Crown lands. For this he was hanged, drawn, and quartered.

With his opponents taken care of, Edward borrowed money and embarked on one of the biggest and most costly castle-building projects in history. One of those he built was Caernarvon on the north-west coast, which cost in the region of £19,000 in 1283 when craftsmen were paid less than 2p for a ten-hour working day.

All the while the Welsh seethed, and the chieftains clamoured for a native prince to take the place of their own dead leaders. So in

1284, according to legend, Edward struck a deal: if they would undertake to keep the peace, he declared, he would give them a Welsh-born prince who spoke no English. Having secured their agreement, he then produced the son to whom his wife Eleanor had just given birth at Caernarvon Castle, and holding the naked child aloft from a window presented him to the Welsh. 'See,' he is reputed to have said, 'a prince born in Wales who could speak never a word of English.'

Edward did not actually create his son Prince of Wales until 1301, when he also conferred on him the earldom of Chester, which borders on Wales. The legend is probably untrue, but the entire episode has remained a source of bitterness amongst certain sections of the Welsh ever since, and many still regard Llewelyn the Last as the last legitimate Prince of Wales.

Since then only one Prince of Wales has been born in Wales. That was Henry of Monmouth, born in 1386, who became King Henry V. Henry Tudor, who became Henry VII, brought Welsh blood into the Royal Family, but he was never Prince of Wales. In fact, such is the nature of European monarchy that only four Princes of Wales have been the offspring of English-born parents. Thirteen have succeeded to the throne, six have died before succeeding, and one, the Old Pretender James, spent his life in exile. Few have had anything to do with Wales; and in over six hundred years only one had been invested in the Principality. That was the future Edward VIII, who was invested at Caernarvon in 1911. Extraordinary as it may seem, the remainder had been appointed unceremoniously in England.

It was the Liberal politician, David Lloyd George, who was responsible for the future Edward VIII being invested at Caernarvon. He was the town's MP, and a famous enemy of inherited privilege, yet he conceived the idea of transforming the ceremony into a Welsh pageant, for which he was roundly accused of political manoeuvring and of using the young Prince as a hapless pawn.

The Scottish Labour leader, Keir Hardie, writing at the time said, 'The Investiture ceremony ought to make every Welshman who is patriotic blush with shame. Every flunkey in Wales, Liberal and Tory, is grovelling on his hands and knees to take part in the ceremony. Funds could be raised for that purpose with ease but when there was money wanted to help the workers gain even a living wage, it could only be found with difficulty.'

Nevertheless, Lloyd George was a friend of the King, and the ceremony went ahead. £12,000 was spent on restoring the ruined castle, and Prince Edward, who was seventeen at the time and a naval cadet at Dartmouth, found the experience appalling, not least because of what he called the 'preposterous rig' he was forced to wear: white satin breeches and a mantle and surcoat of purple velvet edged with ermine. Lloyd George had coached him to say a few sentences in Welsh, which frightened him half to death and which he recited rather lamely in parrot fashion. According to his biographer, Frances Donaldson, when the commotion was over he made a discovery about himself. Whereas he was willing to play his role in the pomp and ceremony, he recoiled from personal homage, and he realized that even the association he had been allowed with the village boys at Sandringham and the naval cadets had made him 'desperately anxious to be treated exactly like any other boy of my age'.

There had been charges of political manoeuvring this time around too, and not just from Welsh nationalists. The English historian A.J.P. Taylor had called the decision to send Charles to Aberystwyth a 'sordid plot to exploit' him. 'Mr Wilson,' he said, 'is imposing on Prince Charles a sacrifice which he would not dream of imposing on his own son.' Activists within the Labour Party disliked the idea of a Labour government spending £200,000 on ceremonial, and in the House of Commons Emrys Hughes never gave up fighting the expense at a time when there was a financial crisis, when the Chancellor of the Exchequer was cutting down local authorities' expenditure, economizing on such things as school milk and school meals and reimposing National Health Service prescription charges. He said the investiture would be 'a parade of snobs and nonentities, flunkies and lickspittles all gathered together at public expense and deluding themselves that they were taking part in an ancient historic ceremony which the most intelligent of them would know to be bunk and hocus-pocus'. The Labour government, he ranted, had got its priorities wrong.

Prince Charles hated being in the midst of such bitter controversy; and he would have shared his great-uncle's regrets about not being treated like other boys of his age. He also looked forward to the ceremony being over, but he was less worried about the event itself than Prince Edward had been; and vehemently disagreed that it was 'bunk and hocus-pocus'. 'I look upon it, I think, as being a meaningful ceremony,' he said, in one of the interviews he gave beforehand. 'One could be so cynical about this sort of thing and think, well, it's only a ceremony . . . it's just a show. But I like to think it's a little more than just that. Perhaps it's symbolizing "Ich Dien", if you like, in some way.' They were brave words for a student who would be back in Cambridge shortly; but he took his responsibility seriously.

He also took his critics to heart. The cost of his investiture had not escaped him.

> Spending £200,000 or £250,000 or whatever it is on an apparently useless ceremony . . . does not get you positively anywhere, unless you think: 'Oh well, we shall get some return in tourism, or investment from interested Americans.'
>
> I think my view of the situation is that if you are going to have a ceremony like this you should spend enough money to make it dignified, colourful and worthy of Britain.
>
> But you should not spend too much, because it can just go on unnecessary things. On the other hand, you should not spend too little because you make it skimped and you debase the whole object of the exercise.

The Prince of Wales was just twenty when he first publicly rationalized the money spent on royal pageantry in this way, and he has faced criticism on this subject on many occasions since.

Charles is sensitive to the conditions around him, yet convinced of the value in maintaining traditions that have been upheld through the centuries. And there was no greater vindication of this than the investiture. He had said he hoped it might 'perhaps take people's minds off the economic squeeze for a moment or two', and indeed it did. An estimated 500 million people watched the ceremony on television screens around the world, and were transported by a curious mixture of ancient and new to a rite that, but for the presence of television cameras, could have been happening in the Middle Ages.

The rite was ancient, but the Earl of Snowdon, in his role as Constable of Caernarvon, saw to it that the medieval spirit was enhanced with ultra-modern materials. Much of the £200,000 had been spent on design, and with designers Carl Toms and John Pound he created a perfect theatre in the round to allow as many as possible of the four thousand people who would be packed into the ruins a view of the centre stage. The effect was dramatic.

The soaring walls of the castle were emblazoned by tall, white banners bearing red dragons – all made of expanded polystyrene. The weathered grey stone walls were brilliantly offset by banks of flame-red seats and a carpet of bright green grass in the middle; and at the focal point, beneath a canopy of clear Perspex bearing the Prince of Wales feathers (weighing over a ton, it was the largest object ever made of the material), stood three thrones of riven Welsh slate on a 28-foot circular slate dais. 'They could be of any date because their design is so simple,' said Lord Snowdon excitedly. 'You wouldn't be surprised to see them at Stonehenge, would you?'

The town of Caernarvon itself had undergone a facelift. A local paint firm called Bradite had offered free paint to the townspeople on condition that they allowed an architect of their choice to direct proceedings. The result was that, under the supervision of Professor Dewi-Prys Thomas of the Welsh School of Architecture, who wanted to recreate a medieval atmosphere, the entire town was a blend of blues, reds and yellows, a perfect match for the heraldic coat of arms.

The ceremony was meticulously stage-managed by the Earl Marshal, Bernard Marmaduke, 16th Duke of Norfolk, the very epitome of an English aristocrat. The office of Earl Marshal is inherited, and by some quirk of the British constitution the task of organizing all state ceremonial involving the monarchy, the foremost Protestant ceremonies in the land, including the Queen's coronation in Westminster Abbey, the shrine of Anglicism, is vested in a family of Roman Catholic dukes. Norfolk was a past-master at the job. He had the day's activities timed to the last second, and it went without a hitch. Prince Charles rode in procession to the Water Gate in an open carriage, escorted by the clatter of the Household Cavalry, while a choir of golden voices selected from all over Wales sang as only the Welsh can. Most of the music had been specially composed for the investiture by the Master of the Queen's Musick, Sir Arthur Bliss. High above, on the ramparts of the Eagle Tower, state trumpeters burst into fanfare.

Travelling with the Prince on the two-mile journey to the castle were David Checketts and George Thomas, who found the narrow seats of the coach excruciating. 'This was Queen Victoria's coach, Mr Thomas,' said Prince Charles, taking him unawares. 'She rode in it herself.'

'I hope she was more comfortable than I am,' replied the Secretary of State.

A far greater distraction during the journey, however, was the knowledge that it would not have taken much for a determined killer hidden amongst the crowds to throw a bomb into the coach and wipe them all out. Before climbing aboard the royal train to greet the family that morning Charles had discovered that they had been held up for two hours at Crewe because the signalling wires had been cut. A bomb had also been reported beneath the railway bridge over the River Dee, but that had turned out to be a hoax. The Queen asked if anything else had happened during the night, and it fell to the Secretary of State to tell her that two men had been blown up while planting a real bomb on the railway line.

Five minutes into their horse-drawn journey from the railway station there was a shattering roar from an adjoining field. An extremist had exploded another bomb, and people watching the procession on television saw policemen run after the culprit and arrest him. In the coach they could only guess.

'What was that, Mr Thomas?' said the Prince of Wales.

'It's a royal salute, sir,' replied the Secretary of State, quickly improvising. When the Prince said it was a peculiar royal salute, he quipped, 'There are peculiar people up here, sir.'

Security was in the forefront of everyone's minds, and back in London obituaries for the Prince of Wales had been updated, and personal tributes recorded by the BBC, where obituaries are prepared for all famous people, just in case an assassin did slip through the net. So it was with some relief that the party arrived at the castle gates and the assembled multitude burst into a welcoming round of 'God Bless the Prince of Wales'.

> Among our ancient mountains,
> And from our lovely vales,
> Oh, let the prayer re-echo:
> 'God bless the Prince of Wales!'

Warmed by their voices, Prince Charles then disappeared from sight into the Chamberlain Tower, where Lord Snowdon and Princess Margaret's young children, Viscount Linley and Lady Sarah Armstrong-Jones, were watching the proceedings on closed-circuit television. The minute they saw him come into the room they leaped up and ran to give him a hug.

The remainder of the day went without a hiccough. On the

A prince is bored. Charles aged five, with Princess Anne on board *Britannia* in 1954.

The nine-year-old. Prince Charles returns to Cheam School after the Christmas holidays.

First day at Gordonstoun, Prince Philip's old school. May 1962.

No one was sure to begin with whether Charles had decided to take up polo to please his father.

On the afternoon of his first day at Trinity College, Cambridge, 1967.

The Queen presents the Prince of Wales. Caernarvon, 1969.

Charles with Lady Sarah Spencer; through this relationship he met Diana.

At the wedding of Lord Romsey, a close friend, and Penelope Eastwood in 1979, Charles was best man.

Prince Charles with Lady Diana Spencer and her friend Sarah Ferguson at Cowdray Park in 1981.

With the Queen and Earl Mountbatten, Charles' much loved great-uncle.

At the theatre with Mountbatten.

The distress is visible. A clenched Charles with Prince Philip after Mountbatten's death in 1979.

Above left:
The picture that introduced Diana to the world. 1980.

Above right:
Lady Diana Spencer's good humour, composure and ease with the press during her engagement was impressive and endearing.

The engaged couple arrive at Goldsmiths Hall, March 1981. Diana's dress caused a sensation.

monarch's arrival, heralded by distant gunfire and the roaring cheers of the crowds, her equerry hammered on the gate and demanded entrance in the name of the Queen. The Constable, also then her brother-in-law, brought the key forward on an oak tray and said, 'Madam, I surrender the key of this castle into your Majesty's hand.' The Queen then touched the giant key, and said, 'Sir Constable, I return the key of this castle into your keeping.'

As the royal party took their seats, the audience sang the emotionally charged words of the Welsh national anthem, 'Land of My Fathers', more frequently heard in Welsh from the stands at Cardiff Arms Park.

> The land of my fathers is dear to me;
> Land of poets and singers, famous and renowned,
> Her manly warriors, devoted patriots,
> For freedom they shed their blood.

It was time for the Prince of Wales to be brought from his dark tower, dressed in the blue uniform of the Royal Regiment of Wales. Accompanied by the Secretary of State for Wales, and flanked by a posse of peers, each bearing an item of insignia, he bowed three times and knelt on a cushion in front of his mother. The Letters Patent, the documentary authority of the Prince's office, were then read out in both English and Welsh, 'And him Our most dear Son Charles Philip Arthur George as has been accustomed We do ennoble and invest with the said Principality and Earldom by girding him with a Sword . . . by putting a Coronet on his head . . . and a Gold Ring on his finger . . . and also by delivering a Gold Rod into his hand, that he may preside there and may direct and defend those parts To hold to him and his heirs . . . for ever.' As the ancient phrases rolled on, the Queen invested her son one by one with these symbols. Still kneeling, with the coronet on his head and a mantle of purple velvet and ermine over his uniform, the Prince of Wales did homage to his sovereign. He placed his hands between those of the Queen and declared, 'I, Charles, Prince of Wales, do become your liege man of life and limb and of earthly worship, and faith and truth I will bear unto you to live and die against all manner of folks.' Then, taking the Letters Patent from his mother, he rose to his feet, gave her the kiss of fealty and took his place on the throne to her right.

This part of the investiture was little different from that of the Black Prince in 1343. An ancient account tells how Edward III 'in a Parliament holden at Westminster . . . created Edward his eldest son surnamed the Black Prince Prince of Wales . . . and invested him in the said Principality with these Ensigns of Honour: a Chaplet of gold made in the manner of a garland, a Gold Ring set on his finger and a Verge Rod or Sceptre of Silver.' It was the Black Prince who adopted the motto 'Ich Dien' ('I Serve') for himself after the Battle of Crécy, taking it from the old blind King of Bohemia who died in the battle. It is a motto which Prince Charles takes seriously, and one which was crystallized for him on that drizzly afternoon at Caernarvon.

After a Loyal Address from the people of Wales, Prince Charles replied in a mixture of English and Welsh. Speaking in Welsh first, he said:

> The words of your address have certainly touched me deeply, and I can assure you I have taken note of the hopes expressed in them. It is, indeed, my firm intention to associate myself in word and deed with as much of the life of the Principality as possible – and what a Principality.
>
> It is with a certain sense of pride and emotion that I have received these symbols of office, here in this magnificent fortress, where no one could fail to be stirred by its atmosphere of time-worn grandeur, nor where I myself could be unaware of the long history of Wales in its determination to remain individual and to guard its own particular heritage – a heritage that dates back into the mists of ancient British history, that has produced many brave men, princes, poets, bards, scholars, and, more recently, great singers and a very memorable 'goon', and eminent film stars. All these people have been inspired in some way by this heritage.

The remainder of the speech was delivered in English; once again he promised to serve the country and hoped that it would go forward without forsaking the traditions of the past.

His triumph had been the Welsh, a difficult language even for those born and bred in the Principality, which he had spoken easily and fluently. In a matter of minutes he had proved to the people of Wales, the crowds who had been waiting long hours to see him, and to the 500 million people around the world watching the proceedings on television, that he took his title seriously, and truly was the first English Prince of Wales ever to speak and understand Welsh.

Next there followed a short interdenominational religious service, conducted in both English and Welsh. This, with the participation of Roman Catholic prelates, was one of the most important innovations since Prince Edward's investiture, and although it was not Prince Charles's own doing he has been very much in favour of ecumenical worship ever since.

All that was left was for the monarch to present the Prince of Wales to the people, and amid a rousing fanfare of trumpets the Queen led Prince Charles first to Queen Eleanor's Gate, which looks out from a great height over the town to the east, and proudly held her eldest son's arm aloft to the cheering, whooping and waving crowd. More fanfares, and they repeated the exercise from the King's Gate to the north, and finally from a point in the Lower Ward for those inside the castle walls.

The Queen, dressed in yellow, looked radiant, and happier than many people ever remember seeing her; and as RAF Phantoms and Lightnings screamed overhead in banshee salute, and trumpets sounded for the last time, the principals climbed back into their coaches for the procession back through the town and along the hedgerows of cheering, waving well-wishers. It had been a far greater triumph than anyone had dared to expect. Every detail of the complicated procedure had gone like clockwork, everyone had played their part to perfection; it had been a glorious, colourful, spine-tingling day. But it was not the pageant that had conquered the Welsh. It was not even the extent of royal attention they were receiving. It was Prince Charles.

A trade union organizer from Mid-Wales must have spoken for hundreds like him. 'I am not a royalist,' he said. 'I am a socialist and I wouldn't cross the street for the Prince myself. But I'll tell you this; that young man has done more for Wales already than we could dream of.'

'Charles is the ace in our pack,' said the mayor of Caernarvon, who had initially been an unwilling host to the whole affair. 'When he stood up . . . and started to speak in Welsh, he wasn't just a boy. He was a Prince. You could have put a suit of armour on that lad, and sent him off to Agincourt.'

CHAPTER NINE

Riding on a tide of goodwill, the Prince of Wales followed up his investiture with a four-day tour of the Principality, the first of its kind he had ever undertaken. Every town and village that he passed through was strewn with bunting, and the children stood out in the streets waving union jacks and Prince of Wales feathers. He saw regattas, carnivals and fetes, heard male voice choirs, brass bands and hymn singing. He attended united services, sacred concerts, swimming galas and football matches. He watched Morris dancing, clog dancing and military displays, fireworks and bonfires, beacons and torchlight processions. And at the end of it all he took off for a well-earned holiday with the Dormans in Malta once again.

The fun didn't last long, however. With the investiture behind him Prince Charles had to get back to the pressing matter of his degree course, which had been seriously disrupted by a term at Aberystwyth. The universities had a reciprocal arrangement with one another, whereby the work he had done there was taken into consideration, but fluent Welsh was not much use in a history paper. So that autumn he returned to Trinity for a final year of hard work, well aware that if he flunked his finals the world would be waiting to jeer, and the critics who had protested that he should never have got into Cambridge on two A Levels would be vindicated. The outcome was only a lower second but his tutors and Lord Butler all felt that without the distraction of Wales he could have done better. The Master was further convinced that if he had continued reading archaeology and anthropology, instead of changing in his second year to history, he might even have come away with a first.

Charles had felt, however, that history would have more relevance to his life. Archaeology and anthropology were fun and he had thoroughly enjoyed his year studying them, particularly the French trip, but after that first year the course became more specialized and since there was no chance he was going to spend his life digging up remains, much as he might have wanted to, it would have been a waste of time.

History, on the other hand, held the key to wisdom. During my conversation with the Prince he said that he believed history was of paramount importance and relevance to us all – particularly people who are involved in world events.

> I honestly believe that the only real way one can hope to understand and cope with the present, is by knowing and being able to interpret what happened in the past. In my opinion one of our greatest statesmen was Harold Macmillan, because he could do that. He was incredibly well read. He had studied history and the classics, so he spoke from a position of knowledge.
>
> I don't think that's true of modern politicians. When all this trouble in the Lebanon flared up the last time, I asked the Foreign Office if they had any books on the subject that would give me some historical background to the friction and they came up with an excellent one, written by Sir Ian Gilmour's son which I read. Some time later I happened to be talking to Lord Whitelaw and I asked him if he knew what it was all about and he said no, he knew very little about the history of the Middle East, so I sent him this book. I had a note back thanking me very much, saying he had read the book and found it fascinating.

The Prince's preoccupation, or as he would say 'obsession', with history has led to some exciting moments, not least of all the tense October day in 1982 when he stood on the deck of a combat support boat in the middle of the Solent and watched with mounting wonder as King Henry VIII's famous flagship, the *Mary Rose*, was precariously winched off the seabed where she had lain for 437 years. It was the culmination of seventeen years' excavation, which Charles had followed with fascination, inspired by Lord Mountbatten who had been a great supporter of the project from its earliest days. In 1976 Charles had dived to inspect the wreck, and in 1979 agreed to the formation of a trust in his name. The Prince was, as the Archaeological Director, Margaret

Rule, says, 'a sheet anchor'. In a tribute to her patron she wrote:

> What can I say of the inspiration and involvement of His Royal Highness Prince Charles, Prince of Wales, President of the *Mary Rose* Trust, Scuba Diver, archaeologist and heir to the throne of the United Kingdom of Great Britain and Northern Ireland? Our confidence in, and loyalty to our President can only equal that of Henry VIII's Admiral to his king who wrote 'I remit all this to the order of your most noble Grace who I pray God preserve from all adversity and send you as much victory of your enemys as ever had any of your noble ancestry' (written in the Downs on board the *Mary Rose*, 22 March 1513).

Another area of history that occupied him for some time was his much-maligned ancestor, King George III, who has long been regarded by historians as insane. Prince Charles became intrigued by reading a book and some pamphlets on the subject of his madness and decided to do some research. So he delved into the archives at Windsor, and after reading through old correspondence and doctors' reports came to the conclusion that the King had suffered not from a psychiatric illness, as had been supposed, but from a physical condition called porphyria. In the course of his research he came upon the historian John Brooke, who was of like mind and writing a new biography of George III. Charles agreed to write a foreword for him which spelt out his own hypotheses.

> As human beings we suffer from an innate tendency to jump to conclusions; to judge people too quickly and to pronounce them failures or heroes without due consideration of the actual facts and ideals of the period. . . .
>
> It is high time the veil of obscurity stifling the King's true personality, known and loved by his contemporaries, should be lifted. . . . Instead of the old spectre of a monarch threatening the constitution by increasing the power of the Crown to the detriment of Parliament, there is revealed a man almost over-dedicated to his duty and to the defence of the British Constitution as he saw it. It was, after all, in George III's reign that the office of Prime Minister gradually evolved – thereby reducing the power of the Crown to the role of influential adviser.

At much the same time Charles was writing to Lord Mountbatten to help him bone up on his history of the Royal Navy, having just embarked upon the final stage in his education. 'I was wondering,' he wrote, 'whether you could recommend me some worthwhile books that might improve my knowledge.'

Charles began his service career with the Royal Air Force, enrolling as a flight lieutenant at the RAF College in Cranwell, Lincolnshire, in March 1971. During his final year at Cambridge he had completed the prescribed number of flying hours in a twin-engined Basset, and was the proud possessor of a Grade A private pilot's licence. Like his father he loved flying, and ideally would have stayed in the RAF, but like the Duke of Edinburgh before him he was dissuaded.

There had been criticism in the media about his going into the services. A training dedicated to the skills of war – particularly in the wake of the Vietnam War – was felt to be inappropriate for the heir to the throne, and to have no place in the modern world. Yet again Prince Charles was left with the task of defending what had initially been a decision foisted upon him by others. The armed forces had nevertheless been a part of his life for as long as he could remember. They were as fundamental to the constitution of Britain as the monarchy, and Charles was sufficiently imbued with his own heritage, as well as the teachings of Earl Mountbatten, to accept without question their worth.

'It is pointless and ill-informed to say that I am entering a profession trained in killing,' he said at a ceremony to receive the freedom of the City of London.

> The Services in the first place are there for fast, efficient and well-trained action in defence. Surely the Services must attract a large number of duty-conscious people? Otherwise, who else would subject themselves to being square-bashed, shouted at by petty officers, and made to do ghastly things in force ten gales? I am entering the RAF and then the Navy because I believe I can contribute something to this country by so doing. To me it is a worthwhile occupation and one which I am convinced will stand me in good stead for the rest of my life.

In particular, he felt, it would teach him about people, which he already recognized was essential for the role he had to play in life. In the time between university and Cranwell he had been halfway round the world on a mixture of royal tours and private visits, including one to Washington with Princess Anne as guests of President Nixon, and a safari in Kenya that took him miles out into the bush; and his ability to talk to people from every walk of life had been crucial.

'In these times this sort of organization [the monarchy] is called into question,' he told reporters when the news that he would be going into the services was released. 'It is not taken for granted as it used to be. In that sense one has to be far more professional at it than I think you ever used to be and I hope that my education and upbringing and all these various schools and establishments will in some way equip me for this role. I think one has to be much more "with it" than of old, and much better informed.'

The RAF was a comparatively gentle introduction to the forces. It is regarded by many as the soft service, although an occupation that involves flying at death-defying speeds, between, not over, mountains so as to elude enemy radar is hardly a game for the faint at heart. Prince Charles was never that. He had something of the devil-may-care attitude that his cousin, Prince William of Gloucester, exhibited. Throughout Prince William's life he thrived on danger, and when he was killed so tragically in a light aircraft less than a month after his brother Richard's wedding in 1972 friends were shocked and saddened, but not altogether surprised.

Prince Charles was not drawn by danger to quite the same extent, but he did find it exhilarating to live on the edge for a while, to pit his wits against the elements and conquer things that frightened him. It was yet another manifestation of the Kurt Hahn ethic. The notion that he was treated differently from other boys of his age, as his great-uncle, the previous Prince of Wales, had remarked, particularly when he was living cheek by jowl with them and supposedly tackling the same tasks, rankled. And when he discovered that certain modifications had been made on the Jet Provosts which he flew, effectively giving him a safety net that was not afforded to his fellow cadets, he became even more determined to push himself to the limit.

Once again he was doing normal things in an abnormal way. The graduate course at Cranwell lasted twelve months; he completed it in five and became the first heir to the throne ever to finish a flying course and earn his RAF wings. In that time he had shown a considerable talent for flying which had impressed his superior officers. He had also qualified for membership of the exclusive Ten Ton Club by flying at more than 1000 m.p.h. in a Phantom scrambled from Leuchars in Fife, which he took over Balmoral before going supersonic off the coast of Scotland.

His station commander was well aware of just what a daunting responsibility he had with the heir to the throne under his care, but just when everyone thought the Prince had survived the course without harming a hair on his royal head Charles insisted on being allowed to make a parachute jump. That, he confessed in retrospect, was 'a rather hairy experience'; but 'I'd always wanted to do it because I wanted to see how I'd react.' He jumped at twelve thousand feet out of an RAF Andover above Studland Bay in Dorset and, far from making a textbook fall, he flipped smartly on to his back in the slipstream of the aircraft and his feet became entangled in the rigging over his head. He made light of it at the time, and said that as he was struggling to free himself he thought he must have hollow legs or something. 'They didn't tell me anything about this,' he quipped, but he actually found the experience terrifying.

Dartmouth was like going back to school and Prince Charles disliked it intensely. He went there in September 1971 as a mere acting sub-lieutenant, a month after passing out of Cranwell with his wings and a glowing report that said he showed a 'natural aptitude for flying . . . excelled at aerobatics in jets', and would 'make an excellent fighter pilot at supersonic speeds'. At Dartmouth he was a new boy again, albeit a graduate cadet, and forced to endure the atmosphere and discipline of school.

It was a school, nevertheless, which had trained not only the Prince's father but his grandfather, King George VI, and great-grandfather, King George V, as well as Lord Mountbatten, and it was the latter's influence as much as anything which made the Navy an inevitable move. His father's was a further voice of persuasion. 'I wanted to go into the Navy,' explained Prince Charles, 'partly for historical reasons, partly because it was a form of tradition in my family, but basically because I felt I had been brought up in the Navy in some ways, heard so much about it. It was the Service I had always known about, having been on the *Britannia* every year as a child.'

A life on the ocean wave was also considered safer than life at the controls of a supersonic jet, although Prince Charles took as many risks during his time in the Navy as he did in the Royal Air Force. He also learned more about life and his fellow men than ever he had in the privileged corridors of either school or university, or indeed the RAF. 'There is,' as Mountbatten had assured King George VI, and his father had assured the King's father, 'no more fitting preparation for a king than to have been trained in the Navy.'

At Dartmouth, where he had a room overlooking the River Dart, Charles took a crash course in all the duties of a divisional officer: basic seamanship, navigation, man management, marine and electrical engineering and administration. After six weeks – once again half the time most cadets spent there – he graduated, and the only member of his family there to watch was Lord Mountbatten, who, realizing that no one else would be present, had flown down to Devon in a helicopter for the occasion. Much to his delight, his great-nephew had come top in navigation and seamanship. 'And that is all we seamen care about,' he said. Next stop was on-the-job training at sea, and that November Charles flew out to Gibraltar to join his first ship, HMS *Norfolk*, currently on routine NATO exercises in the Mediterranean.

For the first time in his life the Prince of Wales was without a detective. For nearly twenty-three years he had had a shadow. Wherever he had lived, the detective lived in the next room, or nearby; whenever he visited friends, the detective came too; whenever he drove his car – at Cambridge a bright red MGB, latterly an Aston Martin DB6 – the detective sat in the passenger seat; whenever he went on holiday, the detective travelled too. Even when Charles was dating girls, the detective might have kept a discreet distance, but he was always there. On board ship the Navy undertook to be responsible for his security, but whenever the ship put into port, no matter where in the world, the detective would have been flown out in advance and would be there waiting on shore to resume his duties. This presence irked Prince Charles from time to time, but having been brought up in a period when security was increasingly important – he was a schoolboy of fifteen when President Kennedy was assassinated – and having never known life without it, he was far less bothered than older members of the family, who having once had a certain amount of freedom found the need for so much security a trial.

Norfolk was a big ship – 5600 tons – with a complement thirty-three officers, so the responsibility on Prince Charles, or Sub-Lieutenant HRH The Prince of Wales as he was known, was not immediately great, and there was plenty of scope for learning the ropes gradually. He didn't always get things right first time, and it fell to his fellow officers to tell him so. 'Sub-Lieutenant HRH The Prince of Wales,' said the Navigator, rather hesitantly, one day, 'I'm afraid that sight is not right, you'll have to do it again.'

'Sir,' said Prince Charles, drawing himself up to his full height. 'Have you ever heard of the Tower of London?'

This sort of quip ensured that the barriers were very quickly broken down, but although Charles was well liked on board, and mixed happily with his colleagues in the mess, he was always slightly at one remove and enjoyed retreating to the privacy of his cabin. That was virtually the only concession made to his royal status. Normally officers of his rank shared a cabin with one other, but Prince Charles was given one of his own. Having somewhere that he could be alone – albeit seven feet square – which with its bunk and little stainless steel washbasin made cadets' quarters at Dartmouth look like the Ritz, was worth its weight in gold.

Charles had always cherished his ability to go off and be by himself. He was happiest in the country: mile upon mile of open moorland at Balmoral – still his favourite place on earth – was his idea of heaven. And it was the lack of solitude which he found the most difficult aspect of life to cope with on board ship; and yet the one which probably did him most good. At sea there is no escape; men who have served in the Navy, who have been enclosed in a steel tomb for weeks and sometimes months on end, putting up with smelly feet and grinding teeth and every other noxious habit known to man, come away with a far greater tolerance and understanding of their fellow human beings than they ever thought possible.

Charles certainly learnt a few facts of life, not least about how the other half lives. He went out of his way to discover. He had never really mixed with ordinary men and women before. Apart from Hwyel Jones at Cambridge, his companions had always been from the middle or upper classes, because he found it easier to make friends with people who shared the same interests and had been through some of the same experiences as himself. He could have done the same on board ship – kept to the upper deck, mixed with the people with whom he felt safe, and drunk in the officers' mess – but he did not. He would socialize in the chief petty officers' mess from time to time, which on *Norfolk* happened to be particularly good, with three or four excellent musicians who performed on mess nights and a comedian. Charles might have a token beer but would swiftly move on to non-alcoholic drinks, which, like most members of the Royal Family, he preferred.

Very soon Prince Charles struck up a friendship with two non-commissioned officers: Chief Petty Officer Writer Michael Colborne, who was president of the CPOs' mess, and the ship's master of arms, George Summers, effectively the head of police on board. As such George was the only member of the lower deck to have a cabin to himself, and every night he and Michael used to have a nightcap together. Jokingly, in the mess one day, they had told Prince Charles he should come down to the cabin and join them one night. They had not been at sea more than two days when, lo and behold, there was a knock on the door soon after 11 p.m. There stood the Prince of Wales waiting to take them up on their invitation. Both were older men, with families, who had been in the Navy all their working lives, and regularly Charles would join them, obviously curious about the way they lived. He would ask them how they spent their time at home, what they did at weekends, where they went on holiday, as well as questions about the Navy. Sometimes they told him the truth, and sometimes they pulled his leg. For a while they had Prince Charles believing that Wren officers never wore elastic in their underpants but kept them up with braces. The relationship was relaxed and easy, and the Prince enjoyed being treated as one of the boys.

He also saw the sights like one of the boys. The ship had put into Toulon in the South of France, where Sub-Lieutenant HRH The Prince of Wales and company went on a comprehensive tour of the red light district, ending up in a bar with all the girls from just about every other bar in town dancing on the tables where they sat, and proffering tantalizing bits of their bodies. Prince Charles was no innocent, but this was the first time he had seen anything of the sort, and he was riveted.

Back on board *Norfolk* his training involved working in every part of the ship, so that he had an understanding of the jobs that everyone did, from the bridge to the engine room; he even had a spell in the galley and became a dab hand at bread-and-butter pudding. He also handled money for the first time in his life. Members of the Royal Family never carry money. On the rare occasions when they need it their detective, or a secretary or equerry, will produce it and make any necessary payment. The only cash the family handle is for church collections. For two weeks on *Norfolk* he was given the job of running the ship's office, dealing with such things as postal orders, records, punishments, small change and, not least, the wages, which had to be prepared every fortnight. Charles was handed £25,000 in a lump sum and told to sort it into pay packets for the ship's company.

The Prince was with *Norfolk* for nine months in all, and some of that time was spent in dry dock at Portsmouth and on shore-based training courses in subjects like nuclear, biological and chemical weapons. With plenty of spare time on his hands, and Lord Mountbatten's home, Broadlands, less than half an hour's drive away, Charles was a frequent visitor; it was during this period that he and his great-uncle grew really close. As Mountbatten wrote in his diary, 'It's lovely having him here, we've had so many cosy talks. What a really charming young man he is.'

Charles used him as a sounding board, as a confidant, an adviser – in matters of the heart as well as his career – and in many ways as a father. There was increasingly an element of competition in his relationship with his real father, and a difficulty in communicating. Criticism from Mountbatten, coming as he did from an earlier generation, was somehow easier to take, and more likely to be noticed. But much as he admired his great-uncle, he did not always follow his advice to the letter.

Before making a speech for the Gandhi centenary tribute in October 1969, Prince Charles had flown down to Broadlands to discuss with Lord Mountbatten what he intended saying. Mountbatten read the text overnight, and came up with a number of suggestions for changes which he thought should be made – all of which Prince Charles ignored. 'He very politely pointed out in each case', recalled the older man, 'that it was not the way he would have phrased it, and so his speech remained virtually unchanged. I thought it was really splendid.'

But if Charles was not a dogged follower of Lord Mountbatten, the same was true in reverse. The former First Sea Lord felt he had a mission in the latter years of his life to prepare the Prince of Wales for kingship: to ensure that he kept duty in the forefront of his mind – which the previous Prince of Wales had not.

Some time later the two men were in the West Indies together. The Prince was serving on the aircraft carrier HMS *Hermes*, and suddenly changed his mind about what to do during a weekend's leave, which involved disrupting the coastguard's weekend off.

'Of course you were legally right,' wrote Mountbatten to Prince Charles after the event (quoted in Philip Ziegler's biography of

Mountbatten), 'the US Coastguards could recall a crew from Easter weekend leave if you really wanted them. An officer was on duty and had no claim for the extra 3 days with his fiancee. But how unkind and thoughtless – so typical of how your Uncle David started. When I pointed this out you flared up – so I knew you had seen the point. I spent the night worrying whether you would continue on your Uncle David's sad course or take a pull.'

Prince Charles reverted to his original plan, the coastguard enjoyed his weekend and Lord Mountbatten breathed a sigh of relief. The two men then discussed philosophy until far into the night. 'What impressed me most', continued Mountbatten, 'was your desire to be generous, kind-hearted, and to think of others before your own interests.'

Lord Mountbatten could never have seriously thought that Prince Charles was going the way of the Duke of Windsor, but he knew that the very mention of the man who had abandoned his country would put the fear of God into his great-nephew. He had, after all, been weaned on tales about the Windsors, and the years had done nothing to soften the Queen Mother's attitude to her brother-in-law. According to her biographer, Robert Lacey, the Queen would have liked to end the feud, and had tried to stretch out a conciliatory hand to the Windsors, but out of respect for her mother's feelings she felt she could never do the one thing that would appease her uncle: accord Wallis, his wife, the dignity of the qualification Her Royal Highness.

Prince Charles had been influenced in the matter by both women. He could not forgive his great-uncle's behaviour but, like the Queen, he felt that a lifetime was too long to have to pay for human frailty. At the time of the investiture, when there was so much comparison with the 1911 ceremony, Charles had inevitably thought a lot about the Duke, the only other living person who had experienced what he went through. Charles became curious to meet him again – they had last met when he was a toddler. He had been at Gordonstoun on the famous occasion in June 1967 when, at the Queen's invitation, the Duke and Duchess had come to England from Paris, where they had lived in exile for thirty-one years, and ridden in the official procession to watch the unveiling of a commemorative plaque to Queen Mary. That had been the first time the Duchess had been publicly recognized by the sovereign, though the Queen had visited them both privately in hospital in London two years previously when her uncle was undergoing an eye operation, and had sent him a telegram on his seventieth birthday in 1964.

So, encouraged by his mother, Prince Charles took the opportunity while he was in Paris in October 1970 of paying the Windsors a visit. He was on a shooting party with Sir Christopher (now Lord) Soames, at the time British Ambassador to France, and his son Nicholas. Prince Charles and Nicholas Soames, a grandson of Sir Winston Churchill, had first met at the age of eleven when they both happened to be fishing the same river in Scotland, and they have been friends ever since. That afternoon their route back to the Embassy was to take them through the Bois de Boulogne, where the Windsors lived, and on the spur of the moment Charles had asked whether Sir Christopher could arrange a visit. After much pressing from Charles and hesitation on his own part the Ambassador agreed, and later that evening the three of them called at the house. They were enthusiastically received, and after greeting the Duchess as 'Aunt Wallis' Prince Charles left his companions to converse with her. Later he retreated to a quiet corner of the drawing room to talk for more than an hour with the Duke, and exchange stories and reminiscences about their respective investitures.

While in HMS *Norfolk* he paid his second and last visit to the Duke of Windsor. He joined his parents, who were on an official tour of France, and they went together. The house was hung with banners and royal coats of arms, and the servants wore royal livery. It was four o'clock, and the Duchess served her visitors afternoon tea before taking them one at a time up to see the Duke. He was close to death, with cancer of the throat, and they knew they were saying goodbye. His emaciated body, weighing little more than six stone, sat upright in a wheelchair, and when the Queen entered the room he struggled to stand. She gently insisted that he should be seated again, and sat at his side. Prince Philip came in next and the Duke apologized for failing to get to his feet. Then came Prince Charles, and as Nurse Shanley, who was caring for the old man, recorded,

> As the Duchess brought Prince Charles in [the Duke's] face lit up and he started asking him about the Navy . . . but, after a few minutes, I saw the Duke's throat convulse, and he began coughing.
>
> He motioned me to wheel him away, the Royal Family stood up and I had the feeling that this was his way of

avoiding any formal goodbyes. It had all been brief, immensely cordial, and very important to him, but he had no reserves of strength left.

Eight days later, on 28 May 1972, the Duke of Windsor was dead, and Prince Charles, who had rejoined his ship and was now in Malta, was recalled to London. It was he, with Lord Mountbatten, who escorted a distraught Duchess to see the body of her husband lying in state in St George's Chapel at Windsor.

The Prince was with HMS *Norfolk*, on and off, until the autumn, when he was posted to the frigate *Minerva*. This ship, less than half the size of the *Norfolk*, had a complement of just seventeen officers amongst the crew. It was a far more exciting proposition, carrying greater responsibility even though he remained a sub-lieutenant.

In the meantime, however, and indeed throughout his time in the services, there were all manner of distractions. Some were royal duties at home or in ports of call – he deputized for the Queen at independence celebrations in the Bahamas and in Papua New Guinea, for example, and at the coronation of King Birendra of Nepal; and just a week before the Governor of Bermuda, Sir Richard Sharples, was shot dead by an assassin in the gardens of Government House Prince Charles and he had been in conversation in precisely the same spot. Some assignments were brief spells in other ships and training exercises. Others were pleasure, including polo whenever he could snatch a game, and holidays with friends, including shooting holidays in southern Spain with Lady Jane Wellesley, daughter of the Duke of Wellington, at her family's three thousand-acre estate near Granada. Lady Jane and Prince Charles had known one another since childhood, but recently the relationship had developed into romance, despite the difficulties imposed by the Navy and press. Nevertheless they became very close over the next two years, and were ideally suited. Lady Jane was probably the most intelligent of all the woman whom Charles came close to marrying; she was suitably blue-blooded and well-versed in protocol to have made an impeccable consort, yet she was pretty and full of fun, and at one point there was little doubt that the Prince of Wales was head over heels in love with her.

He did, it has to be said, wear his heart on his sleeve for a while. At Cambridge he had fallen fairly soundly for a South American history graduate called Lucia Santa Cruz. She was working as a research assistant for Lord Butler, who was then writing his memoirs, *The Art of the Possible* – an appropriate title for their liaison. 'The Prince', remembered the Master of Trinity, according to Anthony Holden, 'asked if she might stay in our Lodge for privacy, which request we were very glad to accede to.'

Passionate as it was while it lasted, Lucia was three years older than the Prince, infinitely more sophisticated, and Roman Catholic: unsuitable in every way. Both soon moved on to pastures new although they remained good friends, as Prince Charles has with a surprising number of his girlfriends; and when Lucia subsequently married and had a child Prince Charles became a godfather. Many of his godchildren are the offspring of former girlfriends.

As girls came and went in his life he was constantly faced with the difficulty of finding privacy. He had an apartment in Buckingham Palace which was safe to entertain in, and for a while he might be able to visit the girl's home, but as soon as the press had wind of a romance they set up camp and life became intolerable. It was Lord Mountbatten who came to the rescue. It had been his solemn advice to Prince Charles to play the field before committing himself to marriage.

'I believe,' he wrote, 'in a case like yours, the man should sow his wild oats and have as many affairs as he can before settling down, but for a wife he should choose a suitable, attractive and sweet-charactered girl before she has met anyone else she might fall for. . . . I think it is disturbing for women to have experiences if they have to remain on a pedestal after marriage.'

The advice was well heeded, and to assist the first half of it Lord Mountbatten made Broadlands available to the Prince as a hideaway where he could bring girls. Over the years Charles brought a succession, and it eased the strain considerably. The press never realized that a trip to Broadlands was anything other than a visit to a favourite relative.

By this time Mountbatten had been promoted to the role of 'honorary grandfather'. 'As you know only too well,' wrote Prince Charles when he left Broadlands one time to embark on a six months' cruise, 'to me it has become a second home in so many ways, and no one could ever have had such a splendid honorary grandpapa in the history of avuncular relationships.' According to Philip Ziegler, his departure left a sad gap in Mountbatten's life. He had grown used to his continual visits and felt lonely and deprived without them. 'I've been thinking of you – far more', he wrote, 'than I had ever expected to think of a young man – but then I've got to know you so well, I really miss you very much.'

Prince Charles was with HMS *Minerva* for the best part of ten months, during which time he gained certificates in bridge watch-keeping and ocean navigation and was promoted to the rank of lieutenant. His next posting, four months later, was to HMS *Jupiter*, also a Leander class frigate. In the intervening months he attended the State Opening of Parliament, saw his sister married in Westminster Abbey, and advanced his own romantic inclinations with a few days in the south of Spain as the guest of Lady Jane Wellesley once again; he returned the hospitality at Sandringham in the New Year.

Prince Charles is hugely fond of his sister, but they are quite unalike. Princess Anne is rough, tough and outspoken, like her father. On one occasion she was held up in the Mall by a gunman, who in the course of trying to kidnap her shot and wounded her detective, her driver, a policeman and a passer-by. Prince Philip, who was in Indonesia with the Queen at the time, remarked, 'If the man had succeeded in abducting Anne she would have given him a hell of a time while in captivity.' Princess Anne was already famed for giving press photographers a hell of a time; it was she who popularized the phrase 'Naff off' and as a result spent many years at the bottom of the Palace Hit Parade.

Though the press may not have liked her much, her father was her number one fan: she was the confident, resilient, forthright son he missed in his first-born. Her upbringing had been far less traumatic than that of her elder brother. She had suffered none of the chopping and changing of schools, and been through none of the ceremonial ordeals. After five years boarding at Benenden School in Kent, which she found far more enjoyable than Charles's experience at Gordonstoun, she had turned to a career with horses and won remarkable success in one of the toughest branches of horse-riding, three-day eventing. She had been horse-mad all her life, much to the delight of both parents. Her husband, Captain Mark Phillips, was appropriately enough a fellow enthusiast. He was a good-looking commoner, the son of a Wiltshire farmer, who had won a gold medal at the 1972 Olympic Games in Munich, and the family warmed to him. Former schoolmates were quick to tell the highest bidder that Mark didn't have a brain in his head, and there were wide reports that privately the Royal Family had nicknamed him 'Fog' – 'because he is thick and wet' – but in truth Mark Phillips is quite a shrewd young man who has conducted himself with enormous dignity since his marriage. Charles liked him, but did not at first have a great deal in common with him. In recent times, however, now that they both farm, have young children, and live in the same part of Gloucestershire, they have become much closer; indeed the Prince's dairy herd provides the Phillips family with milk.

Prince Charles flew out to join *Jupiter* in Singapore, and from there sailed to Australia, where he was mobbed by frenzied girls on a Brisbane beach as he tried his hand at surfing. He has never been classically good looking. His shoulders are too narrow for his hips and his legs are too short for his trunk; and at various times in his life he has been teased for having protruding ears and a weak chin. Nothing, however, is quite so potent an aphrodisiac as power: Henry Kissinger, President Nixon's former Secretary of State, was the living proof of that. And there is no power quite so potent as that of the Prince of Wales. The realization that Prince Charles could have virtually any woman of his choosing, whatever their age or marital status, was heady stuff and open to abuse; Lord Mountbatten was always there to remind his protégé of his duty.

From Australia HMS *Jupiter* continued on its round-the-world cruise home, sailing first to the West Coast of America via New Zealand, where Prince Charles joined his parents for the Commonwealth Games, and several islands in the Pacific. In San Diego, California, Charles was the guest of the fabulously wealthy US Ambassador to London, Walter Annenberg, at his exclusive estate in Palm Springs. Fellow guests included Governor Ronald Reagan, who was to become President of the United States, and his wife, and a number of film stars including Bob Hope and Frank Sinatra. Thinking his royal guest might like to play a round of golf on what was, after all, one of the most famous courses in the world, Annenberg had two battery-operated sit-upon carts ready for the off. The Prince confessed that he knew nothing about golf whatsoever. 'My game's polo,' he told his host.

'Then that's what we'll play,' said the American. 'Show me how?'

Thereupon Prince Charles took up a golf club, sprang into one of the carts and, going at the ball as if on horseback, leaned over the side and struck a winner. The American soon had the hang of it, and before long they were both careering over the immaculately laundered turf of the first tee, wildly waving their improvised mallets.

The ship arrived home in Devonport in August, and a month later the Prince of Wales had moved on to that part of his time in the Navy that he enjoyed most of all: flying helicopters. He did his training at the Royal Naval air station at Yeovilton in Somerset – another base no more than a stone's throw away from Broadlands, particularly by helicopter. Again Charles was forced to cut short the course. He crammed the compulsory 105 hours' flying time needed, including twenty-six hours solo, into seven weeks, where his colleagues, who did not have to dash off to the other side of the world on royal business, took nineteen. It was no chore. 'I adore flying and I personally can't think of a better combination than naval flying – being at sea and being able to fly. I find it very exciting, very rewarding, very stimulating and sometimes bloody terrifying.'

One of the most terrifying times was a spell at the Royal Marine School at Lympstone for a commando training programme. When Prince Edward dropped out of the Marines early in 1987 he would almost certainly have had at least one sympathetic ear within the Royal Family. The programme is one of the toughest and most physically testing there is; and trainee helicopter pilots are put through part of it so that they know something about the skills of the men they are up there supporting.

Prince Charles thrived on this sort of challenge – the more dangerous the challenge the better. He was offered no dispensations and indeed demanded to be put through precisely the same routine as everyone else. Earlier in his sub-lieutenant's training he had insisted on taking part in another highly dangerous exercise that was prescribed for all trainees – the drill for escaping from a sunken vessel. It involved making three dummy escapes from depths of up to a hundred feet in the training tank at HMS *Dolphin* in Gosport. Any thoughts that this 'artificial' setting might have made it safe are ill-founded: over the next two years two men died doing the same exercise.

Charles was not given *carte blanche*, however. There were some exercises at which his superiors drew the line, and some aircraft, including supersonic Buccaneers and Sea King anti-submarine helicopters, which he was not allowed to pilot. Indeed, during his solo flying time at Yeovilton his machine had been tailed by another carrying emergency equipment in the event of a mishap.

He felt cheated at being unable to prove himself as capable as his peers, frustrated at being kept at one remove; and nothing throughout his life has enraged him quite as much as the feeling that he is being wrapped in cotton wool. His patience was frequently tested during those years, and on many occasions he lost his temper over a superior officer affording him special treatment.

By December he had not only qualified, but won the Double Diamond award for the trainee who had made the most progress. Progress he may have made, but by all accounts he was not the most brilliant navigator. He had become friends with a fellow officer in the 'Red Dragons' called Warren Benbow. Sitting in the naval base at Rosyth on the Firth of Forth one day, they hatched a plan to beat up a few selected Scottish castles in their helicopters, which like all the helicopters in the squadron were painted red. Castles are shown on navigation maps as red zones, which means they are out of bounds to all aircraft, but the Prince of Wales made a few discreet phone calls and the regulations were waived. He and his chum set off and had great fun buzzing friends and relatives, who would come outside to see what on earth all the racket was about and find Prince Charles hovering a few feet above their heads, waving like a lunatic. On one occasion, however, his powers of navigation suffered a slight setback, and instead of swooping down on Glamis Castle as he had intended, to surprise the Bowes-Lyon family, he swooped down on some entirely different castle. A gentleman whom Charles had never seen in his life before was left looking rather puzzled as two red helicopters beat a hasty retreat.

On their way back to base Prince Charles suggested dropping in for tea with the Queen at Holyroodhouse, her palace in Edinburgh. After they had set their helicopters down on the grass outside Charles climbed out to make sure that it was all right for them to go in. He had not gone far before an irate face appeared at an open window – the Queen, who not only has an aversion to helicopters and refuses to go near them, but was also engaged in an audience with the Prime Minister. 'Go away, Charles,' she bellowed over the noise of the rotor blades, 'and take those frightful machines away with you!'

His next posting took Lieutenant HRH The Prince of Wales to sea again in the aircraft carrier *Hermes*, with 845 Naval Air Support Squadron, sailing via Canada to the Caribbean. In the

Virgin Islands a group of sixteen sailors and officers, including Warren Benbow and Prince Charles, took some helicopters off on a weekend break to one of the neighbouring islands, not fixing anything in advance or quite knowing where they would stay. First stop was the local pub, the Lord Nelson, where they had a few drinks and got chatting to a rich young American, scarcely a day over twenty, who said he had a house there. How many people were there in the naval party, he asked.

'Sixteen,' said Warren.

'Okay,' said the American. 'Some of you can camp in the house and the rest can go in the garden.'

Relieved to have found somewhere to stay, Warren moved on to the delicate part of the negotiations. 'We have the Prince of Wales here. Would it be possible for him to have a room on his own?' The American was only too happy to donate his own bedroom at the top of the house. After a very good dinner at the Lord Nelson the party went back and carried on drinking at the house, which had a large bar at one end of the living room, as American houses invariably do. There they were joined by a long-haired hippy character who was very laid-back but good company. After a while he and Warren and Prince Charles sat down to play cards, and periodically one of them would go and fetch more cans of beer from the bar. Soon enough it was the Prince's turn.

'Boy,' said the hippy, 'your turn to get the beer. Come on boy, beer.'

Slightly shaken, Prince Charles rose to his feet and did as he was bid. Soon afterwards he got up again to go to the loo.

'Say,' said the hippy to Warren, 'I hear we've got your future King staying in these parts. Don't suppose there'd be any chance of meeting him, would there?'

'You've just been playing cards with him,' said Warren, and still cherishes the look on the man's face.

The next time Prince Charles put to sea he was in command of his own ship. On returning to England he had done a course in captaincy, the last of the courses he would have to endure. They were the part he liked least about being in the forces: he became very easily bored, and if any lecture lasted longer than seven and a half minutes Lieutenant HRH The Prince of Wales would be in the Land of Nod. Evidently the first seven and a half minutes of every lecture was enough to see him through, because on completing the course he was deemed fit to command, and no

Admiral of the Fleet would have risked putting the heir to the throne in charge of so much as a rowing boat if he had not known the man was more than good enough for the job.

It was a splendid finale to five years in the Navy, but not the most comfortable. HMS *Bronington* was one of the smallest ships in the service. Her task was to hunt mines in the North Sea and, buffeted about by the wind and the waves, Prince Charles suffered seasickness for the first time in his naval career. It was nevertheless a pleasing end, and delighted both Prince Philip and Lord Mountbatten. Charles was twenty-seven, two years younger than his father had been upon taking command of his first ship, HMS *Magpie*, and he did not disappoint them in ten months in the job.

HRH Lieutenant The Prince of Wales indeed turned out to be a good commander . . . but he was given a very good navigator, just in case.

CHAPTER TEN

Early in 1977 the Prince of Wales treated himself to a return trip to Kenya for a second safari holiday. He had first been on safari with Princess Anne before entering the armed forces; the idea had come from the naturalist and television executive Aubrey (now Lord) Buxton, a friend of Prince Philip's, whose daughter, Cindy, Charles had taken to a Trinity May Ball one year.

Buxton had just finished filming the *Survival* series for the BBC and, with his own adventures fresh in his mind, suggested that Charles and Anne go on a walking safari in the Northern Frontier district where he had been filming. Setting off into the wild on foot with a string of camels in tow to carry food and equipment, and setting up camp at night wherever they happened to be, was the most thrilling experience. Their guide had been John Sutton, a white Kenyan who knows all there is to know about animals and wildlife, and Charles had so enjoyed it that he longed to repeat the experience. This was the first opportunity he had had, and it was a trip which was to have an important influence on his life. One of the members of the select party that accompanied him into the wild African bush in March 1977 was the South African explorer, writer and mystic Sir Laurens van der Post.

Van der Post was a remarkable companion to have in any setting, but in the bushveld of Africa he was in his element. He had lived a long and eventful life, much of it in the interior of southern Africa, and knew more about the African people and their spiritual heritage not only than any European alive, but more than most Africans themselves. He spoke several native dialects and loved Africa – its past, its present, its people, its wildlife and its wealth of folklore – with a passion that has given his writings on the subject classic status. Every evening when the party made camp – on the banks of a river, maybe, with the sun setting deep into a dramatic crimson backcloth – they would settle down by the campfire, while the camels hobbled about them, and listen spellbound to the wise thoughts on man and nature that spilled forth from the elderly man.

He spoke not only of Africa but of his life, of his years as a Japanese prisoner of war in Jakarta, of his extensive travels and explorations, and of his friendship with the Swiss philosopher Carl Jung, in whom he had found a kindred spirit. The more he heard, the more Prince Charles felt that he too had found a kindred spirit.

He felt in many ways as van der Post once said he felt about his 'wise, stern and upright' old grandfather.

> He was already very old when I was very young. Indeed, the difference in our ages was so great and the span of years between us so long that I can remember him telling me in great detail of a battle in which he had fought against the English in Africa in 1848. It seemed to me that there was almost nothing that could happen to human beings this side of the grave that had not happened to him, things both bad and good which his faith and courage somehow had not failed to contain if not altogether to resolve.

As a child Laurens had had an inordinate interest in dreams, which the grown-ups in his life would always dismiss: 'But my dear boy, it was only a dream.' 'That "but only" of theirs', he later wrote,

> became increasingly discredited when I saw how it was automatically part of their judgement of almost everything that mattered to me as a child. Growing up in the European way began to appear to be not so much a process of growth as a dangerous re-education to a provisional 'but only' state. I feared it accordingly, and so acutely that the fear is still with me, for it is continuously encouraged by the loss of power of increase that I see in men and their societies, because how can there be either growth or renewal in such reductive soil of the human spirit?

Laurens had felt torn between this fascination with the inner self, and 'the tug of the world' which tried to keep him focused on the life outside. His old grandfather had come to his aid. After reading aloud the story of Joseph and his bloodstained coat of many colours from the Bible, which he always referred to with reverence as 'the Book' ('And Joseph dreamed a dream and he told it his brethren: and they hated him yet the more'), he had beckoned the child to him and put him on his knee. 'Laurens Jan,' he had said, 'always remember what the Book says about Joseph and his dreams. Remember that though his brothers hated him for it, had it not been for his dreaming, they would never have found corn in Egypt and would have perished as you have heard in the great famine that was still to come.'

Even the most hardened and cynical of critics, Auberon Waugh, has said that there is no one he would more like to spend five hours talking to than Laurens van der Post. But the writer's popularity is not universal, and has waxed and waned over the years: he has been hailed as both a prophet and a charlatan. Few people who have had the experience of hearing him at first hand, however, have failed to be impressed, and many high-ranking politicians and world leaders count themselves among his friends and admirers. Prince Charles was the latest recruit, and a friendship was formed in those days that has endured and strengthened with the years.

Charles was never more relaxed than on these safaris. Bedding down under the stars, miles from civilization, with all around the intoxicating noise and smell of the bushveld at night, was paradise on earth. At dawn he would waken to the unmistakable sound of lions calling, accompanied by hundreds of different species of bird, insect and animal heralding the first glimpse of the sun and the start of a new day. By this time the Africans would have breakfast cooking over the fire, and never would breakfast taste so good nor its eaters have so hearty an appetite. Thence to the trail: detecting where elephants had been in the night by the freshness of their dung, looking for the prowling big cat that had spooked a herd of zebra or water buffalo, and watching the comical antics of lilac-breasted rollers in the trees above.

The trip was not without its dangers, however, and the party carried weapons just in case they needed to protect themselves. On this second safari they were in the spectacular Aberdare region, where the worst of the Mau Mau trouble had taken place in the late 1950s, and once again John Sutton was their guide. He was an expert in game hunting and the art of survival in this terrain, but they came close to using a weapon more than once. One time they came too close to a bull buffalo: they had not realized until they were only about fifty yards away that he was in among a herd of cows. He looked for a while as though he might turn nasty; and everyone in the party knew that the decision was entirely his. It was a tense moment, but the buffalo decided to ignore the intruders and that particular danger was over.

The privacy, the informality, the excitement and the conversation were all too short, and Prince Charles was soon back to reality with a further ten days of official visits to Ghana and the Ivory Coast. Now that he had left the forces he was considered a fully-fledged member of 'the family firm' and expected to pull his weight.

To this end he had gathered together a small household to organize his life, headed by David Checketts, who up until the time Charles left the Navy had played the part of equerry and personal private secretary rolled into one. Three years before leaving, while stationed at Yeovilton, Charles had approached Michael Colborne, the chief petty officer on board HMS *Norfolk* with whom he had shared so many nightcaps in his first days at sea. Would he be interested, he wanted to know, in joining his staff at Buckingham Palace when he left the Navy in 1977? The invitation came like a bolt out of the blue, but one which Colborne, who had since been promoted to warrant officer, or Fleet CPO Writer, was only too delighted to accept. The Navy, however, were less than pleased, and even with Lord Mountbatten's intervention it took more than four months to secure Colborne's release.

During the next ten years Michael Colborne was mainly in charge of the Prince's financial affairs, as Secretary of the Prince of Wales's office, and enjoyed an unusually frank relationship with him. He is fourteen years older than the Prince, a devout and dedicated royalist but the sort of man – and there are precious few of them about, particularly around the Royal Family – who is not turned by status. He liked the Prince for what he was, and Charles recognized it. Colborne was one of the few members of the Prince of Wales's staff, past or present, who would give the Prince an honest and sometimes unwelcome opinion.

He would quite frequently get an equally honest and unwelcome reply, and many were the times he was to suffer the brunt of the Prince's temper. After lunch one day at Buckingham Palace, just as Colborne had decided he could take no more, Lord Mountbatten sought him out and, with his uncanny nose for trouble, asked whether the Prince had been upsetting him.

'Bear with him, Michael, please,' said Mountbatten. 'He doesn't mean to get at you personally. It's just that he wants to let off steam, and you're the only person he can lose his temper with. It's a back-handed compliment really, you know. He needs you.'

The honorary grandfather was seldom far from hand, and the Queen and the Duke of Edinburgh were only too pleased to have him there as a guiding influence. Occasionally the Prince's staff were glad to have him there too, as someone to turn to, whom they hoped the Prince might listen to. When David Checketts had discovered that His Royal Highness had become addicted to hot-air ballooning, which on top of flying and parachuting seemed the final lunacy for the heir to the throne, he wrote to Mountbatten: 'Your influence on the Prince of Wales is enormous, and he has an immense admiration and respect of your wise advice and guidance. I would therefore be everlastingly grateful for your valuable help in avoiding or restraining some of the more adventurous and dangerous endeavours of this remarkable young man.'

Much as Mountbatten might have wanted to be up there in the balloon too, he did see the need for caution. 'I suppose you realize he is contemplating getting the balloon down to Sandringham,' he replied to Checketts, 'so you will have to act quickly if you want to do something about it.'

David Checketts was not a killjoy. Neither was he a professional courtier of the type that surrounded the Queen. He remained a serviceman at heart, which was perhaps his strength. He was able to take the Prince of Wales through the final stages of his growing up, and help him find his feet in a job that was completely undefined. His own job as private secretary to the Prince of Wales is also undefined, at that time considerably more so than it is today, with the result that in the early years of their association they felt their way together, making up the rules as they went along.

When in 1972 the Prince of Wales wanted to do something to help disadvantaged young people, Checketts encouraged him. An old envelope containing their joint scribblings, which contained the germ of an idea that grew into the Prince's Trust, is filed away for posterity in the Palace archives.

It had all begun by sheer chance. One day in December Prince Charles happened to be listening to the radio when a probation officer by the name of George Pratt was talking about a new scheme of community service for young offenders in London. Charles was deeply moved by what he heard; he had been unaware that there were so many young people growing up in such deprived conditions and turning to crime simply because they had no encouragement from their family or anyone else in their lives to do something positive with their time. He contacted George Pratt, via David Checketts, and asked what he could do to help.

As a result of that telephone call the Prince of Wales, then twenty-four, chaired the first of many discussion groups over the years at Buckingham Palace and later Kensington Palace. It became his favourite way of operating. He would frequently make one contact, explain what he was after and the sort of people he would like to have the opportunity of talking to – latterly people who would not normally have spoken to one another at all, which has made for some potentially explosive situations – and let that first contact do the organizing. Once the group had been brought together the Prince would explain the purpose of the meeting, and the various bodies around the table would be expected to produce the goods.

On this occasion there were representatives of all the professional groups involved with the young, such as the probation and social services, the welfare organizations, the Church and the police, and they were given the task of deciding exactly what the Prince could most usefully do to help. It was not a simple question, because of course all the bodies represented were already doing things, and some care was needed to avoid treading on any toes. Charles's thoughts immediately turned to the Kurt Hahn solution to the problems of youth: give them some physical challenge; but the Duke of Edinburgh's Award Scheme, which Charles had taken part in himself at Gordonstoun, already did precisely that.

Finally, after several more discussion groups involving a wider range of organizations, they reached a starting point. The Prince's scheme, as yet unnamed, would help individuals rather than groups of youngsters, and would give deserving cases the wherewithal to help themselves do something useful with their lives.

At this stage the scheme remained unnamed. Until it was formally made into a trust in 1976, much of the funding had come from the Prince's naval allowance of £5,000 a year, which he gave over in its entirety – and quite anonymously – to young people, initially those who lived in areas with which he had a geographical connection, such as Cornwall or Wales. A small group of advisers was set up in each of these places – people from the Church, the probation service or the social services, for example – and using their knowledge of the local grapevine they asked likely candidates to write and say what they felt would most help them improve their lifestyle. George Pratt administered the scheme, but every application for a grant was sent on in the diplomatic bag to wherever the Prince happened to be at the time, and he selected the most deserving applicants. He also followed their progress, and occasionally went to see the young people who had benefited.

As the scheme gathered momentum, and more and more young people applied for grants, it became obvious that the programme would have to be put on a more formal footing, and in the spring of 1976 it was turned into a charitable trust and formally launched as the Prince's Trust. Its aims and policies had to be clearly defined. Its purpose was still 'To help disadvantaged young people' aged between fourteen and twenty-five. Its policy was

> To provide small grants to young people who: a) produce their own proposals aimed at setting up self-help activities which contribute to their welfare or personal development; these projects may sometimes enable them to help other people; b) make the application themselves, either individually or as a spontaneous group, but not as an existing organization; c) are socially, economically or environmentally disadvantaged or physically handicapped; d) would not anticipate further funding from the Trust after the initial grant.

Its range was now greater: there were seven regional committees, and over the years that number has grown to encompass most of the British Isles, but the scheme still operates along much the same lines. Prince Charles no longer sees every application – over a thousand people a year now receive grants, so it would be impossible – but he wants to be told what is going on. He is in regular touch with the central office, now sited in Bedford Row in London, and he still goes out of his way to meet recipients whenever he can, and visit the regional committees. When royal duties take him to different parts of the country he will find out who the Trust has helped in those areas and have his staff organize an informal visit.

The entire operation bears his personal stamp. He detests bureaucracy and red tape above practically everything else, and the Trust therefore has the bare minimum. This is a gift with no strings attached. Once somebody has been given a grant, which nowadays is normally between £50 and £75 – the maximum ever given is £300 – he or she is left to spend it in any way they wish. It may be to buy a bicycle so they can do a newspaper delivery round, equipment to go on a camping trip, or the fee to enrol on an educational course or to learn some kind of sport. It is always hoped that the money actually goes on whatever scheme they have outlined in their application, but the old Kurt Hahn 'trust system' is central to the philosophy. The money goes straight to the recipient in cash, and there is no checking up afterwards because the object is to give them a gift which challenges their own responsibility, and which shows, perhaps for the first time in their lives, that someone trusts and believes in them.

This attitude has paid dividends; and not because the Trust has chosen the cream of its applicants. Indeed Prince Charles is almost perverse in the way that he gives grants to the most unlikely-sounding characters for fear of missing someone who is genuinely deserving. The toughest cases from the roughest parts take money, and time and again write to say what they have done with it, or what a difference being able to own a bicycle or a pair of roller skates, or to go off on an adventure, has made to their lives. Some of the early beneficiaries have even joined local advisory groups and are now helping to help others – indeed the Prince is keen that the people on the selection committee should all be under twenty-five.

Quite often, however, the recipients are offered more than money. Everyone who receives a grant is visited by a contact maker who, if required, will help the young person with whatever venture or expenditure they have planned. In some cases these contact makers have become deeply involved, stepping in perhaps where there has been no family support.

All this, of course, has become possible with the growth of the Prince's Trust and the additional funds that it has raised, particularly with the star-studded and spectacular pop concerts that it has staged over the last few years. Indeed it is only because of these pop concerts that the general public has known about the Trust, but even then few people know exactly what it does or how it came to be. This is largely because funds have always gone towards people rather than publicity, and until pop stars were involved – who naturally generate media interest – the press paid little attention. Now it is a different story, however, and last year the Prince's Trust had a total of a quarter of a million pounds to distribute. It has now joined forces with the Queen's Silver Jubilee Trust, and that has further increased the number of people it can help.

The Queen's Silver Jubilee Trust was set up in 1977, the year in which she celebrated twenty-five years on the throne; Prince Charles came out of the Navy at the end of 1976 specifically to help set it up. The precedent lay in King George's Jubilee Trust, founded in 1935 by Prince Edward, then Prince of Wales, who raised a million pounds for the Jubilee of King George and Queen Mary. The purpose of that original trust, as laid out in the official terms, was 'to assist the physical, mental and spiritual development of young people' aged between eight and twenty-five. Its policy was 'to provide financial support for voluntary youth projects in specific areas of priority'; in particular, projects involving 'young unemployed, ethnic minorities, people on housing estates, young single homeless, young in rural areas, creative art and outdoor pursuits'.

With the Queen's Silver Jubilee approaching, the trustees of the King's Trust sought permission in 1975 to raise further funds under the auspices of Prince Charles, and the Queen agreed, provided that 10 per cent of whatever was raised went to the Commonwealth. One other stipulation was that the money should not be given for the young to spend on themselves, but should be used to encourage young people to give service to other people in the community, such as visiting the aged, running holiday play schools for children or making tape recordings for the blind. Its official policy was 'to put resources into the hands of young volunteers (aged twenty-five and under) to enable them to carry out practical projects which will benefit others in need and the community at large'. Thus the grants were usually given for 'tools, materials, travel, training, and volunteers' expenses'.

The man appointed as director of the Jubilee Trust was Harold Haywood; a jolly man now in his fifties, he has spent most of his working life with young people and has the wisdom, wit and unquenchable energy essential for the job. He and the Prince of Wales have a mutual admiration society and have worked closely together now for the last ten years. Harold is one of his most trusted advisers and, since George Pratt's retirement, has run all three trusts and been involved in just about every venture that the Prince has ever initiated.

They have grown older and wiser together as the years have passed. One early lesson came in 1977 when they were raising money for the Queen's Silver Jubilee Appeal. The Prince appeared in a series of programmes on the popular BBC early evening programme *Nationwide*. During one programme he was seen visiting an urban farm in London's Kentish Town where they had just completed a skateboarding area, and one of the children asked him if he wanted to have a go. Game for anything, Prince Charles, dressed in the usual suit and tie, borrowed a board and, thanks to the good sense of balance he has acquired from playing polo, conducted himself surprisingly well. It was at the height of the skateboard craze, and the BBC used the clip not only on *Nationwide* but on every news bulletin that night, and sent it all round the world. It seemed like a good piece of public relations for the Appeal and some harmless fun.

The next day the storm broke: how thoroughly irresponsible Prince Charles had been to go skateboarding without wearing a safety helmet; didn't he know how many accidents were caused by children not wearing protective clothing? It was a lesson worth learning. The Prince then did a voice-over to go with the film clip: 'Had I known I'd have the chance to try a skateboard, I would, of course, have brought my helmet with me.' The final salt in the wound came from the Royal Society for the Prevention of Accidents. They were making a big poster, they rang to say, with a photograph of Prince Charles on his skateboard and the caption, 'Don't be a proper Charlie.'

Something the BBC did not get hold of was the story about the day in 1972 when Prince Charles nearly killed himself in a Formula II racing car. Without consulting anyone, he took up the invitation of world champion racing driver Graham Hill to have a spin in one of his cars. In dead secrecy one morning he drove down to Thruxton, the Grand Prix circuit in Hampshire, and putting on the necessary protective clothing – on this earlier occasion he didn't make that mistake – climbed into Hill's car. It had been raining overnight and the track was wet; but Charles was no beginner. He had been driving fast sports cars since the age of nineteen, and was good at it. He was also keen to prove that he was not 'chicken', so he accelerated away from the grid at a reasonable speed. However the tyres were dry, and no one had warned him that dry tyres on a wet road is a recipe for catastrophe, and that in these conditions he should drive even more slowly than in a normal car. He had not gone round two corners of the circuit before he lost control, and the car spun off the track and into the grass. The car was fine and the Prince was fine, but the thought of what might have been was enough to make everyone involved break into a cold sweat for a week. Prince Charles confessed it had been one of the most frightening moments of his life.

He was far from 'chicken', however. There was a moment during the Jubilee celebrations, when he paid a visit to a youth centre in south London, typical of the sort that might have been eligible for a grant from the Jubilee Trust. Called the Moonshot Club, it was in Lewisham, where twenty-four black youths had recently been arrested on mugging charges. There was a great deal of tension in the area, and when the Prince of Wales arrived and climbed out of his car he was greeted by a noisy and threatening rabble of protesters. One standing at the front was wearing a badge saying 'Stuff the Jubilee'. With typical courage Charles stepped from the comfort of his shiny, crested black limousine and walked straight across to the noisiest of the protesters, the one who was sporting the offensive badge. With the innocence of a child he asked the young man what it was all about, and when the man told him about their grievance against the police Prince Charles invited Commander Douglas Randall, head of the division whose men had arrested the twenty-four, to join the conversation, and suggested that the two should get together at a later date to sort it out.

Once again the Prince had overstepped the mark. He had put his nose into sensitive waters, where he had no business – or so he was told. Nevertheless the two groups did get together, and although the question of the muggers was resolved by a court of law, as was proper, the black community and the police did start to talk to one another to iron out their differences. The Prince's Trust gave grants to the Moonshot Club and it has subsequently been helped by the Royal Jubilee Trust.

These experiences led the Prince of Wales to retract his horns somewhat and play it by the book. He did not yet have the confidence that he has developed in the last few years to speak and be damned, as his father had always been quick to do. He found the publicity embarrassing and would agonize over criticism in the press, and for several years after these incidents he tried to see pitfalls before falling into them.

His father's attitude was no help. Far from boosting his son's morale, he would undermine it by heaping criticism upon his head without suggesting any positive means of making amends. Prince Charles scarcely knew how to cope. He so admired his father and was so genuinely fond of him that he could not simply dismiss the things he said and put them out of his mind. He worried about the criticism and he worried about the relationship. He would talk to friends and repeatedly bring up the subject of fathers. What was their relationship like with their fathers, he wanted to know; and he was visibly relieved if they too had difficulty.

Prince Philip may not have handled his relationship with his eldest son well, but his lot has not been an easy one. He is a born leader, everything that Kurt Hahn could have hoped for; yet for forty years he has had to walk one pace behind his wife. Playing second fiddle to anyone, most of all a woman, goes against his entire upbringing and character. He thrives on challenge and physical pursuits. He is intolerant of indecision or weakness, and has little time for people's sensibilities. Subtlety is not his forte. As Robert Lacey remarks, he has 'the blunt outlook of a straightforward naval officer at heart who has always felt easiest in a situation where yes is yes and no is damned well no'.

Yet at the same time he is a talented painter and introduced Prince Charles to watercolours, although he now does practically none himself. He also takes childlike delight in practical jokes, and his off-the-cuff remarks have endeared him to millions and been a hallmark of Queen Elizabeth's reign. On tour with the Queen in India once, he stood patiently for some time while a photographer climbed a pole with his equipment strung about him in order to get a better camera angle. All was ready, and Prince Philip was looking obligingly into the lens, when the photographer lost his balance and toppled backwards into the crowd below, wailing. 'I hope to God', said His Royal Highness, 'he breaks his bloody neck!'

If the press execute their business discreetly and efficiently he will bear with them, but the Duke is famed for his dislike of them and his attacks on British industry; such as the suggestion that it was 'time we pulled our fingers out' have become immortalized. But for the most part he has kept out of the limelight, unlike his seventeenth-century predecessor, William of Orange, who said he would never 'hold on to anything by apron strings' and insisted on the title of co-sovereign with his wife Mary. Philip has concentrated instead on patronage of science, design and technology, and preservation of the world's wildlife. And he has got on with his own hobbies of sailing, polo – latterly four-in-hand driving – and after-dinner speaking.

In any other situation he would undoubtedly have ruled the roost, and within the privacy of the family he does play the role of the old-fashioned paterfamilias. He bullies anyone he thinks will let him, although the Queen can be the tougher of the two; but in public he is consort, number two – although in terms of inheritance, of course, he is not even in the running.

Of all his children, Prince Charles is the one whom he has bullied most severely, and the more disillusioned Charles became in his relationship with his father the closer he grew to his 'honorary grandfather'. Earl Mountbatten was delighted, and furthermore he had schemes afoot with regard to the Prince's marriage. Now that he had done as he advised, and sown his wild oats, the old schemer had a bride in mind who would quieten the unwelcome speculation in the press, take the pressure off Prince Charles, and ensure that the house of Mountbatten should finally and inextricably be linked with the House of Windsor. Charles should marry his pretty young granddaughter, Lady Amanda Knatchbull. But Prince Charles had known Amanda all his life, and although they did start to see a lot of one another, and go on holiday to the Bahamas together to the Brabournes' holiday home on the island of Eleuthera, friends say their relationship was too much like that of brother and sister to have gone much further.

The roll-call of titled and glamorous women whom Charles wooed grew ever longer. He revelled in the appeal of his title to the opposite sex, and exploited his unusual powers of attraction to the full. The press followed his affairs with growing impatience for him to find a bride. As the Prince himself said, 'I've only got to look twice at someone and the next morning I'm engaged to her.' The most absurd example of all was Princess Marie-Astrid of Luxembourg, whom Prince Charles had never looked at once, quite simply because they had never met – or not to his recollection. This did not deter the news hounds, and on the morning of 17 June 1977, after mounting speculation in all the papers, the *Daily*

Express boldly led with the news that Buckingham Palace was to announce the Prince's formal engagement to Marie-Astrid the following Monday. Instead Buckingham Palace announced Prince Charles's first and last personal denial.

He was not helped by the fact that, back in 1973, when rumours were rife that Princess Anne and Mark Phillips were about to become engaged, the Palace had issued a firm denial which the press had taken at face value. Two weeks later the couple were formally betrothed; and not surprisingly the media has never fully trusted the Palace since.

Prince Charles was having a good time as a bachelor, and did not want to give it up until he had to; but enthusiasm for 'sowing his wild oats', as Mountbatten put it, was only part of his reluctance to choose a bride. More serious was the knowledge that he would be choosing someone for a specific role, far beyond that of any normal wife: the woman he married might well one day be Queen. He would also be choosing a partner for life, for divorce, he knew, would be out of the question. The precedent for divorce within the Royal Family had actually been made in 1967, when the Earl of Harewood, the Queen's cousin, was sued for adultery by his wife. He had been living with his former secretary, Patricia Tuckwell, for sixteen months and had a son, Mark, by her. The divorce itself posed no problem, but if the Earl wanted to remarry, which he did, under the Royal Marriages Act the Queen had to give her consent. This had presented her with a dilemma. As Supreme Governor of the Church it was impossible for her to condone divorce because it was contrary to Anglican doctrine. On the other hand, if she had prevented her cousin from remarrying in an age of increasing sexual permissiveness and a general relaxation in the divorce laws, she would have been condemned by public opinion for being chronically out of touch. The Prime Minister, Harold Wilson, came to her aid. He put the question to Cabinet and was then formally able to advise the Queen to consent to Harewood's remarriage, which turned her approval into just another piece of legislation to which she gave the royal consent, and not technically a matter for the Church.

Thus in 1978, when it was clear that Princess Margaret's marriage to Lord Snowdon had broken down irretrievably, the way was clear for them to divorce without undue fuss and without threatening the fundamental security of the monarchy. The Queen, who at one time had not even allowed divorcees into the

Royal Enclosure at Ascot, turned it to her advantage. She happened to like Snowdon personally, and was eager to help both parties through their difficulties, and ensure that the children's suffering should be minimal. So she continued to invite her ex-brother-in-law to family events, including her fiftieth birthday party, and, far from casting the couple out, set a public example of how divorce can be handled in a civilized and caring way.

The monarchy had come a long way since 1936 when Edward VIII had been forced to give up the crown because the woman he wanted to marry was a divorcee; or even 1953 when, before Princess Margaret met Lord Snowdon (then Anthony Armstrong-Jones), she was forced to give up plans to marry Group Captain Peter Townsend because he was a divorcee. Nevertheless, while it might be possible for those members of the family who were never likely to succeed to the throne, divorce for Prince Charles, who was almost certain to, and would therefore one day be Supreme Governor of the Church, was impossible.

Whenever asked for his views on marriage, he had repeatedly spoken of the need to choose someone who would know what they were letting themselves in for. 'I've fallen in love with all sorts of girls and I fully intend to go on doing so,' he had said in 1975,

> but I've made sure I haven't married the first person I've fallen in love with. I think one's got to be aware of the fact that falling madly in love with someone is not necessarily the starting point to getting married.
>
> [Marriage] is basically a very strong friendship. . . . I think you are lucky if you find the person attractive in the physical and the mental sense. . . . To me marriage seems to be the biggest and most responsible step to be taken in one's life.
>
> Whatever your place in life, when you marry you are forming a partnership which you hope will last for fifty years. So I'd want to marry someone whose interests I could share. A woman not only marries a man; she marries into a way of life – a job. She's got to have some knowledge of it, some sense of it; otherwise she wouldn't have a clue about whether she's going to like it. If I'm deciding on whom I want to live with for fifty years – well, that's the last decision on which I want my head to be ruled by my heart.

They were brave words and, in the event, far easier to utter than to carry out. One further criterion was implicit: his bride would have to be a virgin. Incredibly, the notion that well-bred young men should marry virgins, while those self-same virgins were expected to accept husbands who had slept with as many women as possible before coming to the marriage bed, still existed. Even in 1986, when Prince Andrew married Sarah Ferguson, who had had several previous lovers, the tide of public opinion raged against her and for a while looked as though it might jeopardize the marriage. So on top of all the other specifications Charles had to find a woman who was inexperienced.

In the 1970s this was no simple task, particularly since as he grew older the girls he tended to meet were also older, and therefore likely to have had more experience of life. Thus the vast majority of his girlfriends were never serious contenders. Even those of whom he was especially fond, like Davina Sheffield, a soldier's daughter, had to go when her ex-fiancé let it be known that they had lived together.

One girlfriend who met all his criteria was Lady Camilla Fane, daughter of the 16th Earl of Westmoreland who was a lord in waiting to the Queen. She was pretty, full of bounce, intelligent and a strong character who could have held her own in public life; and with a father who worked for the Queen she was no stranger to royalty and to its customs and protocol, and perfectly at ease in its company. The Prince fell deeply in love with Camilla – more so, some friends say, than he has ever been again. She was in love with him, and would have married him at the drop of a hat. Alas, he never asked her. He dithered and hedged his bets, and could not resist the charms of other women, until Camilla gave up on him. It was only when she was irretrievably gone, married to an unremarkable cavalry officer called Andrew Parker-Bowles, that the Prince realized what he had lost. There was no longer any chance that she could be his Princess, but Charles has remained close friends with Camilla. Up until the time of his own marriage in 1981 he was a frequent visitor to their home in Wiltshire – less so now – and they would join him for weekends at Sandringham, Windsor and Balmoral; and the Prince is godfather to their son Thomas.

He is also godfather to Charles Tryon, whose mother, Lady Tryon, is another former girlfriend with whom he has remained friends. Dale first met Prince Charles on one of his trips to Australia in the late 1960s. She subsequently married Lord Anthony Tryon, a man ten years her senior whose late father was

Treasurer to the Queen. She is a larger than life Australian, big-hearted, with a wild and slightly uncouth sense of humour, widely known by the nickname that Prince Charles gave her, 'Kanga', short for kangaroo. She is now even designing clothes under the name.

Anthony Tryon is by contrast a somewhat sombre character. A financier like his father, in his capacity as director of the merchant bankers Lazard Brothers, and chairman of English and Scottish Investors Ltd, he has from time to time been able to give Prince Charles advice in financial matters. As well as a house in London they have a seven hundred acre estate in Wiltshire and a holiday lodge in Iceland. Until the time of his marriage Prince Charles was a regular guest in all three places: in London to dine, in Wiltshire to shoot pheasant, and in Iceland to spend a week or ten days fishing in complete privacy in the remote and rugged terrain near Egilsstadir.

One of the most significant girlfriends whom Prince Charles had in that period was Lady Sarah Spencer. Although Earl Spencer, as Viscount Althorp, had been an equerry to the Queen and lived in a house on the royal estate at Sandringham, Charles had never consciously met his young neighbour until 1977 when Sarah was invited to join the Queen's house party at Windsor for Royal Ascot. She was red-haired, pretty and vivacious, and he was instantly attracted. Camilla Fane was also one of the Queen's guests at the racecourse that week, and it was one of the last occasions on which she was ever seen in public with Prince Charles.

For the rest of that year Sarah occupied a considerable amount of his time, culminating in a skiing trip the following February to Klosters in Switzerland. Speculation that she might be his future Princess was rife when she decided to put the record straight and speak to ardent royal watcher James Whitaker:

> He is fabulous as a person, but I am not in love with him. He is a romantic who falls in love easily. But I can assure you that if there were to be any engagement between Prince Charles and myself it would have happened by now.
>
> I am a whirlwind sort of lady as opposed to a person who goes in for long, slow-developing courtships. Of course, the Prince and I are great friends, but I was with him in Switzerland because of my skiing ability.

> Our relationship is totally platonic. I do not believe that Prince Charles wants to marry yet. He has still not met the person he wants to marry. I think of him as the big brother I never had.

Then, perhaps a thoughtless postscript, she added, 'I wouldn't marry anyone I didn't love, whether it was the dustman or the King of England. If he asked me I would turn him down.'

Apart from doing nothing for the Prince's ego, subsequent events were to prove one of her statements quite wrong. Prince Charles had already met the person he would later want to marry: Sarah's youngest sister, Diana. It was in November 1977, when Sarah had invited Charles down to Althorp, the Spencer family estate in Northamptonshire, for a weekend shoot. Diana was home from boarding school in Kent for half term, and they met initially in the unromantic setting of a ploughed field on a part of the estate known as Nobottle Wood. After a chilly morning out of doors the shooting party returned for lunch in the stable block: a steaming stew with mashed potatoes and brussels sprouts, followed by one of Prince Charles's favourite puddings, treacle sponge. Soon after lunch the Prince drove home to London, and Diana, who was just sixteen, returned to school for a second shot at her O Levels – soundly in love with her sister's boyfriend.

CHAPTER ELEVEN

During 1974 the explorer Colonel John Blashford-Snell led a particularly dangerous expedition up the Zaire River in the Congo. It was an unusual party because in addition to the usual mixture of scientists, explorers, marines and local soldiers, three specially selected young men were in the team: two from the island of Jersey, and one from the United States. None of the three knew the first thing about the jungle.

They were there because they had won a competition. In the midst of his preparations – raising funds and getting together supplies and equipment – Blashford-Snell had had a telephone call from the advertising director of the Royal Trust Company of Canada, a merchant bank based in Jersey. How would he like to run a competition in Jersey to find a young lad to take down the Congo? It was the bank's seventy-fifth anniversary, and to mark the occasion they wanted to do something for the island; they suggested donating money to the expedition by sponsoring a local lad.

Blashford-Snell was initially hesitant; the expedition was no seaside picnic. They were going armed and expected trouble; but after considerable thought he agreed, and a specially devised competition was held to test potential leadership and physical endurance. It involved being subjected for forty-eight hours or more to the most terrifying situations – like being woken in the night by screaming natives – which required both courage and initiative, and out of the sixteen finalists two outstanding candidates remained. They were so close that it was hard to choose between them, but one was a newly qualified police cadet, so Blashford-Snell went to the Commissioner of Police and asked whether he might be able to raise some sponsorship for the boy so that both winners could go. This was achieved. Meanwhile the US Ambassador, Walter Annenberg, said he wanted to help; could they take a third boy from the United States? Thus the expedition departed, and any doubts that their leader may have had about the boys vanished. They acquitted themselves brilliantly.

On their return at the end of the year there was a certain amount of publicity, and the two Jersey boys then began touring schools and youth centres talking about their exploits. News of it filtered through to the Prince of Wales. Shortly afterwards, at a regimental dinner one night, he met his equerry for Wales, Alun Davis, who had been on the Zaire expedition, and another explorer, Colonel David Bromhead. Bromhead had been on John Blashford-Snell's famous Blue Nile expedition in the late sixties, as had a friend of Charles's at Cambridge called Gage Williams. At the time the Prince had said that he wished he could have gone too. During the regimental dinner that night both men spoke of some of their more exciting moments while exploring, and Bromhead told the Prince about the epic battle that had ended the Blue Nile expedition. They had been attacked by murderous tribesmen in the middle of the night, and had Bromhead and one other sentinel not managed to hold the enemy off until the rest of the party woke and found their guns, none of them would have lived to tell the tale.

The next day Blashford-Snell had a telephone call from David Checketts inviting him to come and talk to the Prince of Wales. Sitting in his office at Buckingham Palace, the Prince said he was interested in this idea of taking young people on expeditions. If they could take two or three, why not take more?

Blashford-Snell, who is a serious explorer and one of the most experienced in the world, was dubious about the practicality of it, but they talked through various ideas and he promised to go away and think. Some months later he returned with a suggestion: over the course of two years, a 150-ton British brigantine should sail around the world, taking young explorers on a new voyage of discovery. He could get together servicemen and scientists, who would lead teams of international young explorers – four hundred in all – on expeditions in countries on the way. Each young person would fly out from their home country to join one of the expeditions for two or three months, working on a variety of scientific and community projects. The scheme would combine worthwhile scientific research and community service; it would be a challenge for the young and an excellent opportunity for them to discover within themselves qualities of leadership.

Prince Charles was excited by the idea. He had already made two speeches in the House of Lords about the need for young people to have something challenging to do with their leisure time.

'How much would it cost?' he asked.

Blashford-Snell had worked out that because of the expense of the ships and aircraft involved, they would need roughly £900,000.

'If you can get the money,' said the Prince of Wales, 'I will be patron.'

Next was the question of finding a name, and after some thought they hit on Operation Drake, as the year happened to coincide with the four hundredth anniversary of Drake's circumnavigation of the world. Prince Charles could not do any overt fund-raising because his position precludes it. However he did write an open letter that could be used in a general way, explaining what Operation Drake was all about. 'I seem to remember Sir Francis Drake managed to elicit a little discreet royal support provided there were sufficient rewards for well-planned piracy. Times have changed. Charles.'

Charles took an active interest throughout, and when money came in he wrote many personal letters thanking people from all over the world for their donations. David Checketts sat on the committee. The money that actually got the project off the ground came from his host of yore, Walter Annenberg. The former US Ambassador had, of course, helped to fund the Zaire River expedition, so John Blashford-Snell flew to Palm Springs with his wife and two young daughters to stay with Annenberg and solicit his help again.

They had scarcely been there five minutes before the American swept the two little girls into a golf trolley. 'I don't suppose you play golf?' he said.

'No.'

'Do you play polo?'

'No.'

'Well, I'll show you. The Prince of Wales plays polo on these golf trollies.' Whereupon he set off with the two girls, bouncing over his priceless eighteen-hole golf course and playing polo with golf clubs, just as he had done on the Prince's visit four years earlier.

'How much money do you need to go?' he said when he finally got down to business with their father.

Blashford-Snell mentioned the sum he needed for the seed money in pounds.

'Ah, I can't do it without a calculator. I'll give you $100,000. Will that be all right?'

Thus the *Eye of the Wind* set sail from Plymouth on the first leg of her two-year journey, taking a disparate crew of young men and women aged between seventeen and twenty-four from all over Britain. The only thing they had in common was that they had survived the gruelling selection test devised by Colonel Blashford-Snell. The ultimate test of nerve came at the end of a forty-eight-hour period without sleep. Furnished with nothing but a pair of bathroom scales, they had to find some unspecified animal in a pitch-black hut and weigh it. One coloured boy who had been born and bred in the centre of Birmingham came across a sheep in the darkness. He had never even seen a real sheep before, let alone touched one, yet he picked it up and stood with it on the scales. Another successful applicant was a girl who encountered a nineteen-foot snake in the darkness. Try as she might to keep a grip, it always wriggled out of her grasp and she ended up wrapping it around her body.

The venture was a resounding success, and when it was only halfway through its programme the Prince of Wales summoned George Thurstan, who was coordinator of funds and operations at base, to breakfast at Buckingham Palace. He said it would be a shame to waste all the expertise that had gone into Operation Drake. What about doing it all over again on a bigger scale? So when the *Eye of the Wind* sailed into London's St Katharine's Dock in December 1980, to the cheers of the waiting crowd which included the Prince of Wales and 212 of the foreign young explorers who had been a part of Drake and had come to London specially to welcome the final teams home, plans were already underway for a second expedition that would take four thousand young people around the world.

There was a strong flavour of Kurt Hahn in projects like these – not only because they combined young people, community service and adventure, but also because of the essential international element. Prince Charles was and is a truly international man; and he subscribed to Hahn's vision, shared by Earl Mountbatten, of a harmonious world where nations are so educated that they understand, and so tolerate, one another.

The belief that national barriers could be reduced and

international cooperation fostered by education had been the principle behind an organization first called Atlantic College, and subsequently the United World Colleges, which Hahn co-founded in 1962 with Air Marshal Sir Lawrence Darvall amongst others. Situated at St Donat's Castle in South Wales it was a sixth form college which now has three hundred international students, most of whom are on scholarships, combining two years of academic study with physically demanding activities and service to the community. The idea is that by living, studying and putting their lives in the hands of fellow students of every race, colour and creed under the sun, they will take the message of racial harmony home to their own countries, and bit by bit mankind will learn. The regime was much the same as at Gordonstoun, but where Gordonstoun had been concerned with the perils of puberty, Atlantic College was a preparation for life. The students come for the last two years of their school career, and study for an international school-leaving examination, the International Baccalaureate now recognized by most universities in the world, including Oxford and Cambridge.

Lord Mountbatten had become chairman of the College in 1968, and one of his first acts had been to change its name to United World Colleges, which represented the global nature of the school more effectively. The entire concept was a dream in which he believed passionately, and although well into middle age by then he threw himself with full-blooded enthusiasm into the task of promoting the college and inspiring everyone around him. He travelled indefatigably on its behalf, turned every occasion into an opportunity to slip in a word about UWC, often in the very highest places, and raised money shamelessly but successfully wherever he went. After ten years in the job he had whipped up such enthusiasm worldwide that not only had the College got well and truly off the ground in Wales, but new colleges had been set up in Canada and Singapore.

When he could not be there to spread the word himself, he would get others to do it on his behalf. 'I do hope your lunch with Tito went off all right,' he wrote to the Queen, 'and that you were able to put in a word on behalf of UWC. I am very worried to hear that it may be difficult for you to fit in a visit to the UWC activities in the Singapore International School. . . . Could you not just drive through the school? It would be such a shot in the arm, particularly as you are our Patron.'

On another occasion the President of Zambia, Kenneth Kaunda, was visiting London, and Mountbatten had been invited to an official breakfast meeting at which he hoped to be able to broach the subject of UWC. However on arriving at the Hilton Hotel, where Kaunda was staying, he was told by the Zambian High Commissioner that there would be no chance of a private conversation: the President would have his Minister of Finance on one side of him and the British Government's representative, Lady Llewellyn-Davies, on the other. Undeterred, the old fox slipped into the dining room ahead of everyone else and rearranged the place cards so that he was sitting next to Lady Llewellyn-Davies, just one seat away from the President. As the meal began, he ostentatiously leaned across his neighbour to say that he had a special message from the Prince of Wales which he had promised to transmit. Lady Llewellyn-Davies obligingly suggested they change places. 'I then had twenty minutes' uninterrupted conversation with Kenneth Kaunda and found him really interested in the United World College concept. I gradually worked him up, gave him a brochure and an aide memoire and told him exactly what I wanted him to do. He gave it some thought, then said: "All right, I'll do everything you say." We then stood up and dramatically shook hands on it.'

After those ten hard-working years in the job Mountbatten felt it was time to slow down, so he handed the presidency over to the one person whom he knew he could trust to carry on the crusade with energy and commitment: Prince Charles. In taking up the post the Prince told the Council:

> I did in fact receive some ominous overtures from Lord Mountbatten several years ago and I was somewhat anxious and reluctant due to my age and inexperience, particularly when I now learn that I am at least a generation younger than all of you here, but now I hear that Gordonstoun is about to have a thirty-one-year-old headmaster, I am not nearly so worried as I was before. . . .
>
> I know I was not democratically elected but I feel that having been at least to Gordonstoun, I like to think that I have passed some sort of selection test. . . .
>
> My acceptance of the Presidency was based really on a deep and personal conviction of the intrinsic merits of the UWC concept which I think in many ways is close to the Gordonstoun ideal which essentially is the belief in the importance of human relationships in world affairs. . . .

> And last but not least the Presidency does provide me, in particular, with an ideal topic of discussion with Heads of State and so on, throughout the world, so at least I do not waste their time which is rather what I am inclined to do.

Prince Charles was the natural successor, and only too delighted to take over, but he was not his great-uncle's clone. The style of the two men was quite different: where Mountbatten succeeded by charismatic bullying, Charles took the softly-softly approach. His success took the route of coercion by charm. In addition, where Mountbatten could blatantly raise funds, Charles, being heir to the throne, had to be more subtle. Of his predecessor, the Prince said:

> I've seen him in action all over the world, cornering terrified people during receptions, and last year while he was trapping some unfortunate Commonwealth leaders during a reception at Buckingham Palace in one corner, I was trying to emulate him by cornering others in another corner about the Silver Jubilee Appeal. All I can say is that I have been brought up in a very good school! We are, of course, tremendously fortunate that he has decided to remain on as our International Life Patron in which role his prodigious energy appears to be quite unflagging.

Such was his energy that Mountbatten could not resist the temptation to interfere; however Prince Charles was no longer the fledgling he was, and he responded with a stiff note.

> I agreed to take over as President from you on the understanding (as I saw it) that you wished to cut down on your commitments, etc. From the way you have been tackling things recently, it looks as though you are still going to do too much as Patron. I hate having to say this, but I believe in being *absolutely* honest with you, and when I take over as President I may easily want to do things in my own particular way, and in a way which could conflict with your ideas. So please don't be surprised if, like the other evening at Broadlands, I disagree with your approach or appear to be awkward and argumentative. I am only taking a leaf out of your book after all.

If Mountbatten was chastened it was barely discernible, and his withdrawal from UWC was not immediately apparent; but their friendship continued unimpaired.

Mountbatten's would have been a difficult act for Charles to follow, however he had behaved; and no one was more aware than Prince Charles himself that people would be comparing the two of them to see if he matched up to the great man. He had spent the first twenty-eight years of his life following in his father's footsteps; now for the first time he had to contend with his great-uncle's too.

He took on the United World Colleges, therefore, all the more determined to make a positive contribution, and in nearly ten years he has succeeded. According to their manifesto UWC have two main aims: 'to promote international understanding through education; and to provide a pattern of education adapted to meet the special needs of our time'. In Mountbatten's ten years he concentrated on the former. Prince Charles has seen the need to move with the times.

In the course of an official visit to Venezuela during the year he took over Charles took time off to meet a group of former students, as he does on any visit to parts of the world where there are ex-students. They began talking about the crisis in that part of the world, which relies so heavily upon agriculture. Because of the drift from the land to the towns there was a growing shortage of farmers. Venezuela alone had lost nearly sixty thousand farmers, and the trend was universal. What they should have, the students said, was an international agricultural college, right there in Venezuela, which could tackle the problem of under-productivity and do something for the world.

Prince Charles was immediately taken by the idea, and although he had already seen the President and completed the official side of his programme he requested a second audience. President Carlos Andres Perez, very excited at the thought of a college in Venezuela, sent for three of his ministers and told them to start work on proposals.

By chance there was an eminent Venezuelan agronomist on a sabbatical at Reading University. UWC consulted him, and he was largely instrumental not only in bringing about an agreement between UWC and the Venezuelan government, but also in securing the gift of a seventeen hundred acre farm. Political upheaval in the country worked in their favour. The incoming party decided to decentralize agricultural training, and what had been a regional training centre for farm labourers became redundant at the precise moment that UWC were looking for a suitable site.

Of all the colleges, the Prince of Wales is probably particularly proud of the Venezuelan one, which should be fully operational by 1988. Dedicated though he is to the aims of the other establishments, on the face of it they are sending specially selected bright young people to university. At the Simon Bolivar United World College of Agriculture in Venezuela, however, they have broken away from the traditional curriculum. They are teaching young people agricultural skills specially designed for the developing countries of the world; trying to tackle the problems of poverty, famine and disease; providing a practical training at grass-roots level to meet a fundamental need.

This is a departure from the norm, but the Prince was keen to promote it, not only because it was a subject close to his heart – he believes that change in emerging countries must come from the villages and not from well-educated leaders – but because it was pragmatic. Speaking at the International Council Meeting at St Donat's in 1985, he said:

> If the world could see that, in addition to our more conventional educational efforts, we were playing a significant part in educating young people from across the globe to tackle some of the huge survival problems facing the developing world, e.g. hunger, poverty, conservation of our resources and health, we would surely the more easily and quickly attract the global attention and awareness which are two of our most obvious deficiencies.
>
> Such programmes carry their own intrinsic merit and are worth pursuing for their own sake, but we could help ourselves by positively espousing them, for without a better international image and wider international awareness of our admirable aims and activities, we will continue to experience difficulties in obtaining recognition and support, not least financial support. Without this recognition too, we will not attract the level of support from Governments which we need to achieve.

The charge against UWC has always been that it was an elitist organization, which it unashamedly is; but it is elitist in the sense that it admits no one but the best.

'I am not in favour of an elite if it is solely based on birth and wealth,' said Prince Charles, when challenged,

> but I am certainly in favour if it is based on high standards which provide the student with a challenge that is really

worthwhile. Surely we need individuals who are prepared to set examples by their approach to life and, in the case of ex-UWC students, individuals who have had the privilege of meeting people from all over the world and thus forming a more comprehensive picture of the things that unite us all, rather than those which divide us. Unhesitatingly, I am proud to acknowledge that I am associated with such an elite, and even if we only produce about three hundred such students a year, this is far, far better than none at all.

Wealth and status count for nothing at UWC. The scholarship structure is an essential ingredient, which on top of administrative costs, heating and maintenance bills, staff wages and equipment means that a great deal of money has to be found each year to keep the colleges afloat. At Atlantic College alone the headmaster, former diplomat Andrew Stuart, has to find £2 million.

St Donat's Castle, perched over the south Glamorgan coast, with gardens falling away to the sea, is a dramatic mixture of medieval and modern; the original stonework was magnificently restored by the previous owner, the American publishing millionaire Randolph Hearst I, as a love nest. The round tower, with a sumptuous room at the top where Prince Charles stays if he needs a room overnight, overlooks the jousting field to one side and to the other the Beast Garden, where no matter in which part of the garden you stand one of the mythological stone creatures has its eye on you. From there it is a short walk to the two swimming pools, one outdoor, the other covered, and the slipway to the Bristol Channel beyond, an ants' nest of activity with boats and canoes being hauled in and out of the angry sea. The surprise comes when you realize that the students doing the hauling are every size, shape and skin colour on earth, and they are not in clusters of one particular sort. They are truly integrated. You cannot fail to go there and talk to the students without coming away convinced that there is hope for the world.

The director general, Sir Ian Gourlay, was talking to a boy from Zimbabwe who had been in the college three weeks. He was the first student they had had from Zimbabwe, and he was sharing a dormitory with a Venezuelan, a British boy and one from Peking. Sir Ian asked him for a first impression. 'I'd be interested to hear what you've got to say about the boy from Peking,' he said.

A great smile lit up the boy's face. 'I've made a discovery that he can laugh,' said the Zimbabwean.

Sir Ian was puzzled. 'But we all laugh,' he said. 'That's no discovery.' At this the boy explained that in the newspapers in Zimbabwe the Chinese in their severe uniforms and high Mao collars were not a race who smiled.

A Finnish student spoke of a more commonly felt response: 'When you come into the school you have an idea of how things are. But then you have all your ideas broken down. You start to learn how to pick out the truth. You start to see the truth from other people's points of view. That is how you change the world.'

Prince Charles finds talking to the students one of the most fascinating and rewarding aspects of the whole enterprise. Most years he hosts a party at Kensington Palace for a group from Atlantic College during their London visit, but while he enjoys seeing them it was not entirely his idea in the first place. He had a letter one year from a South American girl from the College. She explained that she and two friends were coming to London and that they were very worried because they had nowhere to stay. She was sure he would agree that it was not very safe for young girls to be wandering around London on their own, and wondered if he might be able to put them up for the night at Buckingham Palace.

Charles sent the note on to Sir Ian Gourlay with a large question mark on it; and Sir Ian in turn rang the College to find out what it was all about. Far from the three girls being cast loose in London on their own, they were already booked into a youth centre, and what the author had failed to mention in her letter was that they were coming in a party with 160 others. Profuse apologies were proffered from the College for this girl's wayward behaviour; they had no idea she had written, and would His Royal Highness please ignore the letter. Charles, however, was amused, and so admired the young lady's enterprise that he invited her to the Palace in any event – not to stay, but to a cocktail party with the rest of the students. It was such a resounding success that he has held one almost every year since.

Having managed to get the Venezuelan college on the road, the Prince of Wales began to look at other likely places where a training centre relating to the needs of our time would be appropriate, and the obvious place was India. It was one of the few major countries that he had never visited in his travels around the world, yet the one with which he was most familiar from all he had heard from his great-uncle. As Lord Mountbatten had written in his diary the day before landing in India for the first time: 'I am not by nature incurably romantic but there is something rather wonderful, rather thrilling at the idea of setting foot for the first time in a country which genuinely belongs to the Far East. India is a country one has heard about, read about, even dreamt about, but up to the present I have found it hopeless to conceive what it is like in real life.'

More than twenty years later he returned with the most controversial and unenviable job in the entire history of the British Empire. He was the man charged with giving India her independence in 1947, and who presided over some of the bloodiest religious massacres in history, that resulted in the partition of the sub-continent into India and Pakistan.

Mountbatten's first trip, which he had written about so enthusiastically in his diary, had been undertaken in the company of the last Prince of Wales in 1921, and he was very keen to come full circle and accompany the present Prince of Wales on his first visit too. He had never lost that initial excitement; he loved the country and knew it better than anyone. He would be an excellent guide as well as a great companion. Plans were underway in early 1979 for a trip later in the year, which would include Lady Amanda Knatchbull in the party; but, according to Mountbatten's biographer Philip Ziegler, the Duke of Edinburgh stepped in. Charles, he argued, should not pay his first visit to India in the shadow of this legendary figure, who would inevitably claim the limelight. Mountbatten promised he would keep a low profile, but argued that his presence would be helpful to the Prince. The Duke was unconvinced, and to make matters worse for Mountbatten his son-in-law Lord Brabourne agreed with the Duke that Charles would be better on his own.

Mountbatten wrote to tell Charles what had happened:

> From a purely selfish point of view I must confess I would be very very sad to have to forgo the great happiness of being with two young people I love so much and showing them the country which means so much to me, but if the price of my selfishness were to spoil the visit for you, then that would be a price I could not even contemplate.
>
> So will you please think this over carefully so we can discuss it the next time we meet?

In the end they reached a compromise. All three would travel out to India together, then split up and go their separate ways, meeting once or twice and for two days' holiday at the end. But David Checketts was still dubious.

'You think I'll take over the whole show, don't you?' said Mountbatten angrily.

As things turned out, the question was hypothetical.

CHAPTER TWELVE

One of Earl Mountbatten's great pleasures in life was spending August with his family at Classiebawn Castle in County Sligo, Ireland. It was a neo-Gothic horror in breathtaking surroundings which had come to the Mountbattens via Lord Louis' wife, Edwina. 'You never told me how stupendously magnificent the surrounding scenery was,' he wrote to her after seeing it for the first time in 1941. 'No place ever thrilled me more and I can't wait to move in.'

The excitement had never worn off, and August at Classiebawn became an institution only ever shared with children, grandchildren and the very closest and oldest of friends. 'It is wonderful to have such a delightful family, and all ten of my grandchildren are absolutely enchanting,' he wrote. 'I am indeed a very lucky person.' There every year the loneliness that had been in his life since Edwina's death in 1960 was abated. For a whole month he was surrounded by the family he adored, doing the things they had all done since infants – shrimping, lobster potting, fishing for mackerel, riding along the beach, building castles in the sand and dams across the mouth of the stream – and Mountbatten was happier there than anywhere else on earth.

The only pleasure he had to forego on this month away, because it was in the Irish Republic, was the company of any member of the Royal Family. Instead they went to their own holiday retreat, at Balmoral, where they substituted fly fishing for mackerel, and stalking for shrimping, but otherwise gathered in a tight family group, inviting only the most intimate of friends to spend six weeks of treasured privacy, enjoying the same routine year after year.

That August the Prince of Wales was spending part of his summer holiday with the Tryons at their fishing lodge in Iceland, which had become a regular trip, but before leaving he had written a note to Mountbatten at Classiebawn, as he regularly did, adding, 'I hope you are having a decent rest in Ireland and are not working unnecessarily hard.'

Mountbatten had known that he was taking a risk with his life every time he went to Ireland. All members of the Royal Family, all prominent soldiers and politicians were obvious targets for the IRA, and as early as 1971 the police had put twelve men on guard outside Classiebawn in case there was an attempted kidnap. Every year Mountbatten would write and inform Scotland Yard of his plans, and the wisdom of going to County Sligo was debated; but each time the considered opinion of the Home Office, the Foreign Office and the Ministry of Defence was that it was a risk which could reasonably be taken.

The Irish Garda provided protection for the family during August. A police escort went with them whenever they left the castle grounds, and men were on guard round the clock, but Mountbatten knew as well as anyone – and as every member of the Royal Family knows – that no amount of protection will stop a determined killer. For the pleasure of his month at Classiebawn Mountbatten was prepared to take the risk.

At about 11.30 on the morning of 27 August, Lord Mountbatten set off to inspect the lobster pots in his twenty-nine-foot fishing boat *Shadow V*, which he kept in the little harbour of Mullaghmore. Accompanying him that day were his daughter Patricia and her husband John (Lord and Lady Brabourne), their fourteen-year-old twin sons, Nicholas and Timothy, Lord Brabourne's elderly mother Doreen, and a local Irish boy called Paul Maxwell who enjoyed helping with the boat. Until recently they had always taken a policeman along with them too, but after one of them was miserably seasick Mountbatten had said there was no real need to have anyone on board. The Garda had remained ashore instead and watched operations from the coast road.

As they reached the first lobster pot, some distance outside the harbour wall, a fifty-pound bomb planted by the IRA and probably detonated by remote control exploded beneath Mountbatten's feet. He was killed instantly. Also killed were Nicholas Knatchbull and Paul Maxwell. The boat disintegrated into sticks of matchwood and mangled metal, and it is a miracle that there were any survivors at all; however both Lord and Lady Brabourne and their other son, Timothy, were pulled out of the sea badly hurt but alive. Lady Brabourne senior also survived the explosion but died in hospital the next day.

The IRA announced that it had been 'a discriminate operation to bring to the attention of the English people the continuing occupation of our country'. Mountbatten's 'execution' was a way of 'bringing emotionally home to the English ruling-class and its working-class slaves . . . that their government's war on us is going to cost them as well. . . . We will tear out their sentimental, imperialist heart.'

The IRA tore out many a heart that day, but none more painfully than that of the Prince of Wales. Only a year earlier he had written to his great-uncle to thank him for some advice and for allowing him to pick his brains: 'As I said to you yesterday, I have no idea what we shall do without you when you finally decide to depart. It doesn't bear thinking about, but I only hope I shall have learnt *something* from you in order to carry it on in some way or another.'

Charles was in Iceland. Michael Colborne got word through to his detective, Paul Officer, who went out to the fjord where the Prince was fishing to tell him what had happened. They flew back to London immediately and Charles went straight to Windsor Castle, where his father came to see him briefly. The Prince was utterly devastated, shocked and frightened, and quite alone in his grief. His display of emotion was anathema to his father, a firm believer in the British stiff upper lip, but Charles was unable to hold back his tears.

Ace strategist that he was, Mountbatten had planned for his death some years in advance and worked out in the finest detail the arrangements for the funeral, including the principal participants and guests as well as the procession to the Abbey. He had discussed it with Prince Charles, asking whether his great-nephew would read the lesson, and had then left all his instructions in a letter given to the Lord Chamberlain in 1972. The funeral he wanted was a blend of military and international, attended by dignitaries from all over the world. He had written:

> To keep the Service short, it is suggested that there be no address, unless the Prime Minister felt he would like to say a word, in which case it is hoped it will be short and mainly confined to Lord Mountbatten's efforts to find peaceful solutions for the emergent nations of South East Asia . . . and to helping India and Pakistan to attain

> independence. . . . His personal leadership, as long ago as 1945, helped to set the line on which the British Empire changed itself into the Commonwealth of sovereign states. . . .
>
> The Royal Marines Prayer and Life Guards Prayer could be omitted, though this would be a pity since Lord Mountbatten had been Life Colonel Commandant of the Royal Marines and Colonel of the Life Guards since 1965.

He wanted the Prayer of Sir Francis Drake; the hymns would be 'Eternal Father', 'Jerusalem' and 'I vow to thee, my country'; and the lesson Psalm 107.

Mountbatten's instructions were carried out to the letter: it was a fitting procession of pomp and ceremony that made its way to Westminster Abbey; and, fighting back the tears like many other people in the congregation, Prince Charles read Psalm 107: 'They that go down to the sea in ships. . . .'

After the service in Westminster Abbey his body was taken on the train to Romsey, accompanied by a select group of friends who had lunch on the way. This too Mountbatten had organized, leaving alternative menus for summer and winter. Everything was timed with military precision. He had told Mrs Shrimati Pandit, sister of the late Indian Prime Minister, Jawaharlal Nehru, that she would be included in this select party, and that she would just have time to finish her coffee before the train arrived at Romsey station. It was not until the day of the funeral that she remembered the conversation. As she put down her empty coffee cup the train drew to a halt and they had reached their destination. Family and friends gathered round the graveside to say their last farewells, and amongst the many hundreds of flowers and wreaths was one which simply read: 'To HGF from HGS' – to Honorary Grandfather from Honorary Grandson.

In a memorial service for the Earl in St Paul's Cathedral on 20 December, the Prince of Wales delivered probably the most moving of all his public addresses, and encapsulated all that he admired most about his great-uncle, much of which he has tried to emulate in his own life.

> Does it not seem a cruel and bitter irony that a man who served under Admiral Beatty in his flagship during the first war, who in the second war was torpedoed, mined and finally sunk by aerial bombardment in HMS *Kelly*, who helped defeat the scourge of tyranny and oppression

throughout Europe and the Far East and finally ensured that independence should be brought to the continent of India – that a man with such passionate concern for the individual and for progressive thought and action should suddenly and mercilessly be blown to bits with members of the family he adored through the agency of some of the most cowardly minds imaginable? Without the heroic efforts of people like Lord Mountbatten this country, and many others like it, might even now be under the sway of some foreign power – devoid of the kind of liberty we take so easily for granted in this day and age. Perhaps the manner of his passing will awaken us – or is it too much to hope for? – to the vulnerability of civilized democracies from the kind of sub-human extremism that blows people up when it feels like it. . . .

Although he could certainly be ruthless with people when the occasion demanded, his infectious enthusiasm, his sheer capacity for hard work, his wit made him an irresistible leader among men. People who served under him or worked on his various staffs invariably adored him. And why? Because I believe that above all else he was honest. He was devastatingly frank with people. There was never any doubt as to where you stood – you always knew what he thought about you, whether it was complimentary or rude. That quality of real moral courage, of being able to face unpleasant tasks that need to be done – and yet to be fair and consistent – is a rare quality indeed. But he had it in abundance and that, I think, is one of the reasons why people would have followed him into hell, if he had explained the point of such an expedition. . . . It is also one of the reasons why I adored him and why so many of us miss him so dreadfully now. . . .

After fifty years of service to the Royal Navy that he loved and after defending his country in two world wars they finally succeeded in murdering a man who was desperately trying to sow the seeds of peace for future generations. Rarely have the immortal words of Laurence Binyon been more appropriate – 'They shall not grow old as we that are left grow old. Age shall not weary them, nor the years condemn. At the going down of the sun and in the morning – we will remember him.'

The only comfort was that Mountbatten, as Prince Charles knew, had dreaded the frailties of old age, which he was now spared. He was nearly eighty when he died, but up until that moment had been as active, autocratic and mentally alert as ever. The tragedy was that two teenagers should have died that day before their adult lives had even begun – one of whom, Nicholas, was his godson. Charles spoke of them too, and of Doreen, Lady Brabourne.

> The fact that two of his family died with him would have appalled Lord Mountbatten. He was, above all, a family man. He was a devoted husband, a deeply affectionate and enlightened father, a wonderful grandfather and a very special great-uncle. He was a man for whom blood was thicker than water – a fact which helped to make him the natural centre of the family and a patriarchal figure who provided advice, frank criticism and boundless affection for all those members of his widespread family, with whom he kept in close touch. . . .
>
> Nicholas Knatchbull . . . had his young life snuffed out so needlessly and so tragically at the age of only fourteen. For his shattered parents and brothers and sisters his death has been the cruellest blow to endure. Here was a young boy of such enormous promise and potential – one minute an innocent, laughing, affectionate personality, the next a lifeless reminder of that dark, inexplicable side of man's nature, which brings death and misery to countless people all over the world.

The events of 27 August irreversibly altered the lives of everyone concerned, but they left Prince Charles with a void that has not yet been filled. He had lost the man who probably meant more to him than any other human being either had or ever would. He had lost a friend and mentor, his principal fount of wisdom and advice, the critic he was prepared to listen to, the shoulder he felt he could cry on, a sounding board for new ideas; and he had lost, above all, the one person who gave him confidence: the one person who so obviously believed in him. Without Mountbatten to ring, write to or call on, Charles felt lost. Life, as he said to his friends, would never be the same again.

CHAPTER THIRTEEN

Prince Charles became deeply depressed after the death of Earl Mountbatten. He retreated to Balmoral and spent many an hour walking the lonely hills, wrapped in thought, with no one but his labrador for company. Mountbatten was such a dynamic force that it had seemed he must go on for ever; he had appeared reassuringly indestructible, and such was his enormous energy and enthusiasm for such a multitude of projects, even at his advanced age, that his sudden departure was all the more shocking. Three weeks after his death the BBC sent a video recording of the obituary they had made up to Balmoral, and Charles sat and watched it over and over again, incredulous. It was not so much what had happened as the manner – the uncompromising swiftness of it all, the finality – and it was some time before he could see his way forward alone.

He drew strength during this period from a number of sources, not least of all his own religious convictions, which were put severely to the test; and it was ultimately there, deep within himself, that he found the courage to continue. He discovered strengths that he was unaware had ever existed.

Norton Knatchbull, now Lord Romsey, was another source. He joined Charles at Balmoral immediately after the funeral with his fiancée, Penelope Eastwood, and through their common grief the two cousins, who had never been especially close before, became firm friends, providing each other with valuable comfort. Norton, like his sister Amanda, had lost not just Mountbatten, his grandfather, but his grandmother and one brother, and most of his family were seriously injured. Day after day they talked it through, talked about Mountbatten and about death, trying to make some sense of it all, and both were no doubt helped in the healing process by doing so.

Charles drew on his friendship with Amanda too, and she in

turn took comfort from him; but any romance between them had died with those four people in the Irish sea. They were like brother and sister again, and so they have remained. Mountbatten's hope that they might one day marry was not to be.

The Queen Mother was the pillar of strength that she had always been to Charles. Theirs had been a special relationship from the very beginning. There was an understanding between them that belongs uniquely to the distance of generation. She understood his sensitivity, saw only good – not weakness – in his artistic nature and his caring and compassionate qualities, and had always been there to listen with a soft and kindly ear to his troubles. Now with the wisdom of age, and the experience of her own bereavement still vivid in her mind even after all the years alone, she was able to offer her eldest grandson patience, support and comfort of the sort that his own parents could not.

Another older person who helped him on the road to recovery was Sir Laurens van der Post, a deeply religious man himself, who with his wife Ingaret took a lost and bewildered Prince into the bosom of his family. He helped Charles to seek the depth and the strength within himself, to use the experience of Mountbatten's death, the suffering, and to learn from it and grow in the spiritual sense. It was this man more than any other who seemed to know so many of the answers to life's mysteries, who helped the Prince of Wales to see clearly again, and to recognize that the ultimate waste of 27 August would be to let Mountbatten down. Charles had received over 2500 letters from people expressing their grief, their sympathy, and their admiration for a man who they felt had in some way belonged to ordinary people, and understood them. He realized he had to keep going for their sake, to carry on where his great-uncle had left off, to work towards democracy and justice in the world and to strive towards peace through knowledge and understanding.

'The United World Colleges movement,' he said in his address at the memorial service, 'was a particular passion of his in the final years because he saw within the scheme a means of bringing peace and international understanding through students from many countries to a world that he had seen pull itself to pieces twice in twenty-five years. He worked long and hard to establish something special for which he held a passionate conviction.' Charles had been left work to do, of which UWC was one small part. If he was to be a leader of men, as Mountbatten had hoped, there was no time and no place for self-pity. In a special tribute he wrote for UWC he said:

> We will miss him more than words can say, but it would surely be his injunction to us now as we stand stunned by his loss, not to slacken the pace for a moment in our pursuit of UWC's great aims and the movement's international development. It is surely by rededicating ourselves to the service of our cause that we can best recognize and salute his inspiring example and keep bright the memory of a rare person indeed.

The Prince was back on course, and it was an older and wiser Prince. The events of 1979, culminating in the death of Mountbatten, had had a sobering effect. During the seventies he had teetered on the brink of excess. He had worked hard, but played harder, he had begun to make politically contentious remarks about matters in which he was insufficiently versed, and he had been seen escorting too many actresses and dallying with the jet set. David Checketts, who had seen him through thick and thin for so long, began to get more and more critical. Charles, who has never taken criticism well, decided he was being nannied and had outgrown the need for one. Matters came to an explosive head, and four months before Mountbatten's death Checketts departed.

The man appointed personal private secretary to the Prince of Wales in his place could not have been more different. Where Checketts was an easy-going family man who enjoyed life and could laugh at himself, the Hon. Edward Adeane was a brilliant barrister, eleven years older than the Prince and older still in demeanour. He is a confirmed bachelor, with no apparent sexuality, meticulously dapper, a corner-stone of the establishment, educated at Eton and Cambridge and a royal courtier through and through. His father, Sir Michael (now Lord) Adeane, had been principal private secretary to the Queen until 1972, and his great-grandfather, Lord Stamfordham, had been private secretary first to Queen Victoria, then to the Duke of York (later George V), in which position he had wielded great power. Edward had himself been a page to the Queen years ago, and was a friend – though never close – of many years' standing. He did not hunt or play polo, but he was a fellow shooting and fishing enthusiast and for several years had been amongst the Tryons' summer party in Iceland.

Adeane was a curious appointment for a Prince who was already well on the way to being a champion of youth and of the common man. He lived in Albany, an exclusive block of flats in Piccadilly, and was a member of Brooks's, the famous gentlemen's club in St James's Street, where he liked nothing better than an after-dinner cigar with his port. The world of tower blocks, dole queues and launderettes was a million miles away. Charming man though he was, and impeccably mannered, he was an intellectual snob; he did not suffer fools gladly, he detested the commercial world and was not immediately sympathetic to the young. It was a relationship in many ways doomed from the start. What is surprising is that it lasted as long as it did.

In addition to the changes in his household, Prince Charles changed addresses. In the autumn of 1979 he moved out of his suite in Buckingham Palace and into an apartment in Kensington Palace, where his neighbours included Princess Margaret, and Prince Michael of Kent, who had just married Marie-Christine von Reibnitz, the former Mrs Tom Trowbridge. It was a match that Lord Mountbatten had fostered, and Charles was not alone among people who knew the couple in puzzling why. Kensington Palace, which lies on the western edge of Hyde Park, was built as a home for William III and Queen Mary, and the early Hanoverian monarchs also lived there. When George III bought Buckingham House in 1762, however, and decided to turn it into a palace, he converted Kensington Palace into apartments for the Royal Family and grace and favour apartments for the royal household.

Charles also owned Chevening, a magnificent seventeenth-century country house in Kent which had become an embarrassing millstone. The house had formerly belonged to the Stanhope family; it had been bought during the reign of George I, by the 1st Earl and handed down in the family until the 7th Earl died in 1967 without an heir. Eight years before his death he had given Chevening to the nation under the Chevening Estate Act, which stipulated that upon his death the Prime Minister should be given first refusal of the house, followed by a Cabinet minister, and finally a lineal descendant of George VI. After meeting Prince Charles in 1965, however, the 7th Earl was so impressed that he wrote a memorandum to the Prime Minister asking that his original stipulations be reversed, so that 'one day the Prince would bring his wife to Chevening and their children would grow up there'.

Two years after the Earl's death in 1969, however, the Queen

What role is there for a Prince of Wales? The dangers of polo provide an outlet for the feelings of anger, frustration and uselessness.

His devotion to the Queen is absolute. They are mother and son, sovereign and loyal subject, and two of the loneliest people on earth.

His grandmother, Queen Elizabeth the Queen Mother, virtually brought him up. It is still a very special relationship, but how well will he manage without her?

A day in the life ... Prince Charles with Edward Adeane and David Roycroft, bodyguards and equerries. 'A woman not only marries a man; she marries into a way of life – a job.'

Below: Lady Jane Wellesley was a likely candidate, but too independent – too bright – to have given up her freedom for the royal circus.

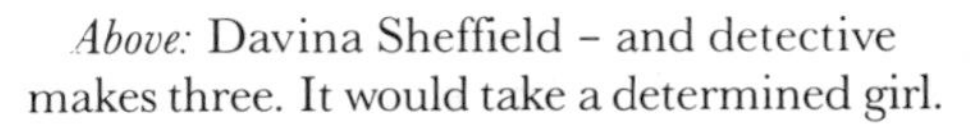

Above: Davina Sheffield – and detective makes three. It would take a determined girl.

Right: Lady Camilla Fane. Charles missed his chance, but some still say he has never been so much in love.

Charles and Diana preparing for the day's events with Sir John Riddell and Anne Beckwith-Smith, Lady-in-Waiting to the Princess. Diana found the discipline of life difficult to accept at first.

With the Reagans at the White House. The Prince was angry that the CBI failed to follow up his US tour.

Fishing, a passion since he was taught by his grandmother at the age of eight.

The garden he created at Highgrove is his sanctuary.

With the Spanish Royal Family on holiday in Majorca. A welcome alternative to Balmoral for the Princess – less so for Charles. Balmoral is his favourite place on earth.

Talking to Rod Stewart and other pop stars after a concert for the Prince's Trust. Some of his staunchest fans are in the pop world.

Cambridge – possibly the best days of his life – and an ambition to play comedy on stage fulfilled.

An honoured guest in New Guinea – next week the front cover of Private Eye?

The family in the wild flower garden at Highgrove.

and Prince Charles went to look at the house, and found it so gloomy and depressing and in such a dreadful state of repair that they turned down the offer. It then passed through several Cabinet ministers' hands, more than half a million pounds was spent to make it habitable, and in 1975 Prince Charles looked again and changed his mind: he would have the house after all. Since then he had scarcely been there, and for many years local people had been angry that the Prince should have accepted the gift and then allowed it to go to waste. He did not even shoot the 2500 acres, but let them out to a consortium.

The real reason was that Chevening was in the wrong county. Although it was only a short helicopter ride from Buckingham Palace, it was a slow and laborious journey by car through the congested and densely populated south London suburbs of Lewisham and Catford. Apart from the Brabournes, Charles knew no one in the county: most of his friends and all his close relatives were to the west of London, in Berkshire, Gloucestershire and Wiltshire. All the polo events were in that area, as was the hunting. Kent was an alien county. If he had had a wife at the time, things might have been different, but in his single state Chevening was simply too big and too grand, and too expensive to maintain.

In 1975 he hadn't really had the time either. He was still in the Navy, and most of his time ashore was spent either at Broadlands with Mountbatten or at one of the royal palaces; but by 1979 he had decided he wanted somewhere of his own at last, and he set a firm of land agents in Woodstock the task of finding him a suitable country house in Gloucestershire. Princess Anne and Mark Phillips had settled in Gloucestershire on an estate bought for them by the Queen as a wedding present. If he lived close to them, he would be able to hunt with his sister, and would also be near Camilla and Andrew Parker-Bowles.

The money for Charles to buy himself a house in the country did not come from the Queen or the state, but from the Duchy of Cornwall. The Duchy is a vast estate, including places like Dartmoor and the Isles of Scilly, which automatically goes to the 'first begotten son' of the monarch, and provides his income. It was with the revenues accumulated during his minority that Edward VII had bought and improved the estate at Sandringham, where the Royal Family traditionally spends the New Year. The title Duke of Cornwall, and the estate to go with it, had been created by Edward III in 1337 in order to give his eldest son, the Black Prince, an income and establishment, and it was he who decreed that it should go to the eldest son. Thus when there is no son, as in the case of George VI, the estate is held by the monarch.

The Duchy is one of the largest estates in Britain: about 130,000 acres in all, of which the greater part – 70,000 acres – is on Dartmoor. The remainder is mostly agricultural land, much of it, as the name suggests, in Cornwall and the West Country, also Wales and Gloucestershire. In fact the Duchy spans more than twenty counties; and also owns forty-five acres in Kennington, south London, which makes the Duke landlord of not only over six hundred urban tenancies in an area that until recently was very depressed, but also the Oval cricket ground, home of the Surrey County Cricket Club.

When Prince Charles came of age in 1969, therefore, and became chairman of the Prince's Council, the governing body of the estate, the Duchy had been in abeyance for thirty-three years and was like a sleeping giant. Farming had been through a great depression; between 1880 and 1940 every estate had become run down and after the war landowners began to modernize, to sell off redundant buildings and pieces of land and plough money back into their farms, so that by the 1960s they had become thriving businesses. This had scarcely happened in the Duchy. For some inexplicable reason, although there had been a Duke of Cornwall since 1952, when Charles became heir to the throne and it was clear that he would almost certainly need the income seventeen years later, few preparations had been made to ensure that the Duchy would provide one. The estate had lumbered along with no specific goal in mind. Land stewards had become autonomous, a number of farm buildings had fallen into disuse, land had been poorly managed, properties had been allowed to run down and rents had gone unreviewed: much of the Duchy was yielding nothing. So when the Prince of Wales reached the age of twenty-one vast resources were waiting to be tapped, but there was one important stipulation: the Duke of Cornwall is never allowed to capital spend; he is only allowed to receive income. Therefore if any of the assets are sold the proceeds have to be reinvested.

Since the Duchy is the Prince of Wales's principal source of income it was imperative that it be revitalized and turned into a going concern. In 1972 a new secretary was appointed – Anthony Gray, who had been treasurer of Christ Church, Oxford – and under his direction that process was set in motion. Charles took very little interest in the business in those days. He chaired meetings of the Prince's Council, which were held three times a year to discuss policy, and was kept briefed about developments; but he was in the Navy, and then he was busy with the Queen's Jubilee Appeal and other interests. It was not really until the end of the decade, with both David Checketts and Mountbatten gone, when Charles began to be concerned about having no role in life and was keen to have a job to do, that he saw the Duchy as the natural solution to his worries. It was the nearest he could come to earning his own living and, largely thanks to the personality of one man within the organization, Charles became genuinely enthused.

Charles had said that he wanted on the Council a practical farmer who knew something about estate management, in addition to the mix of grand and titled financial, military and legal experts; so in 1979 Tony Gray brought in a former colleague of his, the estate bursar at Oxford, John Higgs. There was little about farming, estate management, rural development and conservation that John Higgs did not know; and there was scarcely a contact in any associated organization that he did not know personally. He was a grey-haired dynamo of a man who had yearned to be an academic, and although ideal for the new job in terms of his experience the vision of him as a royal courtier made friends laugh out loud. A man who spoke his mind, he had ruffled more than a few feathers in his time; and there was little chance at this stage in his life that he would be likely to change.

He did not, but he and the Prince of Wales clicked, and when Tony Gray retired in 1981 John Higgs became secretary. Charles enjoyed his prankish sense of humour and admired his tireless enthusiasm, his knowledge, his practical business brain and his inexhaustible fund of ideas. They developed the most extraordinarily close working relationship, where both were utterly in tune, sparked ideas off each other and made one another laugh: once again it was the successful formula of the Prince and an older man. Charles was a complete novice: he knew nothing about farming, although the Queen does have a large farm at Windsor, which the Duke of Edinburgh manages, and another at Sandringham, and she herself is very knowledgeable about livestock and pedigrees. Charles, however, knew nothing about management or business and finance. His education so far had given him no preparation for anything beyond the services.

John Higgs provided a crash course. He inspired Prince Charles, worked alongside him, coached him in the ways of business, schooled him in the art of responsible land management, encouraged him to try out ideas for off-beat alternative methods, to put community architecture into practice, and helped turn the Duchy into the thriving concern which in 1985 made net profits of £1.46 million.

There were three elements to consider in the way the Duchy was run. Firstly, it had to provide the Prince with an income, not just to support his own lifestyle – which was expensive enough – but also to pay for the expenses incurred by the job: his household, his wardrobe, the official cars, the cost of entertaining. The only expense that he does not pay for himself is air transport, since he uses aircraft of the Queen's Flight. And of course there was the cost to be found of running the Duchy itself, which employs one hundred people. Before John Higgs came and injected some verve into the machinery in 1979 there were times when the Duchy scarcely provided enough income to cover it all. So while he was being pressured into finding a wife – the more so after his thirtieth birthday – he did not actually have enough money coming in to support one. Secondly, although the Duchy was made up of land and property, it essentially concerned people, and Prince Charles sensed the need to tread warily. He wanted to show that he was doing more than sitting back and taking money, so he began to involve the tenants in some of the decision making about how their environment might be improved. Thirdly, Charles felt that as the owner of a great estate he had a responsibility to set an example to other landowners.

It was within this framework that they set to work. For administrative purposes the land is organized into five districts, each one made up of manors or estates of between a hundred and four thousand acres; and the day-to-day management of these is handled by local Duchy offices under a land steward. In the past these stewards had been left to their own devices and were not used to interference from London, so the whole system needed a thorough overhaul; although Tony Gray had begun the job, it was not until John Higgs arrived on the scene that reform really gathered momentum.

The first phase was to realize some money for capital investment; this was done by selling off large amounts of surplus housing in the rural areas, farms with vacant possession, and the freeholds of some of the houses and flats in Kennington. In this way they were able to get rid of the poorer property and use the money to improve the better-quality buildings. The remainder was invested on the stock exchange; and it is a measure of their success that in less than ten years the Duchy has ploughed back nearly £9 million into property, and has nearly £14 million invested on the stock exchange.

Next, rents had to be brought up to a realistic level. The farms are let on an annual farm tenancy agreement, and could immediately be brought into line with the Agricultural Holdings Act, which sets a fair rent and reviews it every three years; so dealing with the Duchy's 180 farm tenants, most of whom farmed between 50 and 130 acres, was relatively simple. It was more difficult to adjust the residential rents, over eight hundred of which were paid by tenants in Kennington. Being Crown property, the Duchy was immune from the 1977 Rent Act and only came under its powers in 1980. Bringing up to a realistic level, with no statutory arbiter to hold responsible, the rents of people who had been paying only a few pounds a week was a difficult and delicate business. The Duchy's method was to find out the levels of rent in the area and pitch theirs slightly below. Even so they constantly ran the risk that aggrieved tenants might go to the nearest newspaper and accuse the Prince of Wales of Rachmanism. Many threatened it, and inevitably a few did and received a rewarding amount of publicity, but to no avail. There is no delusion that this part of the Prince of Wales's life is a charity: it is a business. If a tenant does not pay the rent, he or she is evicted and the house repossessed, although if the tenant cannot pay because of illness, unemployment or some genuine hardship the Duchy brings in the local authority and makes certain that the tenant is rehoused.

Having awoken the giant from its deep sleep, the next and most important stage to be tackled was the 'people' side of landowning. It is a basic premiss in estate management that the goodwill of the tenants is any landlord's best asset, and Prince Charles had to set about earning it. He and John Higgs made periodic forays into the countryside, which revolutionized the established style of ducal visits. Prince Charles was adamant that the farms he visited should not be spruced up. He wanted to see real life. The chance to see how the rest of us live is usually denied to members of the Royal Family, and Prince Charles is painfully aware that he seldom sees it. Everyone he meets is dressed up in their best clothes for his visit, factories have always had a coat of paint, newspaper offices have had a new carpet, private houses have had every sign of life removed from view. Nothing is presented as the rest of the world sees it. Mountbatten felt the same frustration, and one day when opening a new College of Nautical Studies in Glasgow he noticed that the tour of inspection omitted the fourth floor. He transferred to another lift and got himself taken there. As he suspected, a dozen workmen were sitting around smoking and drinking and waiting for him to go, so he immediately went up and engaged them in conversation.

Charles wanted to arrive at the farms unannounced, but John Higgs insisted that the tenants be given twelve hours warning so that the wives would not be caught in curlers, for example. The tone of the visit, nevertheless, would be entirely informal. He would be wearing casual clothes, with a pair of wellington boots in the car, and be quite alone except for John Higgs, the local land steward, who was there to make the introductions, and a detective. He had not come to go walking down a line of tenants dressed in their Sunday best, shaking hands and saying how good it was to see them. What he wanted was to find them in the milking parlour or mending a fence; he wanted to talk to them in earnest about the farm, the animals, the work and the problems. What is more, he wanted them to answer him frankly and honestly. The pattern was set on one of the first days Charles spent in the Duchy. He arrived at one tenant's farm and immediately jumped into a Land Rover with the tenant and John Higgs – no one else, not even his detective – and set off across the fields to look at stock and crops. They were gone for two hours; those left behind sat and waited.

A number of people in the Prince's employ spend a lot of their time sitting and waiting. Some also find themselves on call round the clock seven days a week, and will frequently be dragged from a weekend with the family to attend to some task or deal with a change of plan. For a man who is so sensitive, it is surprising to find him selfish. Yet at the same time he can show great compassion. The daughter of one of his employees in the Duchy was killed in a car crash not long ago; the night he heard the news Charles was obviously upset and wrote off a letter at once. At the next Council meeting, unprompted, he asked for news of the man. In the summer of 1986 a tenant in Cornwall (and again, his knowledge of the man was slight) had his leg ripped off by a hay-making machine; Charles sent off a personal letter. He likes nothing more than to feel that everyone involved in the Duchy, both tenants and employees, is part of a large family; and his memory is so good that when he meets tenants for a second time he will remember what they told him on their first meeting and ask about progress, so they do feel as though they belong. One day Charles was visiting a farmhouse in Wiltshire which had severe damp problems, with water literally pouring down one wall. Six months later he found the tenants riding alongside him in the hunting field. 'Ah, Philip,' he said without a moment's hesitation, 'is your house all right now?'

The man charged with the task of finding the Prince of Wales a house in the country was the land steward for the eastern district, one of a new breed of land stewards from the commercial world whom Tony Gray had introduced as part of the initial shake-up in the Duchy. He was the senior partner in the Woodstock firm of Smith-Woolley, and out of several houses that he found the Prince chose Highgrove. Charles had specifically wanted a house with a farm, and Highgrove had 410 acres; he specifically wanted to be within a convenient radius of his friends and relatives, which Highgrove also was. A few miles outside the pretty market town of Tetbury, the house was close to the M4; it was therefore within easy distance of London, Windsor and Wales and would also provide an ideal springboard for visits to the Duchy. It was close to Cirencester Park, and comfortably accessible to Cowdray Park and Smith's Lawn for polo; there was racing nearby at Cheltenham, Newbury, Bath and Chepstow; and, best of all, Highgrove was right in the middle of the Beaufort Hunt country, and the Prince had begun hunting two or three times a week in season.

For all the advantages, there were also disadvantages which made the choice of Highgrove surprising. Even its previous owner, the late Maurice Macmillan, MP, son of the former Conservative Prime Minister, the late Lord Stockton, was surprised that the Prince should have bought the house. He felt it was neither large enough nor grand enough, but considering the Duchy's finances at the time anything grander would have been beyond their reach. It was advertised for sale as 'A distinguished

Georgian house standing in superb parkland in the Duke of Beaufort's Hunt. Entrance hall, four principal reception rooms, domestic quarters, nine bedrooms, six bathrooms, nursery wing. Full central heating. Fine stable block. Easily maintained gardens. Lodge. Farm manager's house. Pair of farm cottages. Dairy unit and farm buildings.' What it failed to say was that the main road ran dangerously close to the house, making it clearly visible to every passer-by, and there was a public right of way, used by about a dozen people a day as a short cut to the village, which crossed into the garden no more than two or three hundred yards from the south side of the house. The farmland was not ideal either. Sixty acres were woodland, and the remaining 350 were in three separate parcels. It was not big enough to justify the cost of employing a farm manager and buying equipment.

One feature that the house did boast, however, which would not be found in a hurry elsewhere, was a large garden planted with the most magnificent trees; it was this above all which appealed to the Prince of Wales. The house had once belonged to the Colonel Mitchell who had founded the arboretum at Westonbirt. He had bought it in 1893 and filled every vista with a dazzling display of ornamental and specimen trees; Charles has since added to them.

The Duchy bought Highgrove in August 1980 for over £750,000, and Prince Charles lost no time in moving in, delighted to have a home of his own at last. He kept on the couple who had worked for the Macmillan family for years – Mrs Whiteland, who took care of the cooking and housekeeping, and her Irish husband Paddy, a real character but a wise old bird. He acted as general factotum and knew all the country lore; he also knew everyone's gossip but gave away none of it. They ran the place, mothered the Prince of Wales and protected him from unwelcome curiosity. Both he and Diana were very saddened by Mrs Whiteland's death in 1986.

Charles was, to begin with, an object of intense curiosity. The road outside was regularly jammed with sightseers' cars, their drivers so intent on catching a glimpse of the Prince that several collided with one another. The footpath through the garden, which has since been rerouted, became a major thoroughfare and the little town of Tetbury was suddenly a thriving tourist centre. It was not long, however, before the locals enveloped their royal neighbour in a wall of silence, as only the British can. They will sell just as many souvenirs and royal mementoes to visitors as they possibly can, they will exploit every commercial avenue possible – of which Prince Charles thoroughly approves – but not a word of gossip, rumour or even fact about Highgrove and all who come and go from there passes their lips.

CHAPTER FOURTEEN

It was not just owning a home of his own at last that so delighted the Prince, it was having a garden too. Neither of his parents has much interest in gardening, and although the gardens at Buckingham Palace, and indeed those of all the royal residences, are immaculate, it is teams of royal gardeners who keep them so. The Queen's forte is fauna rather than flora.

The gardener of the family is Queen Elizabeth the Queen Mother, and both her retreats in Scotland, the Castle of May and Birkhall, have beautiful gardens in which she has taken a personal hand. Hard as it is to imagine the Queen Mother in anything other than organza and feathers, on holiday she is a changed woman, as is the Queen. Both dress comfortably in casual country clothes, and the Queen Mother is never happier than when swathed in mackintosh and waders with a fishing rod in her hand – a passion to which she had introduced her grandson when he was a little boy. Charles came to gardening rather later, but no doubt inspired again in part by his grandmother. He enjoyed beautiful gardens, he loved looking at flowers, and he had a great feeling for trees and the countryside as a whole – but he knew nothing whatever about their cultivation and had no idea how to plan a garden. The matter called for an expect, and one of the advantages of being the Prince of Wales is that experts are only too delighted to help. In this case he sought the advice of a family friend, Lady Salisbury, who had designed several gardens for friends as well as her own at Hatfield House in Hertfordshire, which is open to the public.

What Lady Salisbury, known as Mollie to her friends, does not know about plants is probably not worth knowing. She is a strikingly pretty and elegant woman in her sixties who has gardened without the use of chemicals all her life and fed six children on 'health foods' for all their young lives; having been thought a crank by all her friends for years and years she is now thoroughly fashionable, and amused that everyone should think they have discovered something new.

Charles had originally asked her if she would do the garden for him at Chevening, but the plan to move there had fizzled out before she got started; now he asked her to help him at Highgrove. The 'easily kept gardens' featured in the estate agent's details consisted mostly of lawns, including a croquet lawn. Less easily kept was a walled kitchen garden which had supplied the Macmillans with all their vegetables. Here was an opportunity to create a garden from scratch, and although Charles had no expertise he had a number of strong likes and dislikes. Lady Salisbury could turn his ideas into a cohesive whole; she could say where beds should be sited to enjoy the best aspect, for example, which plants would grow happily alongside which, what combination would give the best show of colour; and in this way they drew up a plan together, which is more or less how the garden is today.

Charles was keen for it to provide a degree of privacy, so he wanted hedges and walls which would divide up the area. Walking round the garden would be an adventure – suddenly coming upon a rose garden, for instance, a pond, or a brilliant display of peonies which had not been visible from the house. He wanted all the old-fashioned flowers traditionally found in an English country garden, like lavender, delphiniums, marigolds, irises and pinks; old-fashioned roses; and scented blooms like phlox. His interest did not stop at selecting what flowers he would grow, however: Prince Charles got into a pair of old trousers and wellington boots and did the digging. He prepared the beds, he manured the ground and he planted the seedlings. Side by side, with the help of just one gardener, he and Lady Salisbury made the garden; and in those early weeks and months Charles discovered a new passion in life. He began to read gardening books rapaciously, and not only did he discover that working the soil was enormously therapeutic, he also discovered it was something he could do rather well. Lady Salisbury describes him as 'a natural plantsman'. He had a feel for what he was doing, and a real love of the soil, and in a short time has become very knowledgeable.

There was something else he wanted to do now that he had his own property: grow wild flowers. Thanks to his father's commitment to the World Wildlife Fund, Charles had grown up with an awareness of the conservation issue, but it was not until 1968 when he was asked to chair the Welsh steering committee for European Conservation Year, designated for 1970, that he fully realized the extent to which our planet was in danger. It was more than man chopping down rain forests on the other side of the world and destroying the natural habitat of the animals which lived there. It was factories and furnaces right here in Britain, all over Europe, and in Canada and North America, emitting chemical poisons into the air; farmers scattering nitrates on to the soil, industry pouring toxic waste into the waterways. If chemical pollution was not going to destroy the countryside, urgent action had to be taken; but because this side of conservation was not glamorous enough to fire the public imagination it had been neglected. It was far easier to win support for an endangered species like the giant panda, for example, than for some species of grass, a nondescript weed or a minuscule bug that nobody but the experts have ever noticed. And it was especially difficult when the subject involved so many political issues and commercial interests.

Prince Charles became absorbed. He made a forthright speech about 'the horrifying effects of pollution in all its cancerous forms' at the Conservation in 1970 Conference, which happened to be the first speech he ever made in public, and at the same time announced the Prince of Wales's Countryside Award for individual enterprise in protecting the environment. Having thus pinned his colours to the mast he became the target for a number of conservation lobbies, and when the designated year came to an end he was persuaded to set up something more permanent to keep up the momentum of the enthusiasm that had been generated during the year. Thus was born the Prince of Wales's Committee, which raised money and gave grants for projects that helped to protect, improve or tidy up the countryside.

One of the organizations that was pleased to find the Prince of Wales taking an interest in conservation was the Society for the Promotion of Nature Conservation (now the Royal Society for Nature Conservation), founded in 1912 by Nathaniel Charles Rothschild, a member of the famous banking family. He was a remarkable man, an all-round naturalist whose views on conservation were fifty years ahead of his day. He travelled the world extensively, listing plants and butterflies, and his knowledge of specialized habitats from the forests of the Austro-Hungarian Empire to the shingle beaches and mosses of the United Kingdom was encyclopaedic. It has been said that he invented conservation. Certainly he was the first person to realize that it was important not just to protect individual rare species that were threatened with extinction, but to protect and preserve their habitats, too, by forming nature reserves. Such was his boundless energy that by 1915 he had drawn up a list of 284 potential reserves in Britain, with details of the rare species and special interests in each, which he submitted to the Board of Agriculture. He had realized that his scheme would require government support and massive publicity.

Sadly Rothschild died in 1923, while his visionary plans were still in their infancy, and for the next thirty years or so the Society slumbered until his daughter, Miriam Rothschild, who had inherited her father's passion for bugs and butterflies, as well as his energy and enthusiasm, brought the whole matter to life once more. But her passion does not stop at bugs. As one of the leading authorities on wild flowers, and an inveterate promoter of her scheme to reintroduce them to the countryside, she travels the world delivering papers at scientific conferences and converting individuals whom she encounters on the way. Betty Ford, wife of the former President of the United States, was one of her converts. She does not conduct her campaign just for the aesthetic value of the result: there is sound scientific sense behind it too. A vast range of plants are used in medical preparations, and as research continues new species are found to have beneficial properties. If a species is allowed to become extinct, however insignificant it may have appeared to be, that is one potential medication lost to mankind for ever.

Prince Charles, however, was taken with the romantic idea of looking out over meadows of colourful flowers, and when he acquired Highgrove he asked Miriam Rothschild if she would come and plant some wild flowers there. She too had known him since he was a child – she was an old friend of Lady Salisbury's – and so, armed with sacks of seed and a rotary strip seeder, she descended on the garden. Over the years her efforts have created the most magnificent wild flower garden, including all the plants that attract butterflies. In a strip between the house and the kitchen garden, which had formerly been a sea of dandelions, she has recreated a flowering hayfield with over ninety species of wild flower. Charles was particularly fond of arable weeds like cornflowers, poppies, corn marigolds, corn-cockle and mayweed – which need bare ground – and so those have gone into a specially prepared strip alongside the drive, with bulbs planted in between to give some colour in spring.

The running costs of house and garden are Prince Charles's and dealt with by his office at Buckingham Palace, but the property itself and the surrounding acreage belong to the Duchy and are consequently administered by the Duchy. Since Highgrove was, as Maurice Macmillan had thought, too small to justify the cost of putting in a farm manager, the local land steward instructed Terry Summers, one of his colleagues from Smith-Woolley, to let the land out to neighbouring farmers under share-farming agreements. They farmed it as their own: the only proviso was that they had to leave grass tracks around the edge of every field for the hunt to use.

Charles kept several of his hunters at Highgrove and has now started breeding from them, but he has never ridden regularly with the Beaufort. Most of his hunting was and still is in Leicestershire with the Belvoir and the Quorn, and he keeps more horses there. His polo ponies lived at Windsor, and still do during the season, although he now brings them home to Gloucestershire for the winter. The Prince's horses are his one major extravagance; they also give him a great deal of pleasure, and provide the element of risk that he feeds on in his life.

The horses on a polo field gallop flat out at between 28 and 30 m.p.h. and it is quite within the rules for one player travelling at this speed to ride into another, who may also be travelling at 30 m.p.h., in order to stop him hitting the ball, provided he hits at an angle of not more than 45 degrees. The rules also state that you can hook someone else's stick to prevent him hitting the ball, which at 30 m.p.h. more often than not means clouting them on the hand or the leg – although deliberately hitting another player with your stick is not allowed. It is not a game for the nervous. It is fast and rough, and inevitably blood is spilt, bones are broken and muscles torn as a regular occurrence.

It also requires tremendous fitness. The game is played in short sessions called chukkas, and depending on the grade of polo you are playing there will be four, five or six chukkas to a match. Each chukka lasts seven minutes, but with fouls and other interruptions, as in football, the seven minutes is stretched to nearer eight or nine. With a three-minute break between chukkas to change horses the whole match lasts for about an hour and twenty minutes, and there will frequently be a second match to play immediately afterwards. For many years Charles played with Guy Wildenstein's team, Les Diables Bleus, where he was playing top-grade polo, and when he is out on a polo field he takes his chances with the rest of them. No one holds back because his opponent is the Prince of Wales, and he has no inhibitions about careering into anyone either.

So much of Prince Charles's life is spent being a figurehead, an ambassador, a public relations officer for the 'family firm', shaking hands, uttering pleasantries, having to show interest in displays, demonstrations and production lines that sometimes bore him stiff; the polo field is a welcome release. For an hour and twenty minutes at least he can forget who he is and what comes next on the agenda. There is no time to think of anything else – if you don't concentrate on the polo field you are a dead man. He uses the game to work out all his aggressions and frustrations, to test his strength, his courage and his physique, and above all to prove himself in a life where he constantly doubts his own worth.

It means keeping a close watch on his weight, being careful about what he eats, and exercising daily to keep himself fit. He does aerobic exercises, as Lord Mountbatten used to do every evening before going to bed, and he swims and cycles, but since he now hunts during the winter, which also requires tremendous fitness, these activities are simply a topping up process.

The season runs from April to August, and Prince Charles plays in tournaments three or four times a week – five or six if he can manage it – and takes part in practices, or 'stick and ball' as it is called, in between times. Since 1985 he has been coached by a former team-mate in Les Diables Bleus, a Mexican professional called Gracida, who has a handicap of ten (unlike golf, the higher the handicap, the better the player), and is rated as one of the best players in the world. Charles admires him enormously and has gained confidence by playing with him, with the result that his game has improved out of all recognition. According to his manager, Major Ronald Ferguson (whose daughter Sarah married Prince Andrew in 1986), who was a top player himself when younger, if Charles had the chance to play as much as most of the people he competes against his handicap would be considerably better than the four it is now. His competitors are a mixture of professionals like Mike Devcich, a wiry Australian who sits on the back of a horse and plays polo day in and day out; gentlemen farmers who have both the time and the money to spare; rich businessmen like Lord Vestey, of Dewhurst the butchers fame; or the Prince's friend Guy Wildenstein, a member of the wealthy family of art dealers and racehorse owners, who can organize their working life around polo.

There is no pretending that it is anything but a very rich man's sport. To play seriously you need at least six ponies, which can cost anything up to £15,000 each. The Prince saves a considerable amount there by using ponies bred by the Queen; his favourite polo mount is a home-bred pony called Happiness. Nevertheless keeping the animals, feeding them and transporting them to and from tournaments all adds up. Prince Charles employs four people to look after his ponies: a senior groom from the Argentine called Raoul, who is a naturalized Briton, and three girl grooms. He is one of the few amateurs playing who pays for everything himself. About 80 per cent of polo players have some degree of sponsorship, by an individual or a commercial organization, but as the Prince of Wales it is impossible for Charles to accept so much as a polo stick. It is a cast iron rule that he cannot receive money from anyone lest he be compromised. He pays his own way, and that accounts for nearly £30,000 a year.

His polo has been through phases. At Cambridge he was playing often and well and captained the university team, but during his years in the forces he played very infrequently and when he did play it was usually on borrowed ponies, with the result that his handicap fell to two or three and his game became indifferent. Since then he has played at every available opportunity, both at home and abroad, and he is playing better now than at any other time in his life. The odds are still stacked against him, however. Most polo players have time to psych themselves up before a match; they arrive at the ground an hour or so beforehand, then go out on to the field and warm up to calm their nerves. Prince Charles cannot afford that luxury. He usually arrives two minutes before the game is due to start, having, say, shaken 150 hands that morning, had three meetings and a state luncheon, and at the end of a match, when everyone else sits down for a cup of tea or a drink to unwind, he usually has to dash off for another engagement. What is worse, when he plays abroad he has to do all that on a strange horse, which will have all sorts of characteristics and habits which are new to him, and in front of a crowd who have come specifically to watch him. Nevertheless he cannot play enough, and every winter when Ronald Ferguson plans his games for the coming season those days become sacrosanct.

The Prince's life is run to a schedule mapped out months in advance, with precious few days or hours he can call his own; in drawing up his plans for the polo season Major Ferguson has to liaise closely with the Prince of Wales's Office at Buckingham Palace to make sure they do not clash with any other engagements. All members of the Royal Family are bound by these schedules, which are laboriously worked out at six-monthly programme meetings held at the Palace. On these occasions they all get together with their senior members of staff, including their press officers, and go through all the hundreds of invitations that have come in, all the state visits that are planned, all the immovable dates and ceremonial occasions like Remembrance Day and Trooping the Colour. They work round those fixed dates to come up with a balanced diary in which no one member of the family overlaps another, nor does any one charity or factory receive more than its fair share of royal attention. One of the accepted wisdoms among Palace staff is to 'treat them like pop stars – never put them on the stage together', which accounts for the fact that the occasions on which they do all appear together in public are very rare.

In the winter months it is hunting that has to be slotted into the schedule, but in 1978 Charles added a further equestrian challenge. He took up cross-country riding, which involves much the same skills as fox hunting, and is organized by local hunts, but lacks the elements of fox or hounds. Competitors race round a rugged, demanding course of difficult obstacles and unpredictable jumps, like those they might meet in the hunting field, while being egged on by crowds of excitable spectators. In the thrill and scramble to get ahead of the field the sport is every bit as dangerous as the real thing. Prince Charles went at it with a determined fearlessness. He then took up an even more exacting sport – steeplechasing under National Hunt rules, which is the top class of amateur racing in the country and fiercely tough and competitive. In all of this he was shadowing his predecessor. As Prince of Wales the Duke of Windsor had also been a fearless horse rider and enthusiastic huntsman, and had done some point-to-pointing and steeplechasing too. Watching him romp home first in the Welsh Guards' Challenge Cup in 1921, Lord Stamfordham, King George V's private secretary, remarked that it was the first time an heir apparent had ridden in such a race, far less ridden a winner, and he hoped that HRH would never take such a risk again. Instead, Edward took up the infinitely riskier game of polo.

Steeplechasing was undoubtedly a dangerous business, none the less, and Prince Charles took some nasty falls – most probably because he was never able to devote the amount of time to training that other riders could. He trained with Nick Gaselee at Lambourn, riding out along the Berkshire downs in the early mornings; then after a quick breakfast he would dash back to London for the day's work.

It was a punishing schedule. When Prince Charles went to dinner with friends or to stay with them at weekends, however stimulating the conversation it was not unusual for him to fall asleep at the dinner table from sheer exhaustion. The workload itself was heavy, as it still is today: there is a daily round of briefings, receptions, meetings, committees, tours of inspection, lunches, visits and dinners – each one in a different place. In addition there is correspondence to deal with and state papers to read. Not all Princes of Wales have had this task. Queen Victoria adamantly refused to let the future Edward VII take part in any affairs of state, and even discouraged him from meeting politicians; as a result he turned his energies to the pursuit of pleasure, became involved in gambling and divorce scandals, and dragged the monarchy into disrepute. Queen Elizabeth II, by contrast, has encouraged Prince Charles to become involved. She has wanted him to meet and talk to as many politicians of as many hues as possible, and in 1977 she made him a Privy Councillor so that he would have access to state papers and begin to know something of what the job involved – the Duke of Edinburgh has never had this opportunity – and she and her son discuss matters and share burdens to which no other member of the family is privy.

CHAPTER FIFTEEN

The news that Prince Charles had finally bought a home of his own and appeared to be settling down aroused new speculation that he planned to marry. He was thirty-two now; it was high time. The question was, which of the many girls that he brought to the polo ground, or invited to Sandringham or Balmoral, or took to the opera, was it to be?

In their quest for an answer, the popular papers grew ever more invasive. Photographers and royal-watchers followed him and spied on him even when he went on holiday; the gossip columnists speculated, and every girl he was seen with was immediately a suspect. Charles grew heartily sick of it, and angry that he should be allowed so little privacy. Unlike his sister, who has never pretended to like the press, Prince Charles had always been polite and cooperative to newspaper men and women, recognizing that they were on the whole responsible people with a job to do, and that they could play a useful part in allowing him to reach a wider audience. During this time he became bitterly disillusioned, however, and has remained so. He now reads nothing but *The Times*, as he explained to me, 'because I get so angry when I read something about me or my wife which is untrue, that I want to ring up the editor and complain, and I'd spend all my time on the telephone, so I've just stopped reading the other newspapers. If I don't know what they're saying I can't get angry.'

He considers his private life nobody's business but his own. Unlike the President of the United States, for example, who chooses to run for office and to put himself deliberately into the public eye, Prince Charles had no choice in the matter. He has devoted his life to the duty that devolved upon him by an accident of birth, and feels that it would not be too much to expect some privacy in return, particularly in the matter of his love life.

How, after all, could he ever hope to find someone to marry if he was never allowed the time to get to know anyone? He had taken one of his girlfriends to Balmoral for a few days, for instance, for a chance to be alone and to relax. The more persistent members of the press followed, and in his book *Settling Down* James Whitaker described the ensuing events with some pride:

> He took her on a secret holiday to Balmoral in Scotland in May 1980. Instead of fishing from morning until dusk, as he usually does, I found him lying on a rug on the river bank with Anna. It was right out of character, certainly at that time of the day. He grew more angry than I have ever known him when I followed them along the river Dee with Ken Lennox, trying to get pictures. He even authorized his friend Lord Tony Tryon to shout a four-letter word across the river 'suggesting' we go away.

The girl was Anna Wallace, known by her friends as Whiplash Wallace. She had once worked as a secretary to the fabulously rich Iranian socialite Homayoun Mazandi, the same job that Marie-Christine von Reibnitz had had before she married Prince Michael of Kent, but Anna was not destined to follow suit any further. She was fiery and independent, and although they enjoyed the best part of eight months together the romance came to a dramatic end soon afterwards. Furious at the way the Prince had treated her one evening, she walked out on him. It was something of a new experience for him, and Prince Charles was left licking his wounds.

However angry the press made him with their obsession that he should get married, he was unable to dismiss it entirely. Even Prince Philip had begun to agitate that it was time he found a wife, and the pressure began to get to Charles.

As he took stock, and looked ruefully at the opportunities he had missed, at the women who had been scared off by the publicity, at the girls who had been so hopelessly unsuitable, he realized that there was one girl in his life whom he had entirely overlooked: Sarah Spencer's younger sister Diana. Lady Diana Spencer had carried a torch for Prince Charles ever since their first meeting at Althorp when he was dating her sister. She had fallen soundly in love with him, with the passion of a schoolgirl falling in love for the first time, and in three years she had not wavered.

Plotting away in the wings in the meantime were two grandmothers, both of whom had acted *in loco parentis* to their grandchildren at various times in their lives, and who shared an especially good relationship with them. The Queen Mother was concerned for her grandson's happiness and thought a loving wife would be the answer; Diana's grandmother, Ruth, Lady Fermoy, was a lady in waiting to the Queen Mother and anxious that her granddaughter should make a good marriage – as she herself had done. As Ruth Silvia Gill, an Aberdeenshire girl studying the piano in Paris, she was just twenty when she had met and married Maurice Roche, 4th Baron Fermoy, who was twenty-six years her senior. The Baron, who had been at various times both MP and mayor for Kings Lynn, was a friend of the Royal Family, and King George V offered him the use of Park House on the Sandringham estate. A firm friendship was struck between the Yorks and the Fermoys, which continued after the accession of George VI in 1936. Maurice Fermoy used to play ice hockey and tennis with the King, and was out hare shooting with him in February 1952 on the day before George VI died.

Not only had Ruth Fermoy done well for herself, but so had both her daughters. Mary the eldest, had married the newspaper magnate Viscount Kemsley's son, Michael Berry; while the second daughter, Frances, had married Viscount Althorp, heir to the Earl Spencer and equerry to the Queen. The only hiccough in an otherwise successful climb up the social ladder was when this second daughter divorced her viscount and ran off with Peter Shand-Kydd, a charming man and a millionaire, but a man in trade nevertheless. So appalled was Ruth by what Frances had done that she turned against her and took her son-in-law's side in the subsequent action; it was many years before mother and daughter spoke again. The fact that her daughter had endured years of cruelty at the hands of her husband before ending the marriage, and had produced five children, was apparently irrelevant.

One of those children, of course, was Diana, who like her mother had been born at Park House. Frances had been born there on the day that King George V died. It is said that the news of her birth was rushed across the park to Sandringham House, where he lay gravely ill, and that Queen Mary told him of her birth before he passed away that evening. Frances had met

Johnnie Althorp at her coming-out ball in 1953. He was fourteen years her senior and quite a catch. Good-looking, educated at Eton and Sandhurst, during the war he had joined the Scots Guards as soon as he was old enough to fight and been sent off to the campaign in north-west Europe, where he was mentioned in despatches. Afterwards he had spent three years as ADC to Sir Willoughby Norrie, the Governor of South Australia, and in 1950 became an equerry to George VI. When the King died, Johnnie continued as equerry to the Queen until 1954 when he married Frances Roche.

It was the society wedding of the year, and at eighteen Frances was the youngest bride to be married in Westminster Abbey this century. Among the guests were the Queen, the Queen Mother, the Duke of Edinburgh and Princess Margaret; but despite its glittering start the marriage was not a happy one. They began their life together in a house on the Althorp estate in Northamptonshire, but Johnnie and his father did not see eye to eye. The son had neither the father's intellect nor his erudition. He preferred farming and outdoor activities, and was an easy-going character, while his father was autocratic and ill-mannered. The Earl was a huntsman who encouraged the fox population, while Johnnie, who had never been interested in horses, liked shooting. His marriage to Frances Roche had not helped, for she was a strong-spirited girl who was not prepared to humour the old man. It came as a relief to everyone, therefore, when after her husband's death the following year Ruth Fermoy suggested they take over Park House, which with ten bedrooms was more than she needed for herself. Thus it was here, in the house built by Edward VII in 1861 when he was Prince of Wales, using income from the Duchy of Cornwall, that Diana Frances was born on Saturday, 1 July 1961.

Diana was the couple's fourth child. Sarah, the eldest, was born in 1955, followed by Jane two years later and in 1960 by a boy called John, who only lived for ten hours and now lies buried in the west corner of the churchyard at Sandringham. To one side of him lies his grandfather, Maurice Fermoy; to the other his cousin, Elizabeth Roche, a daughter born to Frances's brother, Edmund, Lord Fermoy, who died six days after her birth in 1966. Diana was conceived in the year that John died, and so convinced were her parents that she would be a boy that they had not thought of any girl's names; for the first few days of her life she went unnamed. It was another three years before Charles was born and they had the son they wanted.

Johnnie in the meantime had become a farmer. Gone was the glamorous, sophisticated man about town. He had accumulated about 650 acres around the locality and settled down comfortably, with his herd of beef cattle, to the onset of middle age. Frances, on the other hand, was lively, only thirty, and just coming into her prime. More important, however, behind closed doors her husband was not the gentle, kindly man he seemed to neighbours. Frances tolerated his ways until she had provided him with the son and heir he so badly wanted, but when in 1967 she fell in love with Peter Shand-Kydd, and the chance of a new and happy life presented itself, she left Viscount Althorp.

The two elder children had just started at boarding school in Kent when she left. Diana was six, and already adjusting to her sisters' departure. The house that had been full all day long was suddenly very strange and empty with just her and Charles in the nursery. The family had nothing like the complement of staff that had been customary in the Fermoys' day, but it was still a staffed and formal household by most people's standards, with a nanny, a cook and even a governess. The girls had all been taught at home up until that time.

The Althorps tried separation at first, and during that time Diana and Charles stayed with their mother in London. However it was obvious that the marriage was over, and so in December 1967 Frances took them home to Park House to spend Christmas with their father, their sisters who were now home from boarding school for the holidays, and their two grandmothers. She herself left for good, and Ruth, Lady Fermoy, stepped into the breach.

Heartless as it might seem to abandon such young children, Frances would have had every expectation that she would be awarded custody in the subsequent legal proceedings. In the event, she was not. In April 1968 Peter Shand-Kydd's wife, Janet, sued him for divorce because of her husband's adultery with Frances. He let it go undefended and lost custody of his three children. Then in December Frances sued Johnnie for divorce on the grounds of his cruelty. He contested it, and knowing that he would be able to call as witnesses to his good character some of the highest names in the land, Frances backed off and the case was dismissed. He then sued her on the grounds of her adultery with

Peter Shand-Kydd. Since Peter had not contested his wife's claim, there was no way that Frances could contest Johnnie's accusation. The case went through undefended, and the price she had to pay was custody of her children.

She and Peter Shand-Kydd married that same year and went off to live on the Sussex coast. Frances had access to the children nevertheless, and although Johnnie was hurt, shocked and surprised by what had happened he never tried to use the children against his ex-wife, nor to keep them from her. Diana, therefore, began the typically unsettled and nomadic life that the children of divorced parents lead. She remained friendly and cheerful on the outside, but within she developed resilience and toughness, and came through her childhood with the determination that if she did nothing else in life her own marriage would be rock solid and she would never allow her own children to go through the misery and the insecurity she had suffered.

Everyone decided that school would be the best antidote to losing her mother. So within weeks of Frances leaving, the old governess, who had been in the household for as long as Diana could remember, was told that her services were no longer required. Diana was sent to Silfield School in Kings Lynn, a small private day school recommended by her godmother, Carol Fox. Ironically, Diana was the only one of the Spencer children not to have had a royal godparent, although the list of those who were was not undistinguished. There was John Floyd, later chairman of Christie's, who had been at school and Sandhurst with Viscount Althorp; Alexander Gilmour, brother of the former Lord Privy Seal, Sir Ian Gilmour, and a relative; Lady Mary Colman, wife of the Lord Lieutenant of Norfolk and a relative of the Queen Mother; and Sarah Pratt, who like Carol Fox was a well-to-do friend and neighbour.

Diana was a thoroughly likeable little girl; she was neat, well-mannered and perky, but sensible, with a pronounced interest, even at the age of six or seven, in the nursery class where her younger brother Charles was installed. She looked after him with the firmness and devotion of a mother hen, evidently filling in for his own mother. Diana would always dedicate the drawings and paintings she did at school 'To Mummy and Daddy', but never talked about Frances after she had gone.

Diana stayed at Silfield until the age of nine, when it was generally agreed that she might do better academically and emotionally in the more stable environment of a boarding school. Her father had become involved in a number of activities which took him away from home, and a never-ending stream of nannies was unsettling. In September 1970 Diana and her pet guinea pig, Peanuts, went off to Riddlesworth Hall, a small, friendly preparatory school in Norfolk, and into the tender care of Miss Elizabeth Ridsdale. After an initial bout of homesickness she settled down well, and although, as at Silfield, she showed no great intellectual promise, she did very well in both swimming and ballet. She was popular at school, but never a leader; always happy to fit in with whatever was going on, always wanting to be liked.

In 1973 it was time to move on again, and she followed in her sisters' footsteps to West Heath, a small select girls' public school near Sevenoaks in Kent, from which Sarah had recently been ejected for misdemeanours. Jane was still there, however, and a prefect. A member of the lacrosse and tennis teams, she had passed eleven O Levels and was working up to A Levels.

She was the exception to the rule. Girls sat common entrance to get into West Heath, but there was no pass or fail mark. The only qualifications, apart from their parents' ability to pay the fees, was a facility to express themselves neatly and tidily on paper. The emphasis was not on academic success. As the headmistress, Miss Ruth Rudge, once said of their aims:

> What we remember from school are rather the people we met there, the teachers themselves rather than their lessons. The training in the art of living together is the most important part of school-life: the endless variety of experiences including squabbles, accusations, sharing or lack of sharing, clashes of personalities, together with much mutual joy and helpfulness between those of the same and of different generations are the experiences that form attitudes and judgements, and teach tolerance or leave us with a sense of frustration that will affect our lives and our relationships with others far more than the acquisition of three 'A' levels and six 'O' levels.

Diana took the message to heart, and acquired no examination passes whatsoever in her four years and a term in the school. She devoted her time instead to swimming, dancing and tennis and to reading Barbara Cartland's romantic novels, which were all the rage among her friends. They would each buy dozens of them in the holidays, and swap them during the term, reading them in prep periods and after lights-out in bed.

Coincidentally, while Diana was wrapped up in her novels Barbara Cartland was working on a new plot which would be of some consequence to the young schoolgirl. At the age of forty-six her daughter Raine, who had been married to the Earl of Dartmouth for twenty-eight years and had four children by him, had shocked everyone who knew them by deserting her husband for one of his old friends, Diana's father. 'Mummy, I'm madly in love, just like one of your heroines,' she had told her mother.

'What can you do?' said Barbara Cartland. 'You've got to stand by your daughter.'

The Dartmouths were subsequently divorced, and the children – William, Rupert, Charlotte and Henry – remained with their father.

There had been changes in the Spencer household in the intervening time. In June 1975 old Earl Spencer had died at the age of eighty-three, and Johnnie had inherited the title and the Northamptonshire estate. The girls all acquired the title of Lady, and at the age of eleven Charles became Viscount Althorp. That summer they moved lock, stock and barrel from their unassuming family house in Norfolk to the splendours of Althorp, a vast stately home steeped in family history and boasting one of the finest private art collections in Europe.

A year later they had a new mother to go with it. Johnnie and Raine married secretly in Caxton Hall in July 1976, and by the time anyone knew about it this most formidable of women was installed as mistress of Althorp. 'She's not a person,' remarked a somewhat irreverent friend of some years, 'she's an experience.' Or as a former colleague on the Greater London Council, on which she had sat, observed: 'Raine has an iron hand in an iron glove which is so beautifully wrought that people don't realize even the glove is made of iron until it hits them.' The new Countess Spencer moved in and attempted to take over not only the affairs of the house and the estate, but all who lived in it. After years of having their father to themselves, the older girls in particular found it hard to take and chose to stay away; but it has been said, to her credit, that were it not for Raine, the estate would have in all probability been sold years ago. There were crippling death duties to pay after the 7th Earl died, and Johnnie Spencer would not have known where to begin on his own. Raine turned it into a going concern.

Old retainers were retired, and the staff and household budget were pruned to a minimum. She moved the family into the west wing, smartened up the remainder and invited the paying public in. The old stable block was converted into a tea room and souvenir shop, and coachloads of day trippers, who would have made Diana's grandfather revolve in his grave, poured in in ever-increasing numbers.

Diana tolerated her new stepmother far better than her sisters did, but they were complete opposites. The new Countess Spencer played the role to the full. She spent her mornings in bed, attending to a pile of files and papers that were spread about her. Once up she wore smart suits and high-heeled shoes, and every evening would dress for dinner in a long gown, even when she and Johnnie were the only people in the house. Diana by contrast dressed in jeans, wore no make-up, did all her own washing and ironing, and would quite frequently saunter into the kitchen to warm up on the Aga and chat to the cook and any other members of staff who happened to be around. They all adored her, and when, soon after her engagement, she went home for a weekend, she made a point of going into the kitchen to show her ring to the staff. She even took it off and the cook, the housekeeper and the ladies' maid all tried it on their own fingers.

They had all been present on the weekend when Diana had first met Prince Charles, back in 1977. The shoot was on the Monday, but he had arrived the previous day in time for one of the famous Althorp Gala Dinners, a glittering occasion packed with local dignitaries. Diana had come down from her room via the back staircase in order to show off her gown to the kitchen staff before joining the guests, and they had remarked to one another how suddenly that night the schoolgirl they knew appeared to have become a young lady.

Diana had gone back to West Heath after that weekend for her last term, and a second stab at the four O Levels she had failed in the summer. But she had had enough: she was sixteen and bored with school, so after Christmas she was sent off to Switzerland, once again following in Sarah's footsteps, to the Institut Alpin Videmanette, a finishing school at Château d'Oex near Gstaad. It was the first time she had been in an aeroplane, the first time she had been abroad, and the first time she had been away from all her friends and family. She was miserable and bitterly homesick, and after just six weeks she came home to London and refused to go back. All she had learnt in that time was how to ski.

Her mother was sympathetic and so Diana was allowed to stay on in London, living first of all in her house in Cadogan Place and then in a flat of her own which she shared with friends. Her sister Jane, meanwhile, was about to get married to Robert Fellowes, son of Sir William Fellowes, who had been the Queen's land agent at Sandringham. Robert was thirty-six and a member of the Queen's permanent staff – he is now the Queen's assistant private secretary. After a grand marriage ceremony at which Diana was bridesmaid he and Jane, who had always been Diana's closest sister, moved into a grace and favour apartment at Kensington Palace. Thus when Prince Charles moved into Kensington Palace the following year they became neighbours.

Diana spent the next year doing odd jobs in smart houses around Knightsbridge; then she worked as a mother's help in Hampshire for three months, and another three months were passed on a cookery course in Wimbledon. In the midst of that, tragedy struck the family yet again. In September 1978 her father collapsed in the estate office at Althorp with a cerebral haemorrhage and was taken unconscious first to the Northampton General and then to the National Hospital in London, where for three weeks he lay in a coma. It seemed certain that he would die, but Raine Spencer virtually willed him back to life. She kept up a bedside vigil and let no one near him, at times not even his children. She refused to accept defeat, and when she heard of a wonder drug available in Germany she persuaded her friend Lord Cavendish-Bentinck, now the Duke of Portland, who was in the drugs industry, to obtain a supply. It did the trick, but although he made a miraculous recovery people who know Earl Spencer well notice that his speech has been impaired by his illness, that he tires easily and has generally slowed down.

The day their father came out of hospital in January, Diana and Sarah were at Sandringham as guests of the Queen for a shooting party. The two girls were both worried, and the Royal Family was at pains to comfort them. The Queen had known them since they were children and, while they were living at Park House, if ever she saw them in their garden while she was out riding she would stop and say hello. She had been concerned about them after their parents' divorce, and it was only natural for her to include them in the New Year festivities when their father had been so ill.

That weekend heralded the start of Diana's friendship with Prince Charles. He found her delightful company: she was bright and witty and full of laughter, and easy to be with. She made no demands on him. She was just a friend – naïve, unsophisticated and unaffected – who obviously enjoyed being with him, who laughed at his jokes and made him feel good. Back in London he began to invite her out. He would ring her at Cadogan Square, quite out of the blue, and ask her to the ballet or the opera or just to dinner, usually to make up a party; and because she was an acknowledged girlfriend's little sister no one thought anything of it.

Meanwhile she had applied to Betty Vacani, at her famous children's dancing school in Knightsbridge, to ask if she might join as a student teacher. At West Heath Diana had been taught by a Vacani teacher, and Miss Vacani herself had come to the school once to judge a competition. It was also Betty Vacani who had taught Prince Charles to dance all those years ago. Although Diana had not reached the grade Miss Vacani normally required in her student teachers, she agreed to take her on for a fee of £100 a year. Unfortunately Diana did not get past the first three months – she was unhappy and out of her depth, and once again rather than stick it out she turned and fled.

She had arrived there as an unworldly seventeen-year-old, slightly plump and expensively but conservatively dressed in twin-sets and tartan skirts, her hair shoulder-length and nondescript, and wearing no make-up. Her two fellow students were chic and sophisticated, and were not only heading for the West End stage but looked as though they had already arrived. They were not the worst of it, however. Diana could not cope with the large numbers of children, and the audience of mothers and nannies who sat and watched. Each morning the day began with the babies' class, when she had to hold hands and dance 'Ring a Ring o' Roses', mime 'Hickory Dickory Dock', and show them how to touch their heads, shoulders, knees and toes, knees and toes. It called for an extrovert – someone who was not afraid to stand up and make a fool of herself. Diana could not do it. The three classes a week for professional dancers in which she was allowed to participate were another matter; she loved dancing, she had a good natural turn-out of the feet and she worked hard, but it soon became apparent that she was never going to make the grade. If she had kept up the hard work for three years she could have become a qualified classical ballet teacher, but not a professional dancer. She never gave herself the chance. Before the end of the term in March she left without offering any explanation. When someone telephoned to ask what had happened she said she had hurt her foot. A few days later she was skiing in the French Alps.

On her return she bought herself a flat at 60 Coleherne Court in Fulham, using money left in trust by her Fermoy great-grandmother, Frances Work. A considerable sum came to each of the children when they reached eighteen, and on their mother's advice all three girls had bought flats to share with friends. The next few months were spent shopping, choosing wallpaper and fabrics and furniture, which Diana loved. To earn some money she charred for her sister Sarah at her flat nearby, which she also enjoyed. Friends in the chalet on the French skiing holiday had been amazed at how domesticated Diana was, and how compulsively neat and tidy.

In the autumn of 1979 she found a permanent job as a helper at the Young England Kindergarten in St George's Square, Pimlico. It had come via the old school network. The kindergarten was run by two women, one of whom was the sister of a girl whom Jane had been friends with at West Heath. They had just started an afternoon group for younger children three days a week and needed an assistant. Diana's task was to cut up paper for them to paint on, help them into their aprons, supervise them in the garden at playtime, sort out their squabbles and mop up anyone who looked tearful.

At last Diana was in her element. Looking after groups of no more than five children she could cope with them on a one-to-one basis, and gradually became more relaxed and confident than she had ever been. The children adored her, so much so that she was asked to help in the mornings as well with the other children, who went up to the age of five. Diana was blissfully happy and came home day after day full of stories about what the children had said or done.

Flatmates came and went at Coleherne Court, and it was in every way typical of a flat full of girls. The hallway was a jumble of bicycles and tennis racquets, and music of one sort or another was playing most of the time. Fashion magazines lay around the living room, coffee mugs sat here and there, and on the mantelpiece stood a never-ending supply of invitations to parties. They were all girls from similar backgrounds, a clean-living lot who neither drank much nor smoked. Friends who came to supper at the flat would have to bring their own wine if they wanted it. There were boyfriends around, but the girls tended to be more chummy than flirtatious with men, and to go out in a giggling group rather than seriously with a single partner.

Diana certainly had no serious single partner. She had her sights set on the Prince of Wales, as she had since she was sixteen years old, and that summer in 1980, having watched glamorous and tempestuous women come and go, her patience was rewarded. At the very moment when the pressure upon him to marry was at its peak, and Charles found himself taking stock of his life and his duties and responsibilities, he noticed Diana anew. What he saw was not Sarah Spencer's little sister who was good for a laugh and a relaxing night on the town, but a sexy and kittenish young woman, in many ways the perfect woman to make his wife.

They began to see more of each other. She went to watch him play polo, she danced with him at the Goodwood Ball, she was on the royal yacht *Britannia* during Cowes Week, and then she went up to Balmoral to stay with her sister Jane who had just had a baby. In addition to their grace and favour apartment in Kensington Palace the Fellowes had the use of a cottage at Balmoral so that Robert would be on hand while the Queen was in Scotland, and it provided the perfect camouflage for Diana to spend some time with Prince Charles without anyone knowing. It was vital for them to have the time to discover whether the relationship was going to go any further; and by the time the indefatigable Mr Whitaker and his ilk came scanning the salmon pools with their binoculars Prince Charles and Diana had realized that it was.

It did not take the gentlemen of the press long to discover who Diana was and where she lived. What followed between that first sighting and the day the engagement was announced five months later, was the one of the most bizarre periods in the history of both the Royal Family and Fleet Street. Coleherne Court literally came under siege from reporters and photographers who stood watch on the doorstep twenty-four hours a day. Until the couple became engaged, Buckingham Palace could offer no help whatsoever: Diana was on her own. Everywhere she went the press followed and the cameras clicked. Once she struck a bargain with them: she would pose with a couple of children from the kindergarten if they would leave her alone for a while. The result was some of the most memorable royal photographs ever taken. With the light behind her, the skirt she was wearing became totally transparent, and the exquisite shape of her legs was recorded for posterity.

For the most part Diana quite enjoyed the thrill of the chase, finding it exciting to be the centre of attention and the name on everyone's lips. It was a great big game; sometimes she lost, sometimes she won. Her greatest triumph happened one day in December when she packed her Metro car – parked outside the flat – with a coat, an overnight bag and a pair of wellington boots, as if going away for the weekend. She then locked it up and walked off in the direction of the shops round the corner. It was some time before the press realized they had been tricked, by which time Diana was well on her way to Scotland for a secret weekend with Charles at Birkhall. It was the first time the Queen Mother had ever given the Prince the use of her house for a romantic rendezvous, and a clear indication of just where her feelings lay.

But there were less happy times too. One story in particular made everyone very angry, which was another measure of how much they all wanted this match to work. Prince Charles, aboard the royal train on a visit to the West Country, had stopped overnight in a railway siding in Wiltshire. According to the *Sunday Mirror*, which printed the story, Diana had driven down from London and was sneaked on board to spend a couple of hours with the Prince before slipping away and driving home. 'Love in the Sidings', it was dubbed; what made Diana especially upset was that the paper had telephoned her before publishing to check the story, and even after her denial of it they still went ahead. The editor of the *Sunday Mirror*, Bob Edwards, will go to his grave believing the story to have been true, and furthermore regarding it as a harmless illustration of how much Diana loved the Prince; but the Queen took the unprecedented step of instructing her press secretary, Michael Shea, to demand a retraction.

Everyone was growing concerned about how much more this nineteen-year-old girl would be able to take. Her mother even wrote to *The Times* to appeal for a break:

> In recent weeks many articles have been labelled 'exclusive quotes', when the plain truth is that my daughter has not spoken the words attributed to her. Fanciful speculation, if it is in good taste, is one thing, but this can be embarrassing. Lies are quite another matter, and by their very nature, hurtful and inexcusable. . . .
>
> May I ask the editors of Fleet Street, whether, in the execution of their jobs, they consider it necessary or fair to harass my daughter daily, from dawn until well after dusk? Is it fair to ask any human being, regardless of circumstances, to be treated in this way? The freedom of the press was granted by law, by public demand, for very good reasons. But when these privileges are abused, can the press command any respect, or expect to be shown any respect?

Heartfelt though her plea might have been, it fell on stony ground. When the couple met up on New Year's Day at Sandringham, having spent Christmas apart, the place was teeming with pressmen. Prince Charles had had his fill. 'I should like to take this opportunity,' he said, 'to wish you all a very happy New Year and your editors a particularly nasty one.'

Charles asked Diana to marry him, in his apartment at Buckingham Palace, three weeks before it was officially announced. She was due to go on holiday with her mother and stepfather to the Shand-Kydds' sheep farm in Australia, and he was keen that she should think it over very carefully while she was away. There was no thinking to be done. Diana had been frightened at times by the press, upset at times by their methods and their disregard for the truth, but she had never at any time had doubts about her desire to marry Prince Charles – nor about her desire to be a princess.

On the morning of Tuesday, 24 February the headline in *The Times* carried the simple message: 'Engagement of the Prince to be announced today.' It was an appropriate end to a courtship by newspaper that someone should have leaked the news to *The Times*. Sure enough, at 11 a.m. that day Michael Shea issued the official announcement to the Press Association. At that moment the Queen was about to begin an investiture at Buckingham

Palace. Instead the Lord Chamberlain, Lord Maclean, stepped forward and addressed the assembled company:

> The Queen has asked me to let you know that an announcement is being made at this moment in the following terms: 'It is with the greatest pleasure that The Queen and The Duke of Edinburgh announce the betrothal of their beloved son, The Prince of Wales, to The Lady Diana Spencer, daughter of The Earl Spencer and The Honourable Mrs Shand-Kydd.'

CHAPTER SIXTEEN

Diana had survived the ordeal of the previous five months with remarkable coolness. Not only that, she had rightly identified the people whom she most needed as allies – the most important of those being the press – and by a mixture of charm and girlishness had turned even the most hardened cynics into ardent fans. She was meticulously polite to the people who hounded her, never losing her temper, never failing to smile, and by remembering a name or some incident that had happened on a previous occasion managed to make each dogged reporter believe that he or she was singled out and in some way special to her.

As a result they boosted her in print. They presented her in such a way that no one could fail to see that she was young and happy and in love with her Prince, and the British people, who had been hyped to such a pitch by the media's obsession with finding a wife for Prince Charles, went wild. She was the living proof, the public told itself, that fairytales can come true. She was a real rags-to-riches girl, plucked from London's bedsitter land to live in a palace and be happy ever after.

Of course, she was nothing of the sort. Her ancestry was impeccable – she came from the very top drawer of the English aristocracy and could boast as much blue blood in her veins as the Prince of Wales, if not more. They are in fact distantly related: both descended from Henry VII and James I and, depending upon which common ancestor you take, sixteenth cousins once removed, eleventh cousins once removed, or seventh cousins once removed, via William Cavendish, the 3rd Duke of Devonshire. They are also related through Charles II and his brother James II: five lines lead back to Charles's innumerable children born the wrong side of the blanket, and one to an illegitimate daughter of James II and Arabella Churchill, sister of the 1st Duke of Marlborough.

The magic ingredient, however, was not the blue blood but the common touch. Lady Diana Spencer had the distinct advantage of having been brought up as a normal, if privileged, member of the public. She knew what it was like to shop in the January sales, travel by bus, stand in a queue at the supermarket, wait a week for the telephone engineers, wash up after a dinner party and do the laundry. Yet because of her father's previous connections with the Queen, and her grandmother's friendship with the Queen Mother, she understood the workings of protocol and was not daunted by the company of the Royal Family, which so many ordinary people would have been. It was the perfect combination for a princess to take the family into the twenty-first century. A commoner might have debased the role, and a royal princess might have alienated it still further from the people; Diana was the ideal compromise. There have been stories from time to time that have knocked her, that have called her a spendthrift and a tyrant, but the vast majority of her public has remained faithful. In six years she has not only become perhaps the most famous and most frequently photographed woman in the world, but she has helped to bring the institution of monarchy to a new peak of popularity and boosted the image of Britain worldwide.

The most remarkable phenomenon to take place during those six years, however, has been Diana's metamorphosis. In the five months between the engagement and the wedding she underwent a thorough transformation, and has continued to change ever since. By the time she married Prince Charles the slightly plump girl next door had been miraculously turned into a stylish young woman. She had slimmed down and smartened up, her hair was restyled and her face carefully made up. Almost the only trace of the girl who used to cycle to work and mix up the powder paint for the under-fives was the famous walk. She had a habit of bowing her head to one side and looking out from beneath her fringe which had earned her the nickname 'Shy Di'. She had done it for years, and even today there is still a trace of that mannerism left.

Extraordinary as the change in her physical appearance was, it was not entirely mysterious. Diana's sister Jane had once worked as an editorial assistant at *Vogue* magazine, and still knew people on the staff who could be trusted to be discreet. As a leading fashion magazine they regularly had clothes coming in from all the top designers to use for photo sessions. They knew what was around, and what sort of clothes should be worn to which occasions, with which accessories; when Diana found something she liked she would contact the designer, without going through the embarrassment of calling in unannouced. Diana used to go there two or three times a week and learnt much of what she knows today in the *Vogue* office in Hanover Square. The fashion editor, Grace Coddington, once a well-known model, taught her how to walk in front of crowds and cameras – no mean feat – and helped to improve her deportment. The beauty editor, Felicity Clark, taught her about make-up and for formal occasions introduced her to Barbara Daly, one of the best make-up artists in Britain, who did her face on the day of the wedding.

The greatest change of all, however, was not to the face or the walk or the wardrobe. With Prince Charles's ring on her finger Diana found a new confidence. She still had a lot of growing up to do, but for the first time since she was six years old she felt truly secure. The adulation of the press and the public boosted that confidence further. She read every word that was written about her, and was hurt by every criticism.

As soon as the engagement had been announced, the Palace were able to shield Diana from the press. She moved out of Coleherne Court, first of all into Clarence House to stay with the Queen Mother, and then into a suite at Buckingham Palace which it was thought would offer a livelier environment. By comparison with Clarence House it might have been, but the courtiers who roamed the corridors of Buckingham Palace were hardly a jolly crowd for someone used to a flat full of teenagers. So during the Prince's absence on tours abroad and engagements around the country she stayed with her sister at Kensington Palace, or her mother in Victoria, and went shopping for her trousseau and to dress fittings.

The Royal Family was generally pleased with the Prince's choice of bride, particularly if the good effect she seemed to be having on Charles was going to last. None was more delighted than the Queen Mother, who saw in Diana the soft, gentle qualities that would make the perfect wife, combined with a naturalness that could not fail her as a princess. The Queen was amused by her sense of humour and ability to relax and become part of the family, the Duke of Edinburgh was flattered and charmed by her attention, and the two younger princes, Andrew and Edward, both found her attractive and jolly good fun. The only one who was not so taken was Princess Anne, whose life simply revolved in a different orbit.

Winning the approval of the courtiers and the Palace staff was almost as important as having the family's blessing. Diana realized as much, and set about the task with purpose. The most effective weapon in her arsenal was an endearing nature. She bounced about the place chattering and joking with such friendliness and sweetness that even Edward Adeane, who could not begin to understand the workings of her nineteen-year-old mind, had to admit that she was a lovely girl.

Everyone agreed she could not have been more enchanting. Several, however, had reservations about whether she was the right girl for the Prince of Wales. Some of his friends also had reservations, which they expressed. Attractive, delightful, kind and genuine though Diana was, they feared that the pair would not have enough in common to keep the relationship stimulating. For a start there was the age difference: Diana was a very young and innocent nineteen, while Charles was thirty-two and in some ways had had more experience than most men of fifty-two. He was a deep and contemplative character, while she was always on the go. He was an avid reader of history and philosophy; she enjoyed women's magazines and the television. He loved classical music, sang with the Bach Choir, and a treat for him was a night at the opera. She liked pop music – groups like Dire Straits, Police and Wham – had no enthusiasm for opera, but enjoyed ballet. Charles blossomed in the country, while Diana preferred the excitement of London. He could happily spend all day fishing; Diana would rather be in Harrods or Harvey Nichols shopping. His other great love was horse-riding, which Diana abhorred. Her sister Sarah had been a keen horsewoman, but Diana had fallen off and broken her arm as a child and had never had any desire to repeat the experience. Her sport was tennis, which Charles had never much cared for.

Prince Charles could not see that any of these differences would be important. Diana was still so young – it was hardly surprising she spent all day tuned in to Capital Radio. They had fun together: she was frothy and witty and slightly irreverent and teased him for being square and old-fashioned. What they had was a marvellous friendship, the sort that he had spoken about all those years ago in interviews:

> It's rather more than just falling madly in love with somebody. . . . It's basically a very strong friendship. . . . I think you are very lucky if you find the person attractive in the physical *and* the mental sense. . . . In many cases, you fall madly 'in love' with somebody with whom you are really infatuated. To me marriage, which may be for fifty years, seems to be one of the biggest and most responsible steps to be taken in one's life.

Friends feared he had fallen into the very trap he had said he should avoid; but the consequences were something that they would have to worry about if and when they occurred. For the time being, Charles and Diana were happy and in love and the whole nation was being swept along on a tidal wave of romance and jubilation.

The royal wedding on Wednesday, 29 July, was the happening of the decade. The night before, beacons blazed all over England, Scotland and Wales. In Hyde Park fireworks whirred and banged and lit up London's sky with multicoloured stars, showers and shooting balls of fire, while the massed bands of the Household musicians played, the Morriston Orpheus Choir and the Choir of the Welsh Guards sang, and above it all the Royal Horse Artillery fired salvoes from the guns of the King's Troop. It was a night to remember; traffic ground to a halt and millions of people roamed the streets, talking to one another and sharing drinks and food as if they were all guests at one mammoth party.

At 4 a.m. the route between Buckingham Palace and St Paul's Cathedral was closed to traffic. By dawn there was no standing room to be had within a hundred yards of St Paul's. And by nine o'clock, when the first guests started to arrive, more than a million people had taken up their places along the route, determined to have the day of their lives. They had come with camping stoves and thermos flasks, sandwiches and beer and champagne. Dozens in the front row had been there since Sunday, camping out all night in sleeping bags to be sure of a good view.

They were not disappointed. It was a magnificent day, with the full ceremonial works: open carriages – Charles travelled in a 1902 state postillion landau, Diana in a glass coach – jangling harness on the horses, and the gleaming brass of the Household Cavalry.

Most of the crowned heads of Europe were there, and a number of monarchs from Africa, the Middle East and Asia, including the twenty-five-stone King of Tonga, for whom an extra-large chair had to be made. There were over 160 foreign presidents, prime ministers and their wives, amongst them Mrs Nancy Reagan – whom Prince Charles had met at Walter Annenberg's – and who arrived in London with twelve security men and five hat boxes.

Prince Charles wore the full dress uniform of a Royal Navy commander with a splendid blue Garter sash, and looked, as he always does in uniform, strikingly handsome. Diana's dress, made by the Emanuels, was a sensation: an elaborate, billowing ocean of ivory silk paper taffeta, hand embroidered in tiny mother-of-pearl sequins and pearls, with lace-flounced sleeves and a twenty-five-foot train, trimmed and edged with sparkling old lace. The design had been a closely guarded secret, but within five hours of the wedding replicas had been drawn and made up and were in the shops in almost every high street.

Diana was given away by her father, and as they arrived at St Paul's a great cheer went up from the crowds. Then the State Trumpeters of the Household Cavalry, standing in the porticoes by the west doors, sounded a fanfare to wake the marble dead. The cathedral clock struck eleven, the dramatic opening bars of Jeremiah Clarke's Trumpet Voluntary rang forth, and Diana began the three-and-a-half-minute walk down the aisle, firmly clutching her father's arm. It was the start of the most expensive wedding recorded in British history, yet a service that, despite the presence of television cameras and an audience of 700 million people worldwide, was at the same time intimate, beautiful and immensely moving. No one found it more so than Prince Charles himself.

He had taken a considerable hand in its organization, insisting that the whole thing be a rousing musical extravaganza. With the help of Sir David Willcocks, Director of the Royal College of Music, whom he knew from his activities with the Bach Choir, he had chosen all the music and assembled three orchestras, the Bach Choir and the world-famous Maori opera singer, Kiri Te Kanawa. It was he who had insisted that they should be married not in Westminster Abbey, where recent royal weddings had traditionally taken place, but in St Paul's, which unlike the Abbey was big enough to accommodate all three orchestras and many more guests, and where the acoustics were better. 'I can't wait for the whole thing,' he said in a television interview the day before. 'I want everybody to come out, you know, having had a marvellous musical and emotional experience.'

The Lord Chamberlain was not at all happy about the choice of venue. St Paul's was three times the distance from Buckingham Palace as Westminster Abbey, which apart from anything else would mean three times the normal level of security, and therefore much more expenditure, which at a time when nearly 3 million people were unemployed and the British economy was at an all-time low seemed to be an insensitive move. But when he was told that there might not be enough soldiers to line the route properly, Prince Charles simply said, 'Well, stand them further apart.'

He was not to be dissuaded. The soldiers stood further apart; and despite the Lord Chamberlain's misgivings, and despite the grumblings of a few anti-royalists like Willie Hamilton, MP, the additional cost, bringing it to close on £150,000 in all, was well spent. In front of television sets the length and breadth of the country, in homes, hospitals and institutions, young and old alike were lifted from the gloom and despondency of their everyday lives and transported by the marvellous musical and emotional experience that Prince Charles had hoped for. It was the very fillip the country needed, a boost to the national morale at the very moment it mattered most. Also, as a footnote, it raised more than £750,000 for charity by way of profits from the official programmes and souvenirs from the previous night's fireworks display, and from admission fees to St James's Palace, where the wedding presents were on show to the public for eight weeks.

The Archbishop of Canterbury took them through the marriage vows, and after Diana had muddled up the Prince's names and promised to take Philip Charles Arthur George as her wedded husband, instead of Charles Philip Arthur George, Charles made a slip himself. 'All thy goods with thee I share,' he said in ringing tones – rather different from the undertaking to share all his worldly goods with his new wife. It was human touches like these which made the day such a huge success. The crowds loved it. They roared and cheered, especially when later, having made their way back to the Palace in the open landau, waving every inch of the way, the couple went out on to the balcony and the Prince gave his bride a kiss. It was the first time one member of the Royal Family had every kissed another publicly on the balcony at Buckingham Palace, and the thousands below went mad. They shouted, laughed and burst into song, and in their delight turned and embraced their neighbours – even total strangers.

Prince Charles summed up his feelings during a lunch at the Guildhall three months later.

> We still cannot get over what happened that day. Neither of us can get over the atmosphere; it was electric, I felt, and so did my wife.
>
> I remember several occasions that were similar, with large crowds: the Coronation and the Jubilee, and various major national occasions. All of them were very special in their own way but our wedding was quite extraordinary as far as we were concerned. It made us both extraordinarily proud to be British.

They spent their wedding night at Broadlands, which since Lord Mountbatten's death had been Norton Knatchbull's home. Lord Romsey, as he had become on the death of his grandfather, had married Penelope Eastwood that same year, and Prince Charles had been his best man. Charles had initially wanted Romsey to be his best man, but royal protocol required him to have his two brothers as 'supporters'. Instead he asked whether he and Diana might stay at his friend's house for a couple of days before flying to Gibraltar to join the royal yacht for a two-week cruise round the Mediterranean and Aegean. Broadlands was filled with such happy memories that it seemed an appropriate and auspicious place to embark upon their married life. It was also the house in which the Queen and the Duke of Edinburgh had spent the first night of their honeymoon; and when Mountbatten was alive it had been almost more of a home than home itself. The Romseys had moved out to give Charles and Diana the place to themselves, so for two days and three nights they enjoyed their first taste of real privacy amid six thousand acres of rolling countryside and a stretch of the best salmon fishing in England.

When their two weeks on *Britannia* were over the relaxed and sun-soaked newly-weds returned to Britain to join the rest of the Royal Family at Balmoral. A change had come over them both. Now the strain they must have been under during the lead up to the wedding was apparent. Charles looked years younger, and carefree for almost the first time in his life. He gazed at his wife approvingly, touched her, put his arm around her, held her hand – things he had never easily done before. Diana glowed with contentment, and was happy to pose for press photographers and chat to reporters about the honeymoon. Of married life she said, 'I can highly recommend it. It is a marvellous life and Balmoral is one of the best places in the world.'

The Princess was still euphoric, but when the gentlemen of the press departed, taking with them the limelight to which she had become so accustomed, she felt a terrible sense of anticlimax. The whirlwind magic of the last year was suddenly gone, and like a child who has been waiting and waiting for Christmas, Boxing Day was a let-down. As the days at Balmoral passed into weeks, with nothing to do but walk for mile upon mile the treeless, heather-clad grouse moor, she grew bored, and one of the best places on earth became an open prison. Charles, by contrast, was in paradise, surrounded by everyone and everything he loved best. He could not understand his wife's brooding moodiness.

Diana had spent her life moving on when circumstances did not suit her, quitting if she was unhappy or up against a problem, and her parents had always let her do so. This was one instance, however, when she could not do as she pleased. It would have been unthinkable for her to have left Balmoral ahead of schedule, as she knew only too well: there would have been stories of a rift in the marriage. So she had to stay, but it was a difficult time for her and on occasions she let it show.

The early stages of the marriage, once they had returned to London, were also difficult. They were not like any ordinary young couple setting up home together, for Prince Charles was already set up. He had two houses and a well-established pattern of existence. He had friends and acquaintances who went back many years; most of them were either his own age or older. He had his hobbies, his interests and sports, all of which were a part of his routine, and some involved his absence from the house for the best part of the weekend. The remainder of his time was spent working. He awoke early, and stayed up until midnight or beyond dealing with paperwork; even at weekends he would arrive to stay with friends and a pile of work would come too. Charles thought that a wife would comfortably join in and settle down around all these activities. The wife had different ideas.

A further difficulty was his family, closely knit by any standards; they worked together and traditionally holidayed together too. Charles could see no problem with the arrangement; he liked nothing better than the complete relaxation that their company afforded. For Diana, however, his family were her in-laws, and the fact that they happened to be royal did not alter a relationship which is tricky in any marriage. Her husband was devoted to his mother, spoke to her regularly and indeed shared secrets with her that he was not prepared to share with his wife. Rationally Diana must have known this had to happen – his mother was the sovereign, he her heir – but emotionally the Queen was still a mother-in-law to her.

As well as the family there were the servants, some of whom had been with Prince Charles for years and during that time had become close and trusted. His valet, Stephen Barry, was one in particular on whom the Prince relied very heavily. Like many good valets he was gay, but as upright and devoted a man as one could hope to find. As well as taking care of the Prince's wardrobe and the dozens of uniforms he had to wear, remembering which to pack for what occasion in which country, he selected his outfit each day and advised on taste, style and colour, in furnishings as well as in clothing, and did all the Prince's personal shopping.

Diana had married Prince Charles because she loved him, and because she was more than a little in love with the idea of being a princess, but she had also married him because she desperately wanted to be a wife and mother. With so many people dancing attendance on the Prince she found her role was almost superfluous.

Then there were his friends. All so much older than her, the men on the whole were involved in business, finance and politics, things that she neither knew nor cared about; and the women were mature, most of them with children and interests beyond those of a twenty-year-old, and could hold their own in conversation with the men. They posed a threat, particularly the attractive ones, which she feared. Before and during the engagement they had all tolerated one another quite well – the friends had been welcoming and Diana had been pleased to be welcomed and interested in everything around her – but now that the honeymoon period was over, and she and Charles began to settle into a routine of seeing people who belonged to the Prince's old life, she was less happy.

The feeling was not entirely one-way, for Diana had a host of friends too. The men were in their early twenties and starting out in life in the army, banking, the family firm or the stock exchange – typical Hooray Henries with lots of money, fast cars and parents with houses in the country to take friends to at weekends. The girls were mostly like Diana, with no great academic leanings, not intent upon a career, but doing some sort of job to fill in the time between leaving school and marriage, to supplement the allowance from their parents and pay for skiing in winter and a holiday in the sun later in the year. On the whole Charles found their interests and conversation as strange to him as his interests were to them.

These were all problems that were left simmering quietly beneath the surface – erupting occasionally, as the marriage progressed, into blazing rows between the two. It was inevitable that Diana should want to make changes, but it was hardly surprising that her husband should not want to alter what he regarded as a perfectly well-ordered existence, surrounded by friends and staff whom he knew and liked and owed loyalty to. There was a discipline of life too which was new to her, and not altogether to her liking. Prince Charles had grown up with it, and had never questioned the need for his life to be so regimented. There was so much in his life which he took for granted simply because he had known no other situation. Diana had not; she was impulsive and had always enjoyed freedom and flexibility: if she woke up one morning and did not feel like doing what she had planned, she would give it a miss. Likewise if she suddenly felt like taking a train to Brighton, or spending the afternoon at the cinema, she could do it. With a schedule prepared six months in advance, however, with the need for a detective to accompany her and for extensive security precautions to precede every visit, behaving on impulse had become virtually impossible.

What was even more restrictive was the presence of the press. No one could have foreseen the obsession of the popular papers and foreign journals with Diana after the wedding. There was a story about her, either real or imagined, in one paper or another almost every day, and after the announcement in November that she was expecting her first child the following June they were on her doorstep night and day. They were with her everywhere she went: they photographed her in public, in private, in her car and buying sweets in Tetbury; they even used powerful telescopic lenses and took peeping-tom shots of her inside the house at Highgrove. She was back to the siege conditions she had suffered before the engagement – and it was happening despite the best security Buckingham Palace could offer.

Where her mother had appealed for Diana to be given a break before the engagement it was now the Queen who came to her aid, in precisely the same way as she had done twenty-five years earlier when Prince Charles had begun at Cheam. Her press secretary, Michael Shea, invited the editors of every national newspaper and of the television and radio news programmes, and representatives from all the major news agencies, to a meeting at Buckingham Palace. He had had no instructions from the Princess, he made it clear, but she was clearly growing despondent at being unable to leave her own front door without being photographed. There was anxiety about the short-term strain of this on a girl of twenty expecting her first child. He appealed to them to consider regarding the private life of the Princess as private.

With some notable exceptions the pressure did lift, and the bulk of the coverage was restricted to Diana's public engagements. Her first engagement as Princess of Wales was, appropriately, a tour of the Principality. It was an initiation by fire, but a resounding success, and it set the seal on her popularity. In every part of the country, along every stretch of the road that the royal car would travel, hundreds of people stood out in the cold and the rain to catch a glimpse of her. She and the Prince of Wales covered four hundred miles in three days, visiting seaside resorts, historic towns, country showgrounds, leisure centres, hospitals, mining communities and industrial cities. At every stop she stepped from the car – a glass-topped Rolls Royce – or train to an awe-inspiring reception, a sea of faces with outstretched hands, of every size and shape and age, all desperate to see, touch and hear their fairytale Princess.

She did not disappoint them; she looked stunning in brilliantly coloured outfits and stylish hats, with a smile or a giggle for every one of them. Queen Victoria once said, 'Dress is a trifling matter but it gives also the outward sign from which people in general can and often do judge upon the inward state of mind and feeling of a person.' The tartan skirts and twin-sets of 1979 were gone, and the new Diana that had emerged, secure in wedlock, was the fashion industry's dream. She had slimmed to almost distressing proportions, but she wore designer clothes with such flair that she has become a leader of fashion. She began to wear pearl chokers, for example, like Princess Alexandra of Wales in the second half of the nineteenth century – they had scarcely been seen since that time. Suddenly the shops were full of pearl chokers. She wore culottes on honeymoon: culottes returned to fashion; high necks, and they too flooded the market. Her hairstyle was also copied in every high street salon. The people of Wales turned out in droves to be the first to see the real thing.

The tour was not without its risks. Welsh Nationalist slogans were daubed on bridges and road signs, protesters waving banners saying 'Go home Diana' and 'Go home English Prince' met them in Bangor and Swansea, fire bombs were found in Pontypridd and outside Cardiff, and the BBC was sent a letter, written in Welsh, warning: 'We will not forget 1969 – beware Caernarfon.' It was the work of the extremist group Meibion Glendwr (the Sons of Snowdonia), to which the two men who had blown themselves up on the morning of the investiture had belonged.

Security precautions were therefore tight. Manhole covers and letter-boxes by the roadside were checked and sealed over the dozens of miles the royal couple travelled by road. There was the usual escort front and back of police cars and motorcyclists; junctions had uniformed police standing on guard; and at every point where Charles and Diana left their car marksmen were on the rooftops, dog handlers on the ground as well as hundreds of policemen and women who had been drafted in from other parts of the country to reinforce the local ranks. Special Branch officers had even checked the guest lists of every hotel and boarding house in the area. They were taking every precaution possible, and although it was comforting the Princess knew as well as her husband that nothing was foolproof. The recent murder of President Sadat of Egypt, who had dined on board *Britannia* with the Prince and Princess during their honeymoon, was still fresh in both of their minds; but neither seemed unduly concerned.

Far more daunting for Diana was the prospect of going out and talking to the crowds. Prince Charles had not been many years younger when he had done it for the first time on his refuelling stop in Australia with David Checketts. He had been entirely on his own and on a little runway miles away from anywhere. Diana had to begin under the full glare of the media, with television cameras and microphones, reporters and photographers picking up every syllable, and if they weren't close enough to hear they would ask people in the crowd for a verbatim account.

Diana took the plunge with enormous courage. Like Prince Charles she discovered that it was surprisingly easy to begin a dialogue, and that the people who line security barriers and stand for hours in the rain to shake a royal hand are the friendliest of folk and only too eager to respond to whatever is said to them, however banal. Yet Diana did not mutter banalities. From the word go she had a knack of saying and doing the very thing that would most please the individual in front of her; it is a gift which has become better and better over the years.

'My Dad says give us a kiss,' shouted a little boy at her first stop in Rhyl.

'Well, then, you had better have one!' said the Princess, and bent down to kiss him on the cheek.

'What nice shiny medals,' she said to a hunchbacked old soldier at the Deeside Leisure Centre. Then to his beaming wife, 'Did you polish them for him?'

At Caernarvon, where an icy wind from the sea had chilled everyone to the bone, herself included, she eagerly raced ahead of Prince Charles – holding on to her hat to stop it blowing off as she went – to say hello to a bunch of children who had been patiently waiting. She bent down to their level to smooth their blue-cold faces, squatting for the smallest, stretching forward on tiptoes to reach people standing behind, wiggling her frozen fingers to show off her engagement ring, and cupping icy hands between her own to try and warm them. By the second day torrential rain had compounded the cold, and Diana would have been excused for running for cover. At Carmarthen, however, where the streets were awash, Diana battled with an ineffectual umbrella and lingered if anything longer than usual to talk to the crowds, who were literally soaked to the skin. The effect was devastating. The crowds were enraptured, and the more they shouted for her and cheered her the more she enjoyed herself. 'Now I've seen her, she's everything I thought she would be,' said one woman, speaking for a thousand. 'She's the flower in the royal forest.'

Prince Charles was proud and delighted, but he could not help noticing that people were disappointed if they got him rather than her. At each stop they took one side of the street each, so inevitably not everyone had a chance to meet Diana and he was left apologizing for not having enough wives to go round. 'Diana love, over here,' he would say on occasion to try and bring her over; or to people vainly holding out flowers in her direction, 'Do you want me to give those to her? I seem to do nothing but collect flowers these days. I know my role.'

He made light of it, but what happened in Wales was the seed of an even more serious problem to be faced within the marriage than that of friends or relatives. Quite unwittingly, Diana was upstaging Prince Charles.

CHAPTER SEVENTEEN

Whatever problems lay beneath the surface, there is no doubt that marriage did the Prince of Wales a power of good. The security of a wife, of someone with whom he could share the loneliness of his life and the burden of his position, boosted his confidence in a way that was obvious to everyone who knew him. He seemed truly happy at last; he was proud of his beautiful Princess, proud and excited by the prospect of becoming a father, and friends noticed that whenever they were together he would sit and gaze adoringly at her.

Watching his son come into the world the following year was one of the most miraculous moments he had ever experienced, and the final ingredient which, it seemed, would make his life complete. Charles had always loved children, and had always had a knack with them which made his innumerable godchildren long for visits. He had had practice as an adolescent with his own younger brothers: Prince Andrew, born when he was eleven, and Prince Edward, who arrived when he was fifteen. Unlike most boys of that age, who have no interest in babies, Prince Charles was delighted by his young brothers, patient with them and happy to spend time with them. He painted with them, read them stories and even wrote his own story for them, called *The Old Man of Lochnagar* which he subsequently published for the Covent Garden Appeal. He had empathy with children, and a complete lack of self-consciousness. He did not mind looking foolish and making funny faces and noises for the tiny ones. He enjoyed watching them develop, he liked their odd little ways, and as they grew older he was interested in hearing what they had to say for themselves. Children are the ultimate levellers. They are not impressed by rank or status or even age. Thus Charles could be himself with children in a way that was never possible with adults, and he loved it.

Prince William was born at 9.03 p.m. on 21 June, ten days before Diana's twenty-first birthday, and weighed a healthy seven pounds one and a half ounces. He was born in the private Lindo Wing of St Mary's Hospital in Paddington, one of the top teaching hospitals in London, where Mr George Pinker, the Queen's gynaecologist who had looked after Diana during her pregnancy, is a consultant. Princess Anne had had her two children at St Mary's, as indeed had all royal mothers who had had babies in the previous eight years. It was in this unpretentious-looking redbrick building with views over the seamier part of Paddington, in a small, square room with a polished cork floor and regulation iron bedstead, that the newest prince of the realm came into the world, and ensured that the line of succession was secure for at least one more generation.

Charles had taken the Princess of Wales into hospital at 5 a.m. in the early stages of labour, and had spent most of the day by her side, helping with the breathing exercises she had been taught in preparation for the birth. Outside, the narrow back street was filled with well-wishers, some of whom had been standing waiting for the news since early morning. The atmosphere was electric, reminiscent of the night before the wedding, and as soon as they heard on the ten o'clock radio news that the Princess had given birth to a boy over five hundred people began singing and cheering and popping champagne corks. When Prince Charles emerged from the Lindo Wing an hour later he was grinning from ear to ear, physically and emotionally shattered.

'I'm obviously thrilled and delighted,' he told reporters. 'Sixteen hours is a long time to wait. It's rather a grown-up thing I find – rather a shock to the system.'

'How was the baby?' someone wanted to know.

'He looks marvellous. Fair, sort of blondish. He's not bad,' and when asked if he looked like his father, said, 'It has the good fortune not to. . . . Yes, thank you, my wife is fine. Very, very good.'

Names?

'We've thought of one or two, but there's a bit of an argument about it. We'll just have to wait and see.'

The Prince of Wales is the sort of man whom women instinctively want to throw their arms around and protect; and suddenly a woman from the crowd lunged forward and did precisely that, leaving a large red lipstick mark on his cheek. It was just what everyone had wanted to do, and the excited crowd burst into song. 'Nice one, Charlie,' they called. 'Give us another one!'

'Bloody hell!' said the Prince. 'Give us a chance.' With that he was away to leave mother and baby – or Baby Wales, as he was called on the labels around one wrist and one ankle – for a good night's sleep.

He was back at the hospital again first thing the next morning, and at 6 p.m. a very proud father took his wife and baby son home. The frail little creature he carried in his arms, snuggly wrapped in a white shawl, was the most British prince, the genealogists declared, since James I, and the most English since Elizabeth I. He was 39 per cent English, 16 per cent Scottish, 6¼ per cent Irish, and 6¼ per cent American. The remaining 32½ per cent was German. To Prince Charles he was quite simply the best thing that had ever happened to him.

The following week two announcements were made. The Prince would be named William Arthur Philip Louis; and his godparents were to be Lady Susan Hussey, lady in waiting to the Queen, wife of the man who was to be appointed chairman of the BBC in 1986, and who had known the Prince of Wales since he was a child; Natalia, the twenty-three-year-old Duchess of Westminster, who as Natalia Phillips had been a childhood friend of Diana's; Sir Laurens van der Post, now seventy-five, who had been a guest at Balmoral during the weeks after their honeymoon; and three relatives: Constantine, former King of the Hellenes, Lord Romsey and Princess Alexandra, the Queen's cousin and a family member of whom Charles had always been especially fond.

There had been widespread speculation that the elderly Texan multi-millionaire Dr Armand Hammer, chairman and chief executive of the Occidental Petroleum Corporation, might be a godfather, particularly by those who thought that he had taken the place of Lord Mountbatten in the Prince's affection. This was never the case. Prince Charles enjoyed the company of Mr Hammer, who as founder of a giant multi-national corporation was a fascinating man to talk to, and he was indebted to him for his generosity towards the United World Colleges, as well as some of his other charities, but the American could never have begun to fill the void of Lord Mountbatten – much though he might have wished to.

During his presidency of UWC Lord Mountbatten had cherished a dream of opening a college in the United States. By the time he retired in 1978 colleges had been opened in Singapore – the UWC South East Asia – and in Canada – the Lester B. Pearson UWC of the Pacific on Vancouver Island – but there was nothing in the pipeline for America. Prince Charles took up the search and in 1980 tentatively approached Dr Hammer, a noted philanthropist. He told him about the movement and its ideals and the importance of expanding into the United States, and less than two years later a magnificent new college opened in Montezuma, New Mexico, aptly named the Armand Hammer UWC. Dr Hammer had found a site in the Rocky Mountains near the Pecos Wilderness and bought it. At a cost of $10 million he had then renovated the buildings, landscaped the grounds, built tennis courts, walkways and roads, and thirteen months after purchasing the property had opened the doors to 102 students from forty-six nations. It was Dr Hammer alone who had made this possible, Prince Charles told the International Council Meeting in 1985. His quite remarkable generosity had continued on a bewildering scale unmatched in the history of the UWC.

Another college opened in 1982. Waterford Kamhlaba in Swaziland which joined in 1981, the College of the Adriatic in Italy. With the Venezuelan college that opened in 1986, and the original Atlantic College in Wales, the total is now seven; and Prince Charles is still keen to try to get something going in India, convinced that UWC can contribute to the problem of food production and agricultural development in the Third World. 'I believe most strongly', he said while visiting the Canadian college in 1980, 'that better food production and the development of the rural economy in many of the developing countries is vital to the future of the whole world.'

During his various tours of Commonwealth countries, the Prince had become increasingly preoccupied by the problems of the Third World. Like the Queen, he regards the Commonwealth as being of paramount importance and takes his position within it seriously; he is concerned for the people there no less than for the people of the United Kingdom. He had read around the subject extensively, and had been particularly impressed by a book called *Small Is Beautiful*, written by the late economist and philosopher E. F. Schumacher, who to propound his views had founded in the 1960s a small and largely unheard-of charity called the Intermediate

Technology Development Group. Although Charles was always the guest of the President or Head of State when he travelled to developing countries, and was therefore restricted in what he saw, he was well aware of poverty, sickness and the devastating results of drought and mismanagement. His sister had been able to tell him even more from her visits on behalf of the Save the Children Fund. He was convinced that the problem was not a local but a global one, for which we should all share responsibility. Integrating students in United World Colleges was one way. 'It is vital,' he said,

> for students from the developed world to meet and talk with those from developing countries, for in my contacts with the UWC students it is possible to detect a kind of current which seems to run through the Third World – and if we do not take the trouble to heed it and try to understand it, then an immense gulf will arise which could take a very long time to bridge again, with all sorts of appalling miseries in the meantime.

He was desperately keen to find some means of doing more to help, however, and when Dennis Stephenson, the dynamic young entrepreneur who ran Schumacher's charity, discovered the Prince's interest in their work he invited Charles to become its patron. Schumacher believed, as the title of his book suggests, that small is beautiful, that producing things on a small, workable scale is good for the country and good for the community who live in it, and that if the West abandons its old style of life and follows 'people of the forward stampede' – proponents of new technology and mass production – the Western way of life could be destroyed within fifty years. Its application in developing countries was no different. Traditional Western aid, he argued, was ultimately harmful to the Third World, because it merely robbed the poor of the rich countries to give to the rich of the poor countries. If only the rich and powerful were going to benefit, there was little point in passing on modern technology to the Third World. What was needed instead was technology appropriate to the people for whom it was intended: not giant machines that needed specialist knowledge to operate, but simple tools that anyone could use. When Schumacher first set up the group it was dismissed as the eccentric brainchild of an over-idealistic visionary, but since his death nearly ten years ago it has been taken rather more seriously, and quite a number of the mainstream charities such as Oxfam, Christian Aid and the Save the Children Fund now turn to Intermediate Technology for advice.

In the meantime there were problems closer to home. The difficulties and frustrations caused by poor housing, no jobs and racial tension in the inner cities had been gradually building up in Britain throughout the seventies. Because of the work the Prince's Trust did with the disadvantaged young in those areas Prince Charles had a better awareness than most, politicians included, that Britain was sitting on a volcano that could erupt at any moment, and he had taken every opportunity that presented itself to defuse the situation. In 1979, for instance, he had had lunch at No. 10 Downing Street with the then Prime Minister, James Callaghan, and met Len Murray, General Secretary of the Trades Union Congress. The Prince asked Len Murray what the TUC could do to help the young unemployed, and suggested that the Royal Jubilee Trusts might be able to join forces in whatever scheme they thought appropriate. When Prince Charles left the lunch he straightaway put Harold Haywood on to the job, with the result that Trust-funded TUC unemployment centres began to open their doors to the young unemployed as well as to older people.

The problem was clearly growing worse. New unemployment figures showed still greater rises, with no likelihood of improvement. So in 1981 the government asked the army to assess the situation, and John Blashford-Snell was sent to report on what was happening in south London. Prince Charles sent a message asking for information on how bad things were. Blashford-Snell was still officially a colonel in the Greenjackets, despite his recent excursion with Operation Drake, and his commitment to get the next venture off the ground, which Prince Charles was so keen he should do. In the interim he had been asked by the army to file a report on racial unrest in the city, and was shocked by what he found. The atmosphere was explosive. He and a sergeant major in the same regiment had put on their oldest clothes and gone down one night to a couple of clubs in Wandsworth that were filled with Rastafarians. A West Indian introduced him to a couple of his mates who were playing billiards.

'You fuzz?' asked the first.

'No.'

'What do you do, then?'

'I'm a soldier,' said Blashford-Snell.

'What's that?'

'You know,' said his mate. 'He goes around killing people.'

'Oh, you're all right, then. Let's go and have a drink.'

After several visits of this nature, they discovered that the tall council blocks in Wandsworth were virtually tribal areas and that each street served as a strict demarcation line. The various groups, both black and white, were angry and resentful; they were unemployed, frustrated and using drugs; rival gangs tried to beat each other up on a regular basis, and the blacks told tales of how the 'bully boys', who they said were National Front, came down to do them over. None was prepared to consider travelling outside their patch to find work for fear of being robbed and beaten up away from the protection of their own kind. In north London Blashford-Snell found the same syndrome at an Irish club in Kilburn, a few doors away from a club with an all black membership. The leaders of both groups said there was no way you could mix the two; they were bitter rivals. Blashford-Snell went away and wrote a report for his superior, General Sir John Mogg, who was so horrified that he sent a copy of it to the Home Secretary. A copy also went to the Prince of Wales.

Whatever action might have been planned, it was too late. About six weeks later the Brixton riots began, the first of a string of bitter, bloody and unprecedented scenes of hatred and violence on city streets which shocked Britain. There were riots in the slum district of Toxteth in Liverpool; in the Handsworth district of Birmingham, where two Asian sub-postmasters were burned to death inside their post office; and then in Bristol, where more youths went on the rampage, destroying cars and property and anyone and anything that stood in their way. Tensions that had been simmering away for years had come to the boil, and overnight the old image of the tame British bobby was replaced by that of a frightening figure hidden behind a shield and visor, engaged in bloody battle.

In the aftermath the armed forces were asked to set up a number of training establishments to try to defuse the situation by taking young people off the streets and giving them some sort of adventure training. John Blashford-Snell was asked to run one for the Army at Fort George in Scotland, but it soon became obvious that young people living in the inner cities were deeply suspicious of anything to do with the establishment – whether the police or the Army – and the scheme turned into a flop.

At this point the Prince of Wales stepped in; he had been watching events with the greatest interest. Ever since the *Eye of the Wind* had returned he had been agitating for some sort of follow-on organization for the young people who had taken part in Operation Drake. He had already set in motion plans for a second expedition called Operation Raleigh: ten times the size of the first, it was to set sail in 1984. But in addition he wanted something home-based for them so that the good that had been done in their year away and the expertise that had been harnessed was not wasted. Thus emerged the Drake Fellowship, under the directorship of George Thurstan, who as an ex-Marine was well qualified for the job. No sooner had they settled on a name than the purpose presented itself: the inner cities. It thus became an adventure training scheme specifically for those young people whom the armed forces' schemes had been hoping to reach. It was successful where those schemes had failed because it was run by young people who had come from much the same sort of backgrounds themselves, but who had been transformed and enthused by their months with Operation Drake.

Most of the boys and girls taken on to the scheme had never been out of the city in their lives: they were out of work, some were on drugs, and they had hit rock bottom. Suddenly they were thrown into team work, survival training, community service and the sort of outdoor activities that they had never even dreamt about. They became new people with some purpose in their lives, who by becoming confident in themselves became aware of their own potential. At the end of six or eight months broken up into a series of short courses, between 70 and 80 per cent found jobs. The Fellowship now handles about 4500 young people a year.

Some of the participants were pitiful cases. One boy from Liverpool, for example, kept signing on for more, and producing letters from his mother to say he had permission to do another course. Eventually the organizers said he had done enough, and it was only when he had returned to Liverpool, been arrested for burglary and imprisoned that it was discovered that the boy had no mother and had been writing the letters himself. He had been living in a henhouse, and when he went back to Liverpool after his first course he found that the woman who owned it had rented it to someone else while he was away, so he had nowhere to live. He had hitch-hiked back to Fort George and between courses was living rough on the beach, eating rabbits that they had taught him to catch.

Not one was the sort of youth who was impressed by royalty – their circumstances did not allow them the luxury. Yet when Prince Charles went to visit them they were knocked out, not by a prince, but by a man – a bloke – who made them believe he cared about each and every one of them personally. The day of his visit happened to be one of the filthiest of the year, when under normal circumstances they would not have put to sea. Yet because a royal visit was planned they all donned lifejackets and wet-weather gear and launched the boats and canoes, so the Prince could see the sort of activities they were doing up at Fort George. It was blowing a good force 8 gale in the Moray Firth, the rain was driving horizontally into their faces and the sea lashing the decks and drenching them all with every wave, yet Charles insisted upon going out in a small open boat and staying out, bellowing cheerfully above the roar of the elements until he had seen everything. By the end of the day he had been soaked to the skin and frozen by the cold, he had sat through a lunch and he had seen all over the fort, and he was still laughing and joking with the volunteers. In the course of six hours he spoke to each and every one individually, listening intently to what they had to say and making suggestions as to how things might be improved. He had even recognized a girl from Scotland whom he had sponsored personally on Operation Drake, and was especially interested to hear about her experiences.

'What did you think?' asked Blashford-Snell after Charles had gone.

'I thought he was a smashing bloke,' said one of the hardest characters. 'Well, you've only got to look at him to make yourself laugh.'

Puzzled, John asked him to explain.

'You know, you look at him and he smiles and you smile.'

It was more than a knack of breaking down barriers. What they correctly divined in the Prince of Wales was a genuine interest in their lives and a sincere desire to do something to help. The young in the inner cities and the problems of racial tension in Britain are the two areas about which he feels most passionately and most frustrated of all, and where in all the controversy he has raised over the years he has ruffled most feathers. In the House of Commons the Prime Minister, Margaret Thatcher, has frequently attacked his remarks as uninformed and anodyne. His solutions may not be entirely thought through, but this is one subject on which he is certainly not uninformed. In the wake of the Toxteth riots, to give but one example, it was claimed that a Maoist group called the Liverpool Aid Defence League were intent upon turning the city upside down. Charles asked Harold Haywood from the Royal Jubilee and Prince's Trust to try to talk to these people and find out what was going on. Almost everyone on his own staff advised against it, feeling it was too dangerous and politically explosive an area for the Prince to be dabbling in. Even some of the more cautious people working in the Trust thought the approach was unwise. But Charles was not to be put off. 'I get into enough trouble already,' he said. 'If there are any problems come back to me.' As it turned out, because Haywood was from the Prince's Trust and nothing to do with the authorities he achieved his purpose and had a clandestine meeting with the representatives from the Defence League in a dingy cellar in Toxteth. A two-way direct line to the grass roots had been established, and although the Prince did not agree with what the group stood for he was pleased at last to have the opportunity to hear what people really felt without it being filtered first.

Meeting and talking were only a beginning. As his staff have discovered to their cost, the Prince is a man of action and likes men of action around him: people who think quickly, grasp ideas, find ways of getting round the obstacles and work all-out to achieve their goal. He has no time for the nine-to-five attitude, and nothing makes him angrier than to be told the reasons why something cannot be done, particularly if it is because of bureaucracy; he once referred to it as 'cats' cradles of red tape which choke this country from end to end'. If he has an idea he wants to see it implemented immediately, and pesters daily until it is.

One such idea grew, as most of his schemes do, out of the work of the Prince's Trust. With unemployment on the increase, the Trust had decided to allocate to the young unemployed 10 per cent of the money they gave away, and although a lot of small grants went out it was a drop in the ocean. So they decided to focus their attention on those young people who had completed training courses and done everything that could be asked of them in an effort to find work, yet who were still unemployed simply because they lived in areas where there was no work. The plan was to help those people set up in business on their own, and not only create a job for themselves, but with a bit of luck create employment for others.

After lengthy negotiations with the Charity Commissioners the Trust agreed a scheme whereby they would help this group. There would be no simple cash hand-outs; the grant, of up to £1000 per person, would have to be spent on buying items they would need in starting up a business – like equipment, tools, transport and insurance. The Trust would also provide professional advice from people in the field on running a business. Indeed this was one of the conditions. Every applicant would have to have two tutors: one who knew about finance and would provide accountancy skills for the first year; and the other who was experienced in the particular business they had chosen – be it retailing, manufacturing, motor mechanics or whatever. These would both be volunteers, recruited by regional coordinators whose job it was to oversee the entire operation and who would be on full-time secondment from commerce and industry.

It was along these lines that a pilot scheme began in Merseyside, run by a secondee from ICI. It was so successful that the following year, on 1 April 1983, the scheme was officially launched nationwide as Youth Business Initiative; its stated aims were 'To educate, advise and support the young unemployed with a view to their setting up their own businesses'. A national board was set up under the chairmanship of Dr Alcon Copisarow, a distinguished expert in the field of economic development, science and business. Since then nearly two thousand young people under the age of twenty-five have been helped. In contrast to the usual pattern of small businesses, which have a failure rate of 80 per cent, 85 per cent of the businesses funded by YBI are still trading; 20 per cent of those have employed other people; and of the 15 per cent that failed, half of those people who were unable to run a business of their own found jobs with employers soon afterwards.

The type of businesses they have started could not be more diverse. There are textile designers, carpenters, jewellers, graphic artists, rug makers, fashion manufacturers, printers, photographers, plumbers, TV engineers and even a taxidermist, a reggae band, a milk testing service and a girl who sells biological specimens to schools. One of the most successful was set up by two young coloured boys who discovered some old West Indian cake recipes and started to bake them. They now employ fourteen bakers and Harrods in Knightsbridge is one of their major customers.

Nobody could be more delighted by the success rate than the

Prince of Wales. If in recent years he has grown bored of official functions and playing the role of figurehead, it is because this is where his heart lies. Confronted at a trade exhibition in Manchester in October 1986 by a room full of these young people – representing more than a hundred businesses which were all thriving because of YBI – he came alive. If there are such businesses in parts of the country where he is undertaking an official visit he frequently insists on making a detour to see them, which inevitably gives a boost to their trade. Walking round the Manchester trade fair he remembered individuals whom he had met before – not only that, but he remembered the particular difficulty they had discussed on their previous meeting and wanted an update. He buys from YBI people – he has bought toys for his children, for instance, and nursery furniture – and coerces other people into doing the same. When he came upon a partnership making reflective weathergear of the type policemen wear on traffic patrol, he turned to James Anderton, the Chief Constable of Greater Manchester, who was escorting him at the time, and asked why he wasn't buying dayglo jackets for his force from here; and there was more than a hint of seriousness behind the twinkle.

Sitting having drinks before dinner with his old Navy friend Warren Benbow and his wife at their home in Somerset, Charles looked at the bowl of potato crisps on the table beside him and then leaped to his feet excitedly. 'What sort of crisps are these?' he said. 'Can I see the packet?' When Sarah Benbow retrieved the distinctive Phileas Fogg wrapper from the rubbish he was ecstatic. 'That's one of mine,' he said, and proceeded to tell the story of how two unemployed men in the depressed town of Consett in the north-east of England had had the idea of marketing American-style crisps, and with the help of BiC, another of his interests here they were, rapidly growing into a giant company, employing people in the local community and selling their up-market nibbles like hot cakes.

Charles has been an energetic ambassador of the YBI scheme, so much so that in 1986 he entertained a group of Americans who had been struggling in Boston with a scheme called Jobs for Youth and wanted to hear more about YBI. They had been concentrating on college graduates, and it had never occurred to them, they confessed, to offer help to the bottom strata of society. Prince Charles was clearly chuffed. 'It's so nice that at last you've got something from us,' he said. 'Normally it's the other way round.'

He has, indeed always been an admirer of the American example and the spirit of enterprise that flourishes on the other side of the Atlantic.

Not content with the success of YBI as it is, Prince Charles is now agitating for something bigger and better. When it was launched it was wholly funded by the Royal Jubilee and Prince's Trust, but in the early stages YBI had had discussions with Downing Street, and in 1983 the government introduced Enterprise Grants which provided an invaluable boost to the funding and still do. Since then industry and commerce have become involved and they now contribute the largest proportion of income, much of it as Business Bursaries, as well as providing the seconded personnel. A number of charitable trusts and local authorities have also helped with finance. Nevertheless, YBI is looking for more. They are having talks with the Manpower Services Commission to see if the grant system can be stretched still further; and the latest idea is to persuade companies to put up some money. A hundred companies each sponsoring ten young people, say, for £10,000 – an insignificant amount to the big corporations – could have a very significant effect on youth unemployment.

All that is in motion, but the Prince wants to dig deeper. His worry now is what happens to the people at the bottom of the pile that YBI rejects. For every one applicant they take, three are turned down. What becomes of them? If they are keen enough to have put forward an idea for a business in the first place, they should not be abandoned just because they failed to convince the selection board that they could run a company. Turn them away and they will give up hope. So on Prince Charles's express instructions YBI is busy exploring ways of dealing with these people – setting up workshops perhaps – and ways of financing an extension of the scheme.

It is unlikely to be long before they find a way. He does not happily take no for an answer.

CHAPTER EIGHTEEN

Prince Charles was sitting at his desk working on a speech, desperate for inspiration, and wondering whether he had the courage to stick his neck out. It was the 150th anniversary of the British Medical Association, of which he was outgoing President. It would be a prestigious and glittering occasion, with a large audience that included the most distinguished and respected names in the profession. There would be wide media coverage; it was a golden opportunity to say what he really felt about medicine.

'I agonized over what on earth I was going to say,' he told me, 'and then the most extraordinary thing happened. I was sitting here and I happened to look at the bookshelf, and my eyes suddenly settled on a book about Paracelsus. So I took the book down and there was my speech; and the response to it was extraordinary. I've never ever had so many letters. I've been a great believer in intuition ever since.'

The BMA was dealt a body blow when its President told them:

> I have often thought that one of the less attractive traits of various professional bodies and institutions is the deeply ingrained suspicion and outright hostility which can exist towards anything unorthodox or unconventional.
>
> I suppose that human nature is such that we are frequently prevented from seeing that what is taken for today's unorthodoxy is probably going to be tomorrow's convention.
>
> Perhaps we just have to accept it is God's will that the unorthodox individual is doomed to years of frustration, ridicule and failure in order to act out his role in the scheme of things, until his day arrives and mankind is ready to receive his message.
>
> The renowned sixteenth-century healer Paracelsus

> was just such an individual. He is probably remembered more for his fight against orthodoxy than for his achievements in the medical field.
>
> We could do worse than to look again briefly at the principles he so desperately believed in, for they have a message for our time: a time in which science has tended to become estranged from nature.
>
> He maintained that there were four pillars on which the whole art of healing rested. The first was philosophy; the second astronomy (or what we might now call psychology); the third alchemy (or biochemistry) and the fourth virtue (in other words the professional skill of the doctor).
>
> Paracelsus believed that the good doctor's therapeutic success largely depends on his ability to inspire the patient with confidence and to mobilize his will to health.
>
> He constantly repeated the old adage that 'Nature heals, the doctor nurses' – and it is well to remember that these sort of healers still treat the majority of patients throughout the world.
>
> I would suggest that the whole imposing edifice of modern medicine, for all its breathtaking successes is, like the celebrated Tower of Pisa, slightly off-balance.
>
> It is frightening how dependent upon drugs we are all becoming and how easy it is for doctors to prescribe them as the universal panacea for our ills.
>
> Wonderful as many of them are it should still be more widely stressed by doctors that the health of human beings is so often determined by their behaviour, their food and the nature of their environment.

Charles had grown up with complementary medicine, particularly homeopathic cures, which both the Queen and Queen Mother have been using for years. One of the oldest of the healing arts, it involves treating the person as a whole, looking at his or her medical history to find the cause of the specific illness, then administering remedies that are so dilute as to be scientifically indiscernible. Charles had also followed the Kurt Hahn philosophy for most of his life, which was sympathetic to alternative methods too. His was the Platonic ideal of a healthy mind in a healthy body, with the emphasis on exercise, self-help and positive thinking.

The speech nevertheless caused a stink, although it did prompt the BMA to set up an inquiry into alternative medicine. When it was finally published in May 1986 it predictably found no

Lady Diana with Charles, Princess Margaret and the Queen Mother at Sandown before her wedding.

A perfectly framed kiss on the balcony of Buckingham Palace. Wedding day 1981.

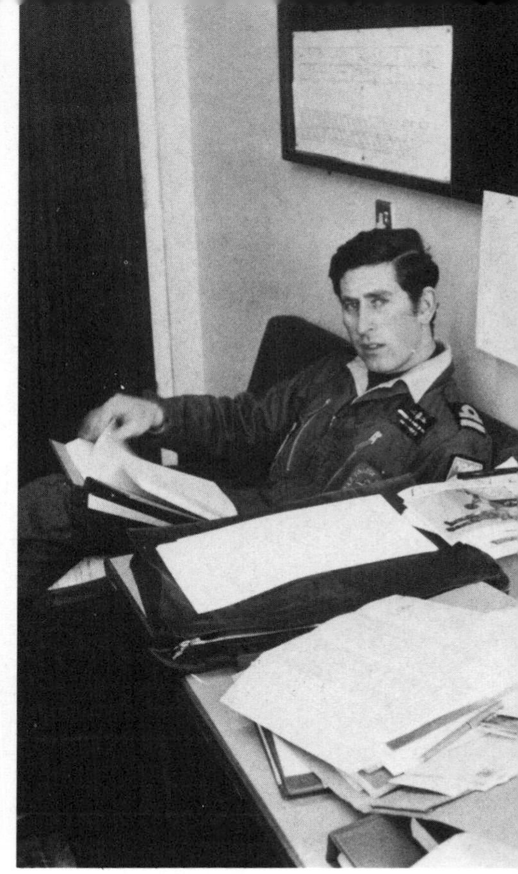
Above left: A Prince in uniform: Royal Navy helicopter pilot, 1975. *Above right:* At ease – with his paperwork. *Below:* At Delhi airport, 1981.

Above left: Keeping your balance with a bearskin on is no mean feat. Charles would practise in his cabin on board ship – sometimes wearing nothing else but a bath towel. *Above right:* Colonel-in-Chief of the Gurkhas.
Below left: Colonel-in-Chief of the Royal Australian Armoured Corps. *Below right:* In New Zealand as a naval commander.

A prince at work. *Above:* With Australian Prime Minister Robert Hawke, Mrs Hawke and Princess Diana. *Below left:* With Mrs Indira Gandhi. *Below right:* With Mother Theresa in Calcutta.

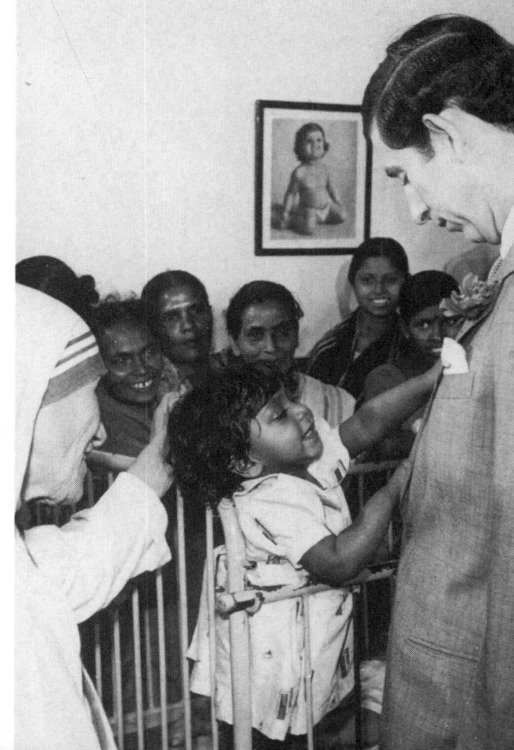

Prince Charles' concern for young people, particularly disadvantaged ones, is tireless and genuine.

During their visit to New Zealand in 1985. The Prince and Princess of Wales went boating.

A Prince relaxes. *Above left:* With Diana look-alikes in New Zealand. *Above right:* Playing polo in Deauville. *Below left:* Strengthening his thigh muscles for steeplechasing. *Below right:* A quiet swim near Perth, Australia: any similarity to Chairman Mao's dips in the Yangtze is pure coincidence.

A Prince at peace. *Above:* In the garden at Highgrove. *Below:* Sketching in Japan.

With Princess Diana and Prince William at Kensington Palace.

On duty.

scientific proof that any of the treatments worked, and said that some, like herbalism, could be positively harmful.

Just as the BMA was recovering its equilibrium, Prince Charles sent more shock waves through its hallowed portals by visiting an unorthodox cancer clinic in Bristol. The Bristol Centre treats cancer patients not by drugs but by a combination of diet, positive attitudes and support from everyone around; their regime is remarkably successful. 'They don't claim any kind of magical cure,' said the Prince after his visit.

> What they claim is that you have to put a great deal of effort as a patient into attacking your own disease, and that those who have the willpower, who are able to adopt the very strict diets . . . who are able to learn the relaxation and imagery techniques and who perhaps have a natural inclination to fight, are likely to do better.
>
> I met people when I went there who had had inoperable tumours on the brain and been given only a few months of life by doctors, who told me they had never felt better.
>
> Those who work at these centres don't say 'There is no such thing as terminal cancer' but 'You should never say a cancer is terminal, because there is always the possibility of defeating it.'

These centres are not designed to take the place of orthodox methods of treatment, but merely to provide an alternative for people who do not want surgery, radiation treatment or chemotherapy; or as a last resort for those whom orthodox methods have failed. Yet the BMA was outraged by the visit, on the grounds that such treatment was unproven and that the Prince's support would only give false hope to people who might be let down. Certain members of his staff also thought that the visit, and Prince Charles's entire attitude, were ill-advised.

The feedback from the public, however, told a very different tale and reassured Prince Charles that his instinct had been right. So the following year, when he was invited to attend a Royal Society of Medicine seminar on the subject, he went further. 'Many, many people in this country are predisposed towards various types of complementary medicine,' he said. 'Increasingly, I think, they are not getting all they want from orthodox medicine. So they are turning in ever larger numbers to people who offer a different approach – with more time and more listening.'

It was instinct again, a year later, which hurled him into more hot water with an equally established professional body. The occasion was the 150th anniversary dinner of the Royal Institute of British Architects. It was a cause for celebration, a gala evening at Hampton Court Palace, and as the Prince of Wales rose to his feet to speak the seven hundred settled back in their seats with their ports and brandies to await a few suitably congratulatory words on the achievements of British architects over the last one and a half centuries.

Instead their mouths dropped open in disbelief as the Prince of Wales quietly tore the profession limb from limb, accusing architects of consistently designing buildings without a thought for the people who were to live in them, and calling the proposed extension to the National Gallery in Trafalgar Square 'a kind of vast municipal fire station . . . like a monstrous carbuncle on the face of a much-loved and elegant friend'. 'A large number of us,' he went on, 'have developed a feeling that architects tend to design houses for the approval of fellow architects and critics – not for the tenants.' The prime requisite for a good architect should be 'to be concerned about the way people live – about the environment they inhabit and the kind of community that is created by that environment.' The development of community architecture had shown ordinary people that they need not feel guilty or ignorant if they preferred traditional designs 'for a small garden, for courtyards, arches and porches'. It had shown them that architects did not necessarily have a monopoly of knowledge about taste, style and planning.

How much better it would have been, he said, if this approach had been used in the Mansion House Square project, which was still subject to public inquiry.

> What have we done to our capital city? What have we done to it since the bombing of the last war? . . . Why can't we have those curves and arches that express feeling in design? . . . It would be a tragedy if the character and skyline of our capital city were to be further ruined and St Paul's dwarfed by yet another giant glass stump better suited to downtown Chicago than to the City of London. . . .
>
> Those who recall it [London before he was born] say that the affinity between the buildings and the earth, in spite of the city's great size, was so close and organic that

> the houses looked almost as though they had grown out of the earth, and not been imposed upon it – grown, moreover, in such a way that as few trees as possible were thrust out of the way.

He faintly sugared the pill by praising some of the work that had been done in designing for the disabled, but the burden of his speech was damning. It was his 'earnest hope', he said, 'that the next 150 years will see a new harmony between imagination and taste and in the relationship between the architects and the people of this country'.

The speech caused a rumpus. The president of the RIBA, Michael Manser, his host for the evening, said through clenched teeth that members of the Royal Family were entitled to their own view, even though he could not share it; but Peter Ahrends, who had designed the 'monstrous carbuncle', was more forthcoming. 'The Prince's remarks were offensive, reactionary and ill considered,' he said. 'He seems to have a rather nostalgic view of buildings, as if they grow out of the Earth, a view of life no longer with us. He seems to be looking backwards rather than forwards.' The Prince, he said, was out of step with the views of the country as a whole, and his remarks had done nothing to further the debate on modern architecture. Once again members of the Prince's staff were dismayed that he should have been so outspoken, not to say downright insulting.

The Prince was not so very out of step, however, as he discovered from the letters of support that poured in. Indeed he had put his finger most succinctly upon precisely what a great many people felt about the proposed National Gallery extension, but had not dared to express for fear of being thought ignorant. The issue of community architecture was based on more than just instinct; it was soundly based on what he had learned from talking to people who had to live in the buildings and environments that planners had created for them. Charles is a great listener: it is his single greatest gift. He asks ordinary people about their lives and their problems and listens while they tell him, and what they tell him goes in. He had not picked up the notion of 'community architecture' from some trendy alternative architect, as his critics suggested.

Community architecture was not a new concept – enlightened architects had been practising it from time immemorial, and during his years as estate bursar at Oxford John Higgs had produced studies on the subject. The Prince had come to it via common sense: he had simply discovered that one of the biggest difficulties for people living in the inner cities was that their housing was unsuitable for their needs. Mothers with young children, for example, were isolated dozens of floors up with nowhere for their children to play. They were dependent upon lifts which frequently broke down, leaving them with hundreds of stairs to climb with prams and shopping and a toddler in tow; and the labyrinth of concrete subways and corridors provided a muggers' paradise, so that even the fit were frightened to leave their homes.

The result was that people became despondent. If they didn't like their surroundings they didn't look after them, and the more run-down they became the more despondent they grew. It was a vicious circle, and with no job prospects, and therefore no hope of ever changing their surroundings or their circumstances, they reached rock bottom and hit out at society. Give them some say in the sort of homes they live in, and you will reverse the spiral, the argument ran. If people are happy in their homes and their environment they will become involved in looking after it and take a pride in what they are doing; this in turn will restore their own self-confidence and alter their entire outlook on life. This surely was the solution, and with this in mind Charles sought out architects who were already working in the field. One of these was Rod Hackney, who had been involved with a successful project in Macclesfield and was very much out on a limb from the main body of RIBA opinion.

The Prince was very impressed with Hackney and took him into his confidence, as he is wont to do with people who strike a chord. He was amazed by the effect that Hackney's work was having in one of the most deprived and run-down parts of Liverpool among people who had had no interest in life, who had been prisoners behind their own front doors, who had no jobs, no hopes, no dreams. By being invited to say how they would like to live, by being acknowledged as human beings and having some store set by what they said they were given a measure of self-respect, a new interest in life, an awakening of sensibilities that had long been dormant, and a community spirit that entirely changed the character of the district.

Surprisingly few intimates break the confidence that the Prince has placed in them. His valet of many years, Stephen Barry, bitter at his sudden dismissal after the wedding, did so, to Charles's sadness, although his revelations were scarcely revealing. So did Rod Hackney. He spoke about the Prince's fear for the future, which was a far more serious indiscretion given the political implications. Charles was furious but also hurt to the core, and quite at a loss to understand why someone whom he thought was a friend should have done such a thing.

He had reached a cross-roads in his life. As the Prince of Wales he was the ultimate symbol of the establishment: he had been brought up as such and for most of his life he had been surrounded by establishment figures, who were concerned with maintaining the status quo and doing their utmost to keep the Prince in step. Yet all his experience over the last six or seven years, particularly with deprived young people, had made him realize that the established way of doing things was not providing the answers.

He was in his mid-thirties, he had become a father and in many ways life had taken on a different perspective. He began to look back over what he had done in his thirty-six-odd years, reassess his life and the world that his children would inherit, and examine some of the conventions and wisdoms that he had hitherto taken for granted. His contemporaries by and large had ceased questioning. Those who had had a youthful idealism about social justice had lost it with their waistlines and the concentration required to accumulate wealth; they were reaching the peak of their careers and settling comfortably into middle age with families and lifestyles to match.

The Prince enjoyed no such contentment. He found it hard to reconcile his lifestyle with the appalling deprivation he saw all around him. He could see very little for all the years' work, and in his less buoyant moments he wondered if there was any point in it all. He had tried to help young people, but all he could see were the hundreds of thousands more who had been missed, who were growing older by the day and would marry and have children and become a forgotten generation. He had become president or patron of this and that, all worthy and good causes, but he felt his only value in life was as a figurehead, turning out on parade in the right set of clothes and making the right anodyne remarks. Every direction he turned there were people in need, and glaring deficiencies – the solutions seemed simple but apparently nobody was doing anything about them. His term as Patron of the International Year of Disabled People in 1981, for example, had introduced him to yet another set of problems affecting hundreds of people, but by the end of the year they had barely scratched the surface.

He longed to be able to do something real: to get down to some hard labour, to feel he was pulling his weight and actually doing what he expected other people to do. This was part of the attraction in gardening, where he really could get his hands dirty and do a day's graft. It was for this reason, too, that he had started going off to a Duchy farm each year, working alongside the farmer for a week and learning what the job entailed: mucking out cattle yards, repairing stone walls, feeding pigs, dipping sheep and milking cows.

Looking at alternative ways of doing things – in medicine, in architecture, even in farming – was a natural follow-on to this feeling that the established means were inadequate; that the greatest profit was not always the best motive for a course of action; that people and the quality of everyone's lives was important for the peaceful future of mankind; and that everyone, no matter what their colour, creed or handicap, has a valuable role to play in the grand scheme of things. The more reflective and contemplative he became, the more he was set at odds with his courtiers and many of his friends and relations.

There was one friend in particular, however, who encouraged him in his new way of thinking – Sir Laurens van der Post. He encouraged Charles to trust his intuition, to listen to his dreams and to pay attention to coincidence. 'It is trained out of us from childhood on,' he told Anne de Courcy of the *Standard*.

> Children are naturally aware – but our whole educational pattern is one where we knock it out of everybody's lives. We are a left-brain society, we concentrate on organizing the denial of the 'intuitive' right half of the brain.
>
> To me it is very interesting to see how primitive societies – though I think 'primitive' is a complete misnomer anyway – are the whole time subconsciously far more aware of their instinctive relationship with the things and people round them than we are in the so-called civilized world.
>
> It's there but buried under a mountain of – what? Anxieties, fears, worries, a feeling that it's something we should be ashamed of as though rational thinking is the only acceptable process. Yet I believe instinct, sensitivity, call it what you will, is enormously important.

Prince Charles was skating on very thin ice. As he himself confessed, intuition is remarkable, but 'You still think, "My goodness, I may be talking absolute rubbish here – how do I know it's right?" But slowly you learn to trust and develop this vital quality.' The media took a long time to learn, and for some time the Prince was held up to ridicule. Stories appeared saying that he had become a vegetarian, that he had given up shooting, that he was dabbling in spiritualism and had been attempting to reach Lord Mountbatten with a ouija board. 'What,' said Prince Charles to Lord Romsey when they next met, 'is a ouija board?'

It was all fantasy, but it was symptomatic of a new problem that was making Prince Charles increasingly despondent. He was not being taken seriously by the media. Whenever he tried to say things, or put forward ideas that he considered important, the press ignored the meat of the speech and highlighted the trivia, the anecdote or the bald patch that was gradually appearing on the crown of his head. If the Princess was with him the entire speech was dismissed, or perhaps mentioned in passing as a background to the main news story which was the fabric and colour of her dress, the change in her hairstyle, or the fact that they smiled at each other and were therefore 'so in love', or they didn't and the marriage was on the rocks.

The obsession with the Princess of Wales had not let up since their marriage, and if anything had escalated. Day after day one trivial story after another hit the headlines, each one more absurd and inconsequential than the last; and Charles began to lose heart. There were so many serious and important issues which needed airing, and yet no one was prepared to listen because they were all looking at his wife instead. He was being eclipsed by her, and on top of everything else the frustration was unbearable. It was as though the world had stopped seeing him as the Prince of Wales and viewed him now as an appendage to the Princess. They printed photographs of him, pinpointing the changes she had made to the cut of his suit and the shape of his hairstyle, and the bits she still had to work on. They talked about the way she had made him change his diet, his sporting activities, his friends and his servants. The wife who had at first given him so much confidence and pride now appeared to have emasculated him.

The more obsessive the media grew, the more Diana became obsessed with reading what they had to say about her. She was elated by being a superstar, she loved the adulation, delighted in the stir she caused, and revelled in being the most famous, most photographed, most sought after woman in the country, if not the world. But it was too much, too soon, and she began to believe her own publicity and enjoy the power of her position. The upsetting aspect was the criticism, the sniping stories that said Diana was temperamental, for instance, that she threw her weight around, or that it was she who had stopped Charles hunting and shooting, hurt her to the quick. She took each story to heart and became depressed or angry. Thus her moods swung like a pendulum with the morning papers, and Charles was not alone in being worried about her.

He decided to try to reason with the press, and invited the editors one by one to an intimate lunch with them both at Kensington Palace in the hope that, if the editors knew the true picture, saw how the Princess felt, heard what the Prince was trying to achieve with the youth of the country, they would stop printing the trivia and the lies. Flattered though they undoubtedly were by sitting down to a simple lunch for three, and being taken into the confidence of the Prince and Princess of Wales, the effect was minimal. What Prince Charles failed to appreciate was that, however sympathetic the editors may have felt personally, they were in the business of selling newspapers. The simple fact of the matter was that their readers were more interested in reading about gossip from inside the Palace than about worthy schemes for the inner cities, and if people didn't get it in their usual paper they would change to another.

The problem seemed insurmountable, and for a while those close to Charles feared he was giving up. He cancelled engagements and wanted to spend increasing amounts of time with his children. He now had a new baby in the house, Prince Harry, born on 15 September 1984, and the wonder and excitement had begun all over again. He was very close to both children, far closer as a result of having been present during their births, than his father had ever been to him; and he was determined to keep the relationship close – to be with them as much as he could and to take an active part in their everyday care. His staff even had to rearrange his daily schedule so that the Prince would be home for bathtime.

'Have a good weekend, sir,' Harold Haywood had said to him one Friday night.

'Well, I was hoping to do some digging,' came the reply, 'but it's so hard I can't get the spade in. So I expect I'll be nappy changing instead.'

Nappy changing he was, as his detective confirmed, while the nanny had the weekend off. He enjoyed the mundane business of children. It was relaxing, it was a legitimate job that needed to be done, an area where he could get 'stuck in', and where there was some positive feedback to reassure him he was worthwhile, where he could reap the rewards of the work he put into it. Everything else he did in his life was so questionable and always brought him back to the nagging feeling that he had no real role to play.

From every quarter he heard advice about how he should behave, what he should be doing with his life and where he should spend his time – and it was all conflicting. The teachings of Sir Laurens van der Post were not universally admired. Charles's father had no time for soul-searching and even less for men minding the babies. He told his son to pull his socks up. The press had calculated that in the same three-month period Prince Charles had fifteen engagements while Princess Anne had fifty-six, Prince Philip forty-five and the Queen twenty-eight, and they were calling him work-shy and lazy. Edward Adeane shared the Duke of Edinburgh's sentiments. He disapproved of the direction in which the Prince was heading, disapproved of all his controversial interests, disapproved of his preoccupation with the young. He felt that Charles should be doing the more traditional tasks that would attract respect for him as His Royal Highness rather than 'a smashing bloke'. Michael Colborne, on the other hand, was pushing the opposite way, telling him to forget what the previous Princes of Wales had done: these were the 1980s. There was a social revolution going on outside the Palace gates, a whole generation of young people who needed his leadership, and he should stop feeling sorry for himself and go out and do it.

It was a fractured and unhappy household which could not go on as it was. Something inevitably had to give, and at the end of 1984 both Edward Adeane and Michael Colborne left. First to go was Colborne, who handed in his notice in July. He had been with Charles for ten years, they had a unique relationship and the former Chief Petty Officer would have walked through fire for the Prince; but he had endured one row too many, he had battled with the Old Guard within the Palace long enough and was tired of the fight. He was fifty, he had a wife who never saw him, and had decided that it was time he devoted some attention to his own family for a change. The Prince was mortified, and loath at first to accept his resignation, but when it was obvious there was no way to change his mind he organized a job for Colborne with a friend in the City. In the New Year's Honours List he was awarded an LVO (Lieutenant of the Royal Victorian Order).

Edward Adeane's departure was less of a shock. He and the Prince had clearly been walking out of step for some years, and the day after Colborne left in December matters came to a head – they had a blazing row and that was that. Adeane returned to the bar.

CHAPTER NINETEEN

One of the projects that Adeane had opposed, and which the Prince of Wales was especially enthusiastic about, was Operation Raleigh; set up in 1981, it was finally launched in November 1984. The most ambitious international expedition ever mounted, it represented a colossal achievement on the part of John Blashford-Snell and a team under the chairmanship of Vice Admiral Sir Gerard Mansfield, former Deputy Commander of the North Atlantic, who had been on the council of the Queen's Jubilee Trust. It was the result of an extraordinary feat of organization and fund-raising, in which once again Walter Annenberg featured prominently. It was another sponsor – the captain of a polo team whom Prince Charles played against in Texas – who had suggested the name to commemorate the four hundredth anniversary of Sir Walter Raleigh's voyage to America in 1584. Thus it was aboard the *Sir Walter Raleigh*, a 1900-ton flagship, that the Prince of Wales was launching the venture with a few well-chosen words about physical challenge and the Gordonstoun ethic – 'Dammit,' he said, 'if it can do me good, can't it help other people?' – when he accidentally found himself putting to sea. 'I think it's time to be going,' he said, as the boat began to ease away from the pontoon. 'We seem to be departing and I haven't even said "Cast off" yet.'

Operation Raleigh was very similar to the previous expedition, but on a far bigger scale than Drake, as Charles had wanted. It was still fully international, but instead of taking four hundred applicants there were to be four thousand, each spending up to three months in the field; in addition the whole venture was to last not two years, as before, but four. The expeditions comprised the same blend of scientific and community projects and adventure, designed to give the participants the 'challenges of war in peacetime', and to bring out the latent potential for leadership in people who came from all sorts of backgrounds, including the inner cities. One expedition, for example, took place in Australia. They were based near Darwin, and the schedule read as follows:

> *Science*: Palaeontological survey; archaeology survey including aboriginal rock art; fauna survey in national parks; buffalo ecology; feral horse survey; bioresources. *Community*: Work with aboriginal community on projects on Bathurst and Melville Islands; work in national parks; construct playground Bathurst. *Adventure*: Descent of Drysdale river by canoe; desert survival; canoeing Victoria River.

At the same time a second team was in Papua New Guinea, based at Port Moresby. Their schedule:

> *Science*: Landsat ground analysis; bioresources; snake collecting. *Community*: SEE international clinic work; building church; medical help. *Adventure*: Jungle patrols; mountain walking; sailing/boating.

Soon after Operation Raleigh was on its way, the Prince of Wales had another idea – a dream that he wanted to put into practice, an opportunity for young people to give service to their country. Most people, he felt, have an altruistic streak in them, but they are either too shy or don't know how to set about using it. So he wrote to George Thurstan, who had organized the Drake Fellowship, telling him of his dream and asking why it couldn't be achieved. Why was Britain the only country in Europe that did not have some form of national service? There must be a way of introducing something – not a military service in any way, but a voluntary service to the community.

The area he had chosen was a political minefield. The question of community service was not new, but it had always fallen foul of two arguments; first, that if you put young people to work clearing drains and digging ditches you keep others out of employment; and second, that these sort of community jobs were bogus, and what young people needed was real work. The same arguments were voiced again, and a dozen reasons cited as to why it wouldn't work and why the Prince ought not to become involved in it, but he was not to be put off. This was the sort of negative attitude he hated most, particularly when he was aware that a whole generation could be lost while everyone sat down and argued the rights and wrongs of the case. Finally he suggested setting up a pilot scheme. Discussions were held with everyone concerned: both sides of industry, the employers and the unions, the voluntary organizations, the government and the local councils which would have to host the venture; just six months after the Prince's letter landed on George Thurstan's desk a pilot scheme opened for business in Sunderland.

It was called the Prince of Wales Community Venture, and the literature and application forms briefly explained his philosophy: 'I believe that we should all have the opportunity at one stage in our lives to make a contribution to our community. It is also vital that we find ways in which people from all walks of life and backgrounds can operate together for a limited period in their lives. Ours is one of the very few countries where this does not happen.'

The man chosen as project leader was Harry Charles, an enthusiastic and unshockable sort of character seconded from Rank Hovis McDougall where he had been a general manager. His characteristics were to be well tried. No sooner had he arrived for his first day's work in a set of empty rooms above the social services department in Thomas Street than he had a message. The Prince of Wales was planning to visit Sunderland on 23 September to see how his venturers were getting on. It was then 2 September; he had no furniture, no team leaders and no venturers – just a set of guidelines. Miraculously, by the time Prince Charles arrived twenty-one days later the first team of twelve young people has just completed their first week.

They had to be between the ages of seventeen and twenty-four, broadly trainable and physically capable of joining in team activities. Unlike Operations Drake and Raleigh this scheme was not looking simply for potential leaders. The ideal was to have two people who might be natural leaders in a group, two who were reliable, seven who were 'Indians, as distinct from chiefs', and one borderline case who might or might not be employable. New teams began every three months – Sunderland is now into the second year of the pilot – and the scheme has been so successful that there are plans afoot to repeat the exercise in Llanelli, Pembroke and Birmingham, and if those work – in two very different types of community – the scheme will be launched nationwide.

Being unemployed was not an essential criterion, although since the pilot was undertaken in the north-east, where unemployment is worse than in any other part of the country, it was not surprising that the majority of venturers have been so. They are paid £38 a week and do a mixture of community service and adventure activity, with a strong accent on teamwork. Most of them have never been out of Sunderland before, so it is something of a culture shock. On day one they go off on an outward bound type of course with the Drake Fellowship, which involves camping and hiking in the Cheviots, to give them a chance to get to know each other and their team leader. The next two weeks are spent visiting community centres like old people's homes, the Salvation Army, spastics' schools, and fire and police stations – all places where they will be seconded later on in the year for an eight-week stint. They are shipped off to Atlantic College in Wales for a week's course in first aid, coastguard and lifeboat service, and cliff rescue. They work with the fire brigade for a month; they clean up and improve some derelict site within the city; work in some branch of the local health authority; and for two months go away again to work in a distant community, such as Pembrokeshire in South Wales, where the first team did conservation work like fencing, scrub clearing and tree planting. Three-quarters of the year is taken up with community service, but the remainder is adventure and enterprise. Each team has to plan and organize a group expedition for themselves, such as climbing Ben Nevis – which the first group chose – or a canoeing trip in the Highlands of Scotland, taking tents and all their food and equipment along with them. Their final task is to work on some project for the community and raise the necessary funds for it, on top of the £50 per group starter they are given by the scheme. One group restored a caravan and bought a second one as holiday accommodation for the elderly; another found a twenty-seven-foot catamaran from Shoreham-by-Sea in Sussex, took it back to Sunderland, renovated it and gave it to the Council for the Disabled; and a third team built an adventure playground for a day nursery specially for children at risk.

The original idea was that the venturers would be interviewed by a personnel manager at the beginning and end of the year to assess their growth. Harry Charles couldn't see this working, so he devised an adoption scheme, and with some trepidation invited managers from twelve local companies to a meeting at which he suggested they might take on a number of volunteers each and meet them periodically towards the end of their year to advise and guide them on how to set about finding employment when it was over. He was asking them to give up time, and for three-quarters of an hour he hedged around while the twelve sat stony-faced. Then all of a sudden they realized what he was trying to say, and became so enthusiastic about the idea that he nearly didn't have enough venturers to go round. They now have one manager looking after every three venturers; he introduces them to the world of business, given them a visit to the works, teaches them how to fill in job application forms and how to present themselves in interviews – some have even videoed a mock interview for their venturers to look at.

By the end of the year the first team had grown immeasurably. They were keen, bright, interested, forthcoming and all able to express themselves well; but the unemployment crisis in the north-east had not gone away and the problem of finding a job was just as real as ever. The only advantage was that they were now infinitely more employable, they were optimistic, and where previously they would only have worked in Sunderland, after a year with PWCV they were prepared to consider moving south or west or wherever there were jobs to be had.

To kill that spirit, to send them back to square one on the dole queue, seemed criminal. In the intervening year the Manpower Services Commission had started a scheme with a branch in Sunderland called Job Clubs. It was a centre which admitted a limited number of people and gave them stationery, stamps and free use of the telephone so they could answer job advertisements and generally try to find themselves employment. The snag was that they would only take people who had been unemployed for six months, which automatically excluded people from PWCV. So Harry Charles did a deal with the local branch and they agreed to take his venturers if they had been unemployed for six months before they did the year's service. For the others he set up his own Job Club on exactly the same lines. It is run by his wife Marjorie, and gives those who have left – even if they have no job – somewhere to go and people to meet who are all interested in finding work.

So far the scheme has been a resounding success: it has been described as the finest project in the country, and an independent assessment carried out last June by the Centre for Employment Initiatives concluded that, with a couple of caveats, the PWCV should be extended nationally. 'Given that the success or failure of schemes, like any product or service, ultimately depends on the reaction of the consumers,' it said, 'rather than on the abilities of designers, the views of the venturers are the surest general guide to whether the scheme works. It does.' Nobody could have been more delighted than the Prince of Wales, not just that another group of young people had been taught to care about others and to taste some adventure in their lives, but because he has been proved right to all those bureaucrats and negative thinkers who at the outset said it would never work.

While all this was going on in Sunderland, the Prince was busy seeing the first stage in another project reach fruition. At the end of the International Year of Disabled People everyone involved had thought it a pity to let all the good work and public awareness that had been created disappear, and had been discussing ways of capitilizing on it. Prince Charles had been eager to make a contribution himself, but needed advice on the best way to set about it. He had been very moved by his year as Patron, impressed by the courage of the disabled and by the activities they were able to do – he had been camping and canoeing with them – and had come to appreciate the problems of living in a world designed for the able-bodied. A committee under Lord Snowdon, who had been President during the year, had originally been suggested, but there had been objections from some quarters and he had bowed out. Royal involvement had been an enormous boost to the disabled, however, and so it was suggested that Prince Charles should set up an advisory group which would not duplicate the good work already being done by other organizations in the field, but rather support them, pinpoint areas of weakness and act as a catalyst in getting things done.

Thus under the chairmanship of Bill Buchanan, a large, jovial Canadian, former Vice-President for Europe of Canadian National Railways and now confined to a wheelchair, the Prince of Wales's Advisory Group on Disability had been formed. Of the twenty advisers, which include Jimmy Savile, Baroness Warnock, Mary Glen Haig, disabled Olympic gold medallist Stephen Bradshaw and Nancy Robertson, who is now director of the group, they have highlighted the five major areas of neglect: access, housing, employment, independent living and prevention, and are systematically working through them.

The first area to be tackled was access, and in February 1985 Prince Charles gave a lunch at Kensington Palace at which he brought the top private house builders, designers and architects in Britain together with members of his advisory group, and talked to them about their failure to meet the needs of a large group of consumers. They called for four basic changes in modern house building: that where there were changes in level in the surrounding landscape they should build gently sloping paths rather than steps; that the high concrete threshold to houses should be lowered; that the width of doors should be increased from 850mm to 900mm, which would be no more expensive to build but would allow more turning space inside; and that there should be a downstairs loo. These were not just requirements for the disabled, the group pointed out, but for everyone – people with elderly relatives, people with young children and prams to accommodate, any one of us who might break a leg, and of course people with friends or relatives who are disabled and might want to visit.

One of the house builders present at the lunch immediately saw the sense of what was being said, not to mention the mileage. He was Sir Laurie Barratt of Barratt's Homes, who was just six months away from the launch of a new Premiere Project in Bracknell. He set his architects to work at once to incorporate the Group's suggestions and invited the Prince to the launch. Alas, it had all been done in too much of a hurry, and was not quite the model community they had hoped for. One bungalow, for example, while perfect in every particular with sloping path, low door sill and wider entrance, stood next to a house with steps and a high sill and all the features that made it impossible for someone in a wheelchair. While a disabled person could live perfectly happily in one, there would be no chance of popping in to their neighbour's house for a cup of tea.

'Ah,' said the foreman, 'but that's not one of the houses designated for the disabled. If you build them all with ramps, you know, no one will want to buy them.'

Sir Laurie Barratt recognized that this was the very point that the Prince of Wales Advisory Group had been trying to make at their lunch – that it was housing for people they were after, not housing for the disabled. After the launch he gave the Group a grant to run a workshop at Bracknell where they could do a systematic evaluation of people suffering from a wide range of disabilities and produce a report on their needs.

Since then the Prince has given several more lunches at which he has confronted the people making the planning decisions with members of the advisory group. It is one of the joys of his position. People at the top of their profession who are inaccessible to anyone else always accept invitations to Kensington Palace, and if they are asked by the Prince of Wales to do or consider some course of action they find it very hard to refuse. Another of the lunches was for senior management of British Rail to discuss the lack of facilities for disabled people travelling by train. Another was for the deans of medical schools and directors of nursing schools. This followed on the heels of the publication of a booklet called *Living Options*, which the group co-produced with a number of other organizations, about the services available and the needs of severely disabled people who require full-time care. Concern was felt that medical staff in general hospitals were not being sufficiently trained to recognize the special needs of disabled people who required treatment for conditions other than their disability.

In his foreword to the leaflet the Prince of Wales summed up his feelings and those of the group as a whole: 'Whether or not we are affected by disability, we are all individuals.' We must, he said:

> Recognize that those who are affected by disability are people first and disabled second, and have individual attitudes, likes, aspirations, fears and abilities.
>
> Understand that although there may be special areas of need, people with disabilities wish to have the opportunity to live in the same way as other people.

The Prince practises what he preaches: there is a lift at Kensington Palace for wheelchairs – also prams and pushchairs – which was a wedding present and, according to his staff, one of the best he had; when it is not in use a bookcase is pulled across the entrance. So entertaining disabled guests such as his chairman, Bill Buchanan, the director, Nancy Robertson and her husband, all of whom are wheelchair-bound, is no problem.

Prince Charles is instinctively thoughtful with disabled people. Whenever he talks to someone in a wheelchair he sits down beside them, which makes them instantly more comfortable, and he is very happy to sit and talk to even the most severely handicapped people. He had a free half day one week when he was going to be in the Hampshire and Gloucestershire area, and consulted Nancy Robertson to see if there was any home for the disabled which he could visit that day. She selected the National Star Centre in Cheltenham, a training college for the severely handicapped, and during the recce with David Roycroft, who was acting as temporary private secretary at the time, suggested the wards they might cover. 'That's no good,' said Roycroft, 'he'll want to see everyone,' and he was right. The Prince stopped and talked to everyone in the place.

One young man had cerebral palsy, and thus in addition to crippling disablement he had great difficulty speaking. Charles squatted down beside him, nevertheless, and struck up a conversation. Where was he living, he wanted to know, and what did he do with his time?

The boy said he did a lot of painting and writing.

Charles said he would like to see some of his work; would he please send him some.

'You're not a bit like *Spitting Image*,' said the boy, referring to the popular television programme which caricatures famous people, including members of the Royal Family.

'You wait till you get on the other side of it,' said Prince Charles. 'You won't think it's so funny then, I can tell you.'

During the spring of 1985 Charles and Diana went to Italy for three weeks. It was the first time either of them had ever been there, and his first official visit to a non-Commonwealth country. It was a place he had been yearning to see for a very long time, and as a devotee of fine art and opera he felt that his education had been sadly deprived. He had heard so much about the country from the Queen Mother, who used to go there every year as a child because both of her grandmothers had villas there. He longed to listen to some Verdi, Puccini or Donizetti in their home settings, to see – and perhaps sketch – the glories of Venice, the splendour of Rome, the buildings, the paintings and sculpture, the countryside of Tuscany and the towns and cities nestling in the hillsides, intact after hundreds of years.

Charles had decided to take his artist friend John Ward along. 'If my grandmother can take Sir Hugh Casson to Venice,' he had said, 'can I take you?' John Ward had first met the Prince through Sir Michael Adeane, the Queen's secretary, at Balmoral in 1962. There was a considerable age difference yet again, but they had got on well together, and when Bobby Chew was retiring as headmaster of Gordonstoun Charles asked Ward to do a drawing of the school for him as a present. Edward Adeane then joined the

Prince's staff and took him to see an exhibition of Ward's work at the Maas Gallery off Piccadilly. A couple of years later Ward and Adeane were dining at a club together when Adeane pushed a packet of cigarettes across the table. Written on the back were the words, 'My boss wants you to draw his wedding.' A little later came a request to paint the Princess. 'Will you *really* paint the Princess?' said Charles, and supervised. Ward was called upon yet again for Prince William's christening, and finally to paint the Prince himself. Once again there were long discussions about the stance he should adopt and the clothes he should wear. All of the works hang in pride of place privately in the Prince's homes and give him lasting pleasure.

So John Ward flew out to join the royal yacht at Catania in Sicily; Charles and Diana arrived from Rome and they sailed up the coast to Venice together. Every day they went off to look at churches and hospitals and meet people, and the minute Charles got back to *Britannia* he would change into a shirt and trousers and be up on deck with his sketchbook, drawing and washing with watercolour, which is his favourite medium simply because it is so mobile and readily available. It is not the easiest. He finds drawing a tremendous relaxation and would sit for two or three hours without moving, right up to the very last minute before the bell for dinner, then whizz below decks and appear at the table as immaculate as if he had spent half an hour getting ready. He has worked a lot with Bryan Organ, another artist whose work he admires and whom he has also sat for and learnt from; he himself is a very, talented painstaking artist who brings to his drawing the same desire to understand as he does to life.

The canvas fishing bag in which he carries his gear is never far from his side, and he draws whenever the opportunity arises. His sketchbook is filled with scenes of lonely moorland at Balmoral, with seascapes from the deck of *Britannia*, with views of buildings that have taken his fancy; and of the rugged Italian countryside. He so enjoyed his visit in 1985 that he went back the following year on a private trip, specifically to paint, with his cousin and fellow artist Lady Sarah Armstrong-Jones. 'The light is so marvellous there,' he explains; 'and the scenery. It's quite breath-taking.'

Finding a successor to Edward Adeane was no easy business, and in the months before one was found David Roycroft, a career diplomat from the Foreign Office who had been assistant private secretary to Adeane, stood in. The Prince had very definite ideas about the sort of person he wanted for the job: someone of a high calibre with business and administrative skills, who could run his office efficiently, who was outside the traditional courtier mould yet compatible with the people already working in the Palace, and, most important of all, someone who was sympathetic to his aims and interests and who would not be over-protective. The person had to be not only of the calibre Charles wanted, but also someone prepared to take a drop in salary. The Prince's staff, like all those in royal employ, are paid significantly less than their counterparts elsewhere.

Efficiency was of paramount importance. Buckingham Palace is notoriously inefficient – a strong contender for the most inefficiently run business in Britain. The right hand has very little idea of what the left hand is doing. People get through to the Prince who shouldn't, and those who should, can't. Letters get lost, the Fax machine breaks down, and time and again Charles discovers that his staff have turned down some invitation on his behalf or withheld some document or letter that he should have been shown. Few things make him more incensed. When Lord Mountbatten was alive he would make himself very unpopular. He had learnt long ago the need to circumvent the Palace, and would ring Prince Charles directly wherever he was in the world and say, 'Your staff have cocked it up again.'

It was a 'head hunter' in the end who came up with three possible candidates, and of those Prince Charles chose Sir John Riddell, a successful investment banker of fifty-one, a director of the Independent Broadcasting Authority and the Northern Rock Building Society, who filled all the necessary criteria. As 13th Baronet from an old Northumberland family, and educated at Eton and Oxford, he had a suitable pedigree; he had no previous experience of the Royal Family, therefore no preconceptions, and was frankly stunned and flattered to have been offered the job. He is a delightfully gentle man, humorous and unassuming, and although fifteen years older than the Prince, he is married with two young children, one just a year or so older than Prince William, so can well understand the problems of coping with wilful young gentlemen.

There was much speculation about how the relationship would work out. The Prince is not an exceptionally good judge of character and has made some serious errors in the past, on occasion backing people because he has become inspired by their ideals and failing to see that beneath the ideals was someone using his friendship for their own ends. So far, however, the indications are that Sir John Riddell was a good choice. Since he has been in the job, the Prince of Wales appears to have taken on a new lease of life. Freed at last from the constraints of the Old Guard, he has become immersed in work that he enjoys with people he admires. Yet still the doubts remain.

CHAPTER TWENTY

Prince Charles has often said that if he had not been a prince he would be a farmer. His love of the countryside, of trees and flowers and wildlife of all sorts, makes it his natural environment; and with so much of his working life in the Duchy taken up with farmers he is well aware of their problems and the work involved in making a living. Wearing his other hat, as Patron of the Royal Society for Nature Conservation, and with the encouragement and influence of Lady Salisbury and Dr Rothschild, he is a passionate conservationist, angered by the way man has plundered the natural habitat of plants and animals all over the world and caused the extinction of so many species as a result, and dismayed by the rape of the land due to the excessive use of chemicals and the fashion for tearing out hedgerows.

Towards the end of 1982 Lawrence Woodward, director of Elm Farm Research Centre, a small charity set up two years before to research and develop organic agriculture, wrote to Prince Charles to ask if he would speak at the first organic food conference at the Royal Agricultural College at Cirencester in January. The Prince said he was unable to, but would be very happy to send a message instead. It was a highly controversial subject in those days, and Lawrence Woodward was delighted to receive some measure of support. He duly drafted a letter for the Prince of Wales, taking care to say nothing extreme. But the Prince ignored what he had written and instead sent a forthright note of support, which rocked the assembled audience on their heels.

> For some years now modern farming has made tremendous demands on the finite sources of energy which exist on earth. Maximum production has been the slogan to which we have all adhered. In the last few years there has been an increasing realization that many modern production methods are not only very wasteful but probably also unnecessary.

> The supporters of organic farming, bio-agriculture, alternative agriculture and optimum production are beginning to make themselves heard, and not before time.
>
> I am convinced that any steps that can be taken to explore methods of production which make better and more effective use of renewable resources are extremely important. Even if it may be some time before they are commercially acceptable, pioneer work is essential if our planet is to feed the teeming millions of people who will live on it by the twenty-first century. I hope that you will seek solutions which can have practical and economically viable results within a comparatively short space of time. I shall be watching the practical results with interest to see what might be applicable to our work in the Duchy of Cornwall, for I am sure that there will be lessons that we can learn.

It was another two years before he was able to experiment himself, but Charles had already embarked on programmes in the Duchy to reverse the more destructive trends of modern agriculture. Working in tandem with John Higgs he had brought in both the Farming and Wildlife Advisory Group and the Nature Conservancy Council to look at all the farms on the estate to make sure they were farming with conservation in mind. He was anxious about the future for farmers and commissioned a survey on part-time opportunities. If farming was not going to provide a living indefinitely, farmers should be looking at ways of diversifying: turning surplus milk into cheese, for example, selling a proportion of the wheat harvest to a stone grinder to sell to the 'muesli belt', and opening up farm shops to sell direct to the public. He was also concerned about the gradual disintegration of country communities; and to stop the rot had begun a programme of renovating redundant farm buildings on the estate and turning them into workshops to encourage industry back into the villages. It was not a new idea: the first landowner to convert farm buildings was one of Princess Margaret's former boyfriends, Christopher Loyd, who had set up workshops on his Berkshire estate nearly ten years earlier; but Charles's interest gave the principle an added boost.

Speaking to the Norfolk Branch of the Country Landowners' Association in February 1985, he said:

> Forty or fifty years ago most of the jobs available in the village were either in, or directly associated with,

> farming. . . . Those who shoed horses or fashioned ploughshares now work in urban industry making tractors and machinery. The job opportunities in rural communities are few and far between and the social fabric of communities is suffering. Schools, post offices and shops close, bus services dwindle and the homes of those who actually worked in the village are taken over by the retired or the commuter.
>
> It was with this state of affairs in mind, coupled with the fact that I minded dreadfully about the disappearance of really attractive old farm buildings made of natural materials, that led me a few years ago to consider what we might do to preserve these buildings and to create more jobs actually in the community.

By that stage forty such buildings had been converted on Duchy property, representing employment for a hundred people. Some old Cotswold stone buildings at the bottom of the garden at Highgrove, for instance, called the Street Farm Workshops, became operational in May 1984 and now house a carpenter, a cabinetmaker, a graphic designer, a textile industry tool cutter, an artist and a china restorer.

The return on doing up dilapidated old buildings, and renting them at between £1 and £2.50 per square foot, is obviously less than selling the site to a property developer, but it is all part of a conscious policy of wanting to be seen as a responsible landlord. Not that all decisions are entirely philanthropic; but where hard financial interests have had to come first, such as development in the sleepy Somerset village of Curry Mallet, rather than steamroller local objections he has involved the locals and put community architecture to the test. There was a conflict of interests: the Duchy wanted to develop part of the village – to build four houses on orchard land – and 22 per cent of the residents objected on the grounds that it would spoil the character of the village. Having seen how well consulting the community about the sort of housing they wanted worked in Macclesfield, Prince Charles suggested bringing in a community architect to Curry Mallet. As a result the Duchy is going ahead with its development, but the residents are to get a new village hall out of it and a scheme for old people's housing.

A similar saga is unfolding in London too. The Duchy has been gradually disposing of its interests in the Kennington estate, and as property falls vacant selling it off. There is one building, however, called Newquay House, which consists of seventy-six flats, two-thirds of which still have tenants who want to stay, and under the Housing Act are protected. To sell the building without vacant possession would be to leave Duchy tenants, who have lived in these flats all their lives, to the mercy of a developer – which some landlords in similar circumstances do. The alternative was to wait until the entire building was empty and then sell, which could take years – which again some developers do so they can realize its full value. The Prince would do neither. He felt he had a responsibility to the tenants who were still there, and wouldn't contemplate leaving empty flats in an area where there were acute housing problems, no matter how much economic sense it made. So early last year the Duchy commissioned a community architect to produce a study of the options, and once his proposals had been passed by a Council Meeting in July the Prince went down to Newquay House in person to discuss the plan. The tenants were simply told on the morning of the visit to be home by 4 p.m. for a meeting, and had no idea the Prince would be there until they were all gathered together and in he walked.

The Prince explained the scheme they had approved in Council, whereby the tenants would become tenants of a housing association which would buy the property from the Duchy and manage it. There followed a lengthy discussion at which everyone spoke their mind and aired their views and anxieties, while the Prince and Duchy staff did their best to reassure the tenants; by the end of the day most people were happy. The tenants appreciated having been included in the plans, and the Duchy were pleased to have found a humane solution to a difficult problem.

A large part of his role in life, Charles feels, is to be an example to others, to take the humane or the conservationist route, but invariably, as with Newquay House, this is far less profitable than any other. This is why his example is not always guaranteed to be appreciated or faithfully followed by the herd. His appeal to farmers to ease up on the finite resources of the earth, for example, and turn towards alternative agriculture, fell on deaf ears – quite simply because the commercial incentive to continue using chemicals was too great. The only way to convince anyone, therefore, was to try it out for himself and see if it could be made viable. He had wanted to farm ever since he moved into Highgrove, and his land agent had been on the lookout for more land to make it worth taking on a farm manager. Charles also wanted his sons to be able to watch nature at work on a farm. So when a property on the other side of Tetbury called Broadfield Farm came up for sale at the end of 1984 the Duchy bought it, thus giving the Prince a total of 710 acres with which he could experiment.

After his message of support to the Organic Food Conference at Cirencester Prince Charles had held a seminar at Kensington Palace to air the issues, and he and John Higgs subsequently went down to Elm Farm to see the possibilities for employing organic methods on the home farm. The principles of organic agriculture are practised in forty different countries in the world, and called, at the last count, by sixteen different names, including 'natural', 'biological' and 'bio-ecological', as well as a variety of derogatory names by its opponents, such as 'muck 'n' magic'. The basic philosophy is the same the world over. It involves farming as far as possible within a closed system – crudely, growing crops to feed the animals, and fertilizing the soil to grow more crops with the manure the livestock produce. The use of soluble chemical fertilizers is banned, as are antibiotics and hormone stimulants, and animals must be reared in humane conditions, which means that intensive operations like battery henhouses or veal units are forbidden. The ideal is to work as a self-sufficient unit, using the age-old system of crop rotation to grow nutritious foodstuffs free from pesticides; to process, distribute and market as much as possible on the farm or in the neighbouring community; to create a system which is aesthetically pleasing; and to preserve wildlife and its natural habitat. The aim is to reverse, in fact, the damage that has been done to the environment by excessive use of agrochemicals since the Second World War; to improve the quality of food; to avoid the hazard of consuming dangerously high levels of nitrates, which are found in chemically grown food; and to rear animals in a way that is ethically acceptable. It would do away with surpluses overnight.

All of this appealed to the Prince of Wales. He liked the idea of producing, processing and marketing within the community instead of the conventional method of sending everything produced on the farm away to some giant marketing board; it fitted in nicely with his desire to bring life and industry back into the villages. He also realized that the current policy of subsidized overproduction was going to put the small farmer out of business, which was a worry for the Duchy in the future; and he found the ever-increasing grain and butter mountains that resulted from such policies obscene. If it could be made commercially viable, organic agriculture would do away with all of that. He was also sympathetic to the basic philosophy: where the conventional farmer endeavours to dominate nature by using chemicals that will ensure growth and deal with any problems, the organic farmer works *with* nature, recognizing the intricate and holistic properties of agriculture, so that growth is encouraged and problems avoided not by bringing in any outside agent, but by structuring and adapting the system.

Britain surprisingly lags behind the rest of the world in this field, and still regards organic farmers as a bit of a joke – as either cranks or bearded hippies. Surveys have been done in other countries, however, which have all arrived at the same broad conclusions: that even in its underdeveloped state the organic system has demonstrated its potential at least to help in solving some of agriculture's current problems and possibly to provide the basis for a viable agriculture for the future. As a result, there is now official funding from government, state or the universities for direct research into organic farming in Sweden, the Netherlands, West Germany, Switzerland, Austria and the United States. Britain has virtually ignored the findings, and relies upon charitable trusts like Elm Farm to do the research. Thus the Prince of Wales's decision to experiment with an eighty-acre block at Broadfield Farm was a massive boost to the organic movement.

John Higgs was enthusiastic too, but not without a hint of scepticism; he felt a lot of hot air was talked by some purists. Nevertheless at the Prince's behest he went across to West Germany to look at an organic project there and was presented with a ten-pound carrot and a massive pumpkin, which he sent it to Prince Charles with a memo attached: 'We found as much wind in Germany as there is in this pumpkin.'

Wind or not, the Prince was prepared to give it a go, but the bulk of the land at Broadfield and Highgrove had to pay its way from the start, so the remaining 630 acres were farmed along more conventional lines. Terry Summers continued as farm manager and is involved in planning and overall management, but a young manager called David Wilson was appointed to run the farm on a daily basis, and he moved into the farmhouse at Broadfield with his wife and small child in the summer of 1985.

Charles visits the farm at least once, if not more, every weekend when he is in the country. He either rides across country from Highgrove, or drives over in his Land Rover with Prince William – more frequently referred to by his father as Wombat – to find out what has been going on during the week, and what progress has been made with any project he has instigated; then he goes off walking around the fields or inspecting the animals.

He has a dairy herd of 110 Ayrshires which he chose in preference to Friesians, for instance, because he likes their brown and white colouring. Ideally he would have liked Jersey cows, but because they are so much smaller than the common dairy breeds which had been farmed at Broadfield by his predecessor, it would have meant entirely refitting the milking parlour with new equipment, which was uneconomic. He didn't want the black and white cows that you see everywhere at any price, so the Ayrshires were a compromise. Their calves will be kept to replace the mothers and cross with beef bulls, and their calves, two generations on, will go into a beef unit of thirty to forty animals. There are also four hundred Newlands sheep, which lambed for the first time in the spring of 1987. In addition there is a normal arable crop, which provides food for the livestock, and oats and hay for the Prince's horses at Highgrove; and last year, tempted by the discovery from Miriam Rothschild that he could make a £1000 an acre by growing wild flowers, and selling the harvested seed, Terry Summers planted two areas at Highgrove with a mixture which were a terrible failure, while those that Dr Rothschild planted along the driveway to the house were a brilliant sea of colour, full of butterflies of every kind imaginable!

Prince Charles stays completely out of decisions about which crops to grow where, or when to spray with what, because he has no real knowledge of the technicalities of farming, but he takes a lively interest in everything else. He has firm ideas about the shape of the place – the height of hedges, for example, the clearing of scrub, the restoration of dry-stone walls and the planting of trees – and insists that all the machinery used on the farm is British-made.

He is also very sold on the idea of processing everything that is produced on the farm locally – of decentralizing farming. He refuses to add to any food mountain, or sell his milk, for example, to the monolithic Milk Marketing Board. Farming is so structured, however, that it is very difficult to sell it in any other way, but the Prince is not shy about using his position to buck the system. He has been experimenting with making cheese from his milk; several batches were sent off to the West Country for the purpose, and if it had been successful, and the cheese is good, then there are plans to make it on the spot and market it, bearing the Prince of Wales feathers, through Marks and Spencer. Unhappily it was not a success, but the Prince is confident that they might take organic wheat grown at Broadfield – which will be 20 tons if they are lucky. His managers are amused at the thought, but say that the Prince is the first person to admit that his ideas are a bit off-beat. His latest wheeze is to sell pick-your-own apples at Highgrove, and have carrier bags emblazoned with the Prince of Wales feathers again.

Amongst less fanciful projects he has been running scientific trials on game conservancy in the last year, which have been monitored by a research group. The idea is that by not spraying the headlands you improve the partridge stock, because the weeds continue to grow along the edge of the crop and encourage the bugs, beetles and butterflies which the partridges feed on. So by improving life for the partridge, you are also preserving other forms of wildlife.

It is the latter rather than the former that the Prince is interested in. He doesn't shoot at Highgrove at all, and nowadays shoots only very rarely anywhere. He hunts the land, however, and encourages foxes to stay in a wood not far from the house, which he insists should remain in a state of disarray so that the foxes are left in peace and can breed. He loves watching them, particularly the vixens and their cubs, which often come trotting round the house at night in the hope of finding a chicken still out and about, and he can see them through the security cameras which scan the grounds. Badgers come sniffing around too; moles and rabbits are less welcome visitors, and arrive in far greater numbers; but to his delight he has just discovered a tawny owl in one of the woods. He had brought in a couple of barn owls, and put boxes out for them in the hope that they might stay, but they didn't. The only domesticated animal is a young Jack Russell which came from Lady Salisbury in September 1986.

Her involvement with the garden is now far less than in the early days. The structure is virtually complete, and all that it needs is digging, weeding and tidying up as the seasons demand. The walled garden is filled with vegetables and fruit – a wedding present from the Royal Society of Fruiterers – and supplies not only Highgrove but Kensington Palace too, and there is not a chemical in sight. The herb garden was another wedding gift – from a women's institute in Sussex, whose members came and planted it. And now Charles also has a greenhouse where he grows scented plants for the house, like stephanotis, jasmine, hyacinths and narcissus. Last year he made a small patio garden with a fountain, because he loves being able to hear the sound of running water from the house; all that remains now is to find the right site for a good water garden further away.

Another sound he thought would be romantic to wake up to in the mornings was the tinkling of cowbells. During a painting trip to Italy in 1986 he saw some cows with bells around their necks and said he would like some for Highgrove. In due course a consignment of antique brass cowbells on wooden collars arrived. The cows, however, thought the idea considerably less romantic than their owner, and bolted in terror when the contraptions were first attached. No sooner had they settled down than a neighbour began to murmur about the dreadful racket; however the Prince is now intent upon finding some smaller bells so the sheep will softly tinkle as they graze beneath his bedroom window too.

He is an exhausting man to work for, and not just on the farm. He constantly has new ideas which he brings back from trips abroad, from conversations with other people, from books or research that he has read, and wants them implemented immediately. His energy and enthusiasm are unremitting, and he gets very impatient with anyone on his staff who is slow to take up the challenge, who tries to put him off, gives an imprecise answer to a question, or displays woolly thinking in an argument. They have to be on their toes twenty-four hours a day, because he is quite likely to telephone from his desk at any time of the day or night and on any day of the week. Even on trips abroad his mind is still on home, be it Highgrove, the Prince's Trust or the Duchy, and he will ring from the other side of the world to check whether a problem has been resolved, or to add a thought or suggestion that has suddenly occurred to him.

No one found the experience of working with the Prince more stimulating than John Higgs. Their minds were completely attuned to one another: if Prince Charles had the vaguest bones of a scheme, the older man would take it up immediately, know what he was after, add to it, embellish and modify until between them they had a sound project – and had had a considerable amount of fun in the process. It was a unique relationship. John Higgs, who was not a young man when he began at the Duchy, worked flat out and put his heart and soul into it. He had found a job that satisfied him completely, and it was he, almost single-handed, who enthused the Prince and by guiding him and pushing ahead with reforms and improvements made the Duchy of Cornwall the buoyant and progressive estate it is today.

When he died after a very short and sudden illness in June 1986 Charles was mortified. He had lost another close companion, guide, support and friend – another who could not be replaced. Before his death the Prince knighted John Higgs, and went specially to St Thomas's Hospital to perform the investiture at his bedside. Afterwards he agreed with Elizabeth Higgs that there should be a service of thanksgiving for her husband, which was held in the Queen's Chapel in St James's Palace. The Prince of Wales read the lesson.

CHAPTER TWENTY-ONE

One of the greatest frustrations of the Prince's life is never being able to get stuck in, as he would say, to any real work in the way that ordinary people can. He is patron and president and colonel in chief of innumerable societies and regiments, and won't take on such roles unless he feels he can be more than a name on the letterhead, but in the end, in practice, his most valuable role is that of figurehead. His sheer presence turns a mundane event into a major celebration, swamps a factory with orders, ensures that a charity gets a sudden flush of donations. He has done nothing, he has proved nothing, he has stretched himself in no way, and he is denied the satisfaction of having done a day's work for a day's pay. This has been the biggest obstacle in his entire life – it is this that sets him apart from the rest of mankind and it is this that leaves him saying even now that he has no real role to play. In 1985, however, he became President of a very different sort of organization, one which has brought about a very significant change in his outlook.

A catalyst organization called Business in the Community, it has been going for almost six years, combines almost all the ideals and attitudes that the Prince holds most dear, and has taken under its wing a number of his own schemes and projects. In the character of its chief executive, Stephen O'Brien, he has found, if not a replacement for John Higgs, at least someone of equal industry, enthusiasm and vision, a man who is not impressed by the Prince of Wales because of his title but who is impressed because of the man he is, because of his gift for talking to people, his sensitivity, his tenacity and his courage in confronting problems that most men would shy away from.

They first met towards the end of 1984. One of the schemes that came under the umbrella of Business in the Community was a training programme for young unemployed blacks in the inner cities called Project Fullemploy. Knowing that Prince Charles was interested in this problem, Stephen O'Brien went to see him to try and drum up some support for Fullemploy and was heartened by how much the Prince obviously knew about the black community. He said he wanted to do something serious about youth unemployment in the black communities – did Stephen have any ideas? If he really wanted to do something that would make a difference, said Stephen, then yes, he did have an idea: the Prince should call a conference for leaders in the business community to meet leading members of the black community. The Prince jumped at it.

The subsequent conference on race and deployment, known as the Windsor Conference and held quite privately over two days at a hotel in the town, was a gamble the like of which had never been seen before. Gathered under one roof were the chairmen of sixty major companies in Britain and a crowd of bright, articulate members of the black community. For two working days and a night they mixed, talked and ate together, and discussed the problems of unemployment among black youths. Prince Charles addressed the conference by saying that racism was a problem of the white society and not the black. It was a failure to recognize the potential of the black community and a failure to use it. When bankers protested 'but we don't discriminate' they were simply laughed at, and such was the success of the experiment that by the end, when someone from the Bank of England said they had a minimum requirement of five O Levels for Youth Training Scheme employees, the other banks wanted to know why.

That conference is widely regarded as one of the most significant advances in race relations ever made, and is still talked about today. The black community came away saying they had had no idea that there were people in the white hierarchy who were seriously interested in their unemployment problems; and the white establishment, on the whole, admitted they had never realized there were intelligent members of the black community. Without the Prince of Wales such a confrontation would almost certainly never have taken place.

Stephen O'Brien had been so impressed by what had been achieved that he put up the idea of inviting Prince Charles to become President of Business in the Community. An approach was officially made through Sir Charles Villiers, Chairman of the British Steel Corporation, who had been involved with the Prince over BSC's enterprise agencies, and in September 1985 the Prince of Wales accepted.

It was a fortunate cycle of events, and the timing could not have been better. Such was his despondency, his boredom and general frustration that just a year before he had been saying that all he wanted in life was to be a country squire and spend the winter hunting and the summer playing polo. Friends thought he was in danger of wanting to run away from it all. A tour of America which he had just undertaken had depressed him still further. He had been promoting Britain and British industry at every step and met enthusiastic responses; he had endured a vulgar fund-raising dinner where people paid five thousand dollars each to dine with the Prince and Princess of Wales; yet he returned to discover that the Confederation of British Industry had done nothing to follow it up with any kind of sales drive, nor did it have any plans to do so. He was thoroughly dejected. 'What was the point?' he asked. 'I'm no good at anything. It's all a waste of time.'

The invitation to join an outfit where there was no such establishment lethargy, where there was some point in it all, was the fillip he needed. Here was a group of people who shared all his ideals, who had the financial support of government and industry, yet was sufficiently energetic to make real waves in society; and it was still young enough as an organization and innovative enough for him to make a positive contribution.

'The day you think I am not useful,' he said to one of BiC's directors, 'tell me. I want to be involved in the growth of something. I don't just want to open things and be seen trundling around. I can go to all the dinners and banquets on earth, but it's not going to make any difference to the world. What I want to do is be part of something that does.'

Business in the Community had been set up in 1981 to try to breathe life back into Britain's dying towns and cities, largely as a result of what was happening in America. In the United States, cities with high unemployment and economic depression were given a massive jolt by a drive to get the companies that operated in those communities to become involved in them, to invest in them, to train and recruit young people from within them – with the result that the community itself became prosperous once more and the people living in them had more money to spend on the goods and services provided by the companies. The intention was that everyone would come out a winner. BiC was set up to try to encourage the same pattern of events in Britain. It embraces business, central government and local government as well as the trades unions, it is non-party political, and is a charity in all but name, funded by contributions from each of its members. One of its greatest achievements, because of its neutral political stance, is its ability to draw together people who would not normally meet – as at the Windsor Conference.

Basically, BiC persuades companies that it is in their best interests to put money into making the community prosperous. Having solicited that money, it then sets about directing it towards means of creating employment, be it by funding training schemes, as with Project Fullemploy, setting up individuals in business, rescuing companies to save jobs, creating managed workshops, or exploring ways of boosting the job prospects for those groups who find it hardest of all to find work, like ex-offenders and the disabled. To organize all this BiC has opened local Enterprise Agencies – there are now more than 250 in the United Kingdom – which act as job creation agencies and are run by personnel on secondment from industry. Donations from companies are thus directed into worthwhile projects, and unemployed people seeking to set themselves up in business have the support and free advice of qualified people. A recent survey conducted by BiC showed that each agency assisted roughly ninety people a year to set up in business, and that within the first year those new businesses employed a further ninety people. BiC also takes under its wing independent job creation schemes like the Prince's YBI scheme, which have been funded by either the private or the voluntary sector. It acts therefore as a general sorting office for the work being carried out which loosely falls into the bracket of economic regeneration, prevents duplication and overlap and makes sure that any available funds are fairly evenly spread.

Charles was able to bring into the fold all his own schemes such as Youth Business Initiative, the Duchy of Cornwall workshop scheme, his Advisory Committee on Disability and the Prince of Wales Community Venture, so in becoming President he was already contributing more than just his name to the organization. In turn, his own projects were given much more shape and focus than they had ever had when operating on their own, and they had the benefit of BiC's clout in the business world and a network of highly experienced staff. BiC, for example, raised two-thirds of the finance needed to launch the pilot of the PWCV in Sunderland – it managed to get the support of more than eighty members and associated companies.

Prince Charles threw himself into the job with renewed enthusiasm. The combination of his name and BiC's solid reputation in all the areas involved presented a powerful partnership for the future; the crusading light was back in his eye. Gone was Edward Adeane, gone was David Roycroft, who appeared to have worked as hard as his predecessor at wrapping the Prince in cotton wool, and he was starting out afresh. Sir John Riddell was joined during the course of the next year by Rupert Fairfax, an able young whizz-kid of twenty-five on secondment from the Hanson Trust in the City, as assistant private secretary; his primary function was to advise on industry. Humphrey Mews, the only serviceman in the team – to appease the traditionalists – came in as deputy private secretary.

Having embarked on his career with BiC on the problem of black unemployment, Charles wanted to see what good had come out of the conference in Windsor. Bringing people together and addressing them with a few words was just a beginning; as always he wanted to follow through. So a special unit called the Black Economic Development Secretariat was set up at the BiC offices in City Road, to report back to the Prince every six months on progress; and progress was noticeable, at least behind the scenes. Companies had begun to review their recruitment policies, for example; a black support system had been established for black businesses, as well as black Enterprise Agencies specifically for, and staffed by, black people.

Prince Charles was eager to have a black face on his staff. Quite apart from wanting to set an example to other employers, or indeed show his awareness that racism is the single most explosive issue in British society, he has an affinity for black people. He comes alive in their company in an extraordinary way, and they respond to him. The day he visited a training scheme in north London is just one of many examples. One room was full of tough black teenagers learning to operate word processors. They were deeply sceptical. 'Who does he think he is?' 'What does he know?' were the sort of comments circulating. Charles went straight in and engaged each and every one in a real conversation. He didn't ask how they were enjoying word processing. He asked about their lives, their difficulties, their feelings. One girl, for instance, was pregnant with her second child and had no husband. He realized, he said, that this was a tradition in the black community – and there was a lot to be said for traditions – but how did she find it worked in the society in which she found herself? He spent several hours in this one small room, and when he finally gave in to his equerry, who had been trying to move him on to his next appointment, the young black people spontaneously rushed to the windows and hung out waving and cheering at him in the street below until his car was out of sight.

This was not the first time that Charles had wanted to employ a black person at Buckingham Palace, and in fact several years before a black secretary had been taken on, but such was the opposition from other people at the Palace that it had been a failure. He would dearly love to see black people admitted to traditional white strongholds, like the Brigade of Guards and the Household Cavalry, and caused a storm in 1986 for saying so. It was a wish that Lord Mountbatten had cherished. He had jokingly suggested creating a regiment called the 'Blackguards', but it was a real enough sentiment and one which Prince Charles has taken up. The only job available for the moment, however, was that of junior secretary, and Stephen O'Brien advised against filling it with someone black. It was too much of a risk, he thought. The salary was too low to attract anyone who was well qualified, and if the candidate turned out to be no good, which at a junior level might be the case whether black or white, the publicity would be very damaging. It was better, he counselled, to wait until a more senior job became available.

BiC has become for the Prince a consuming interest to which he has committed himself for five years, although it is likely that he will be involved for longer. Amongst many other things he has set up a new charity. It is called the Prince's Youth Business Trust, and has brought together three separate schemes: YBI; a similar scheme started by the National Association of Youth Clubs two years after the Prince's, called the Youth Enterprise Scheme, which provides low interest rates on up to £5000 for young people setting up in business; and one of the oldest initiatives of this sort in Britain – the Fairbridge Society, founded in 1909 to provide education and training for deprived young British people on farm schools in underpopulated parts of the Empire.

A week never goes by without some form of contact. At one point he and Stephen O'Brien were speaking on the telephone every day. Charles would ring Stephen at home at about 7.30 a.m. – HRH is regularly at his desk by that time, and it is only worth ringing him before 8 a.m. Now, if he doesn't himself ring someone from the office is in contact two or three times a week. 'I don't want to just open things any more,' he had said. 'I want to be involved in the planning of projects at the beginning as well as at the opening.' In the midst of a vast reception in Boston, USA, where dozens of people were waiting their turn for a word with him, Charles spotted Stephen. 'Ah, I'm so glad to catch you,' he said. 'Do tell me what's been going on with that regeneration scheme we had words about the other day?'

One project they have been working on recently was the question of how to get money into the hands of small-scale would-be entrepreneurs who are refused loans by the banks because they have no security to offer. It is the very problem at which Youth Business Initiative and the Prince's Trust is directed, but what they can do is a mere drop in the ocean. Prince Charles suggested talking to the bankers, and asked Stephen to get together for dinner at Kensington Palace everyone who might be useful. The chairmen and chief executives of all the main banks duly arrived and immediately began defending themselves. Each one trotted out his current statistics, and talked about the millions of pounds he put here, and the hundreds of millions there, and how he never turned down a good proposition. The Prince listened very carefully and patiently until they had finished.

'You are entirely missing my point,' he said. 'I'm not talking about what you are doing. I'm talking about what you're *not* doing.' He then quietly pointed out the lunacy of a situation in which they were each putting up a lot of money to support BiC's Enterprise Agencies; then when the agencies had done all the work in filtering the good risks from the bad – a job that the banks were in effect paying them to do – the banks' branch managers then turned down every application for a loan.

Charles feels spiritually at home with BiC. He has a high regard for Stephen O'Brien and trusts his judgement. When he was running into trouble with some Duchy property in south London it was to Stephen that he came for advice. He had decided that it would be a good idea to convert some property in Kennington into small units to house single teenagers, traditionally the group that has the greatest difficulty in finding accommodation in London.

He thought he was being philanthropic, yet he had caused an outcry in the borough. Local residents and left-wing politicians were up in arms at the proposal and had objected most vociferously to planning permission for the conversion. Charles was baffled. Much as he often sympathized with their motives, he said, he simply couldn't understand the attitude of the extreme Left. Stephen said he must talk to one of his fellow directors who had been selected specifically for her left-wing views. So one day soon afterwards Cathy Ashton's secretary told her, 'Cancel everything you're doing tomorrow night – you're going to the Palace.' Sure enough, the next night she and Stephen O'Brien were ushered into the Prince's study at Kensington Palace to await his arrival. A moment later the door opened and in came a blonde-haired woman dressed in a skirt and jumper. Cathy thought she looked vaguely familiar.

'Good evening, Your Royal Highness,' said Stephen, springing to his feet. 'How nice to see you again.'

'Oh, I'm sorry,' said the Princess of Wales, obviously surprised to find anyone in the room. 'I'm looking for William. It's bedtime, so he's vanished. Will you give me a shout if you see him?' Cathy was left musing on how one might give the Princess of Wales a shout when the gales of giggles from upstairs indicated that the game was up.

Shortly afterwards the Prince arrived. 'Of course you know about Cathy's CND background?' said Stephen.

'Yes,' said Prince Charles, 'it sounds really fascinating.' Cathy, an active member of the Labour Party, had once been a full-time employee, then treasurer and finally vice-chair of the Campaign for Nuclear Disarmament. They were curious credentials for an adviser to the Prince of Wales, and from her point of view such a meeting seemed bizarre. The next two hours were spent discussing politics, and the particular issue in Kennington which still puzzled the Prince. He had thought that providing somewhere for these people to live was the right thing to do.

'The trouble is,' said Cathy, in her frank Liverpudlian way, 'that you are inevitably in the position of people being able to say "It's all right for you, you don't have to live next door to those punks and weirdos", which is what everyone thinks teenagers are. And don't forget, a high proportion of MPs have their second homes in the area, so you're dealing with a very vocal group.' Both observations appeared to have been factors the Prince had not previously thought of.

That night the three of them talked for nearly two hours about the specific problem and about politics and politicians, and Cathy has continued to advise the Prince and, as she would say, make him a little more 'streetwise'. Whenever he telephones a voice says, 'It's Sir John Riddell', or 'It's the Prince of Wales's Office. I have the Prince of Wales for Cathy Ashton', and only when she says that it is she speaking does he come on the line. It is standard practice for a busy man, but she was convinced that it was the same voice. One day she challenged him. 'It's not Sir John Riddell, it's you, Your Royal Highness, isn't it?'

'Yes,' he admitted. He said he had a terrible problem: nobody ever took him seriously when he said it was the Prince of Wales speaking. There was certainly one occasion years ago, when he rang Nicholas Soames's office after he had left for the night. 'Could I speak to Mr Soames please,' he said. 'It's the Prince of Wales.'

'Yeah, yeah, and I'm the Queen of Sheba.'

Cathy's left-wing expertise was called upon again some time later when Charles travelled incognito to look at housing in the Labour-controlled boroughs of Hackney and Tower Hamlets in the East End of London. He was horrified by what he saw: damp, decaying houses unfit for human habitation, and the residents he talked to all blamed the local councils. He determined to do something about it, so on his return he asked Cathy to organize a lunch so that he could get builders from the private sector together with the local left-wing politicians to see if they could find a way of improving the situation. Cathy met considerable opposition to the proposal, not least of all from the Palace. Sir John Riddell was very concerned that the left wing might publicize what was said at a private meeting. The Labour Group in Hackney refused to attend on the grounds that the Prince of Wales owned property which was mismanaged, and until he had disposed of that, and improved his own act, they were not prepared to discuss their own management ability.

It was a long and laborious process, but three months later she had brought together twenty senior people, including a Liberal and a Labour MP and the chair of the Housing Committee at Tower Hamlets. The lunch was set for 13 July, but only a week before the invitations had still not been sent out. Cathy began to agitate. 'Well, frankly,' said Sir John, 'we've never had a refusal.' They had none on this occasion either.

Thus twenty unlikely bedfellows gathered in the pretty drawing room at Kensington Palace, with family photographs on the grand piano, to sip sherry and prepare for battle. No sooner had Cathy been given a glass of sherry than she was whisked next door to brief the host. There was the Prince of Wales wrestling with a seating plan, swearing quietly as he tried to push name cards into a flat holder that was proving awkward. Lying on the floor close by was a large cushion with a picture of a frog wearing a crown and the words, 'It's no fun being a prince.'

The Prince sat down to lunch with the assumption that the appalling conditions in the East End were the fault of local government. It was a revelation to him when the chair of housing at Tower Hamlets said that the borough was desperate to build new houses. The cost of keeping the homeless in bed and breakfast accommodation had risen from £13,000 to £1.5 million in two years, and there was nothing they would like more than to house them. The reason they couldn't build was because central government had cut back grants, and wouldn't let them touch the money from the sale of council houses. 'So what can we do?' It was a catch-22 situation: the ownership of the land was in the hands of the local council, but they couldn't build because they had no money, and couldn't give it away either.

Out of the lunch came a deal which has yet to be put into operation. The council would give the private sector a proportion of their land for development; in return the private sector would put up on the remainder of the land houses designed for the local community – inexpensive houses, therefore, and rented accommodation. The local community would do most of the physical building work themselves, under the supervision of the private sector builders, which would mean they could build a flat or a house for £20,000, as against £70,000 for the average house in Tower Hamlets, and at the end of the day the community would have a trained workforce. The scheme would house people, create employment and regenerate the community in one fell swoop, and because it involves job creation may well qualify for Manpower Services Commission grants. If this trial scheme works, the idea is to produce a blueprint and get all political parties to study it and promote it through their own local councils. The concept of community self-build groups is not entirely new – it has been done in Lewisham in south London – but securing land from the council and involving the private sector in this way is an innovation.

Prince Charles is always the first person to admit that his knowledge on a subject is slight, and he learned a considerable amount from his encounter with the left wing, but from his keynote speech to the National Association of Housebuilders in October 1986 it was clear that he had not yet learned it all, and that his back-up in terms of research at the Palace is still wanting.

'It always seems crazy to me,' he said, plunging himself into more controversy,

> that the building industry spends a great deal of energy in trying to secure greenfield sites which, from an overall national economic point of view, are far more costly to develop than a derelict site, although on the face of things they may appear to be cheaper.
>
> It is extremely worrying, I think, that the second land utilization survey has shown that farm land is being lost at a rate which would see its total disappearance in two hundred years.
>
> Concentrating efforts on greener pastures and leaving the inner city to fester results in an ever-increasing spiral of decay, failing infrastructure, under-developed social and public facilities, poorer housing, schools and hospitals and other social manifestations, such as poor physical and mental health and a general low morale.

The logic of what he said was absolutely right, but what he had failed to appreciate was the pressure of market forces: that people prefer living in pleasant green areas, and if you build luxurious private-sector houses in the decaying inner cities no one is going to buy them. It was a speech straight from the heart, but somewhat naïve, and in some ways encapsulates the Prince of Wales. He is idealistic, but not fully in tune with the ways of the world. Most people have the idealism of their youth knocked out of them by the time they reach middle age. They have accepted that there are forces at work in the world, mostly economic, which are too big and too well established to conquer; and have succumbed to the old adage, 'If you can't beat them, join them.' By living at one remove from the world, however, by not having punks and weirdos as neighbours, the Prince has retained his vision of a better world. He has not, as Lord Northfield, head of a building consortium, claimed, been 'hi-jacked by the loony Green brigade'.

CHAPTER TWENTY-TWO

Prince Charles does not willingly say what he envisages for the future when – and if – he becomes King. To talk about the way he views the role, the changes he might make or the plans he has, is to imply criticism of the Queen; and he is completely uncritical of his mother. His respect and admiration for her are unqualified.

He is not complacent, however. King Farouk of Egypt, deposed by a military coup in 1952, once predicted that by the year 2000 there would be only five monarchs left in Europe: the four kings in a pack of cards and the King of England. He could yet be proved right – this century has so far despatched four emperors and eleven kings. No one is more conscious than Charles of the need for the monarch – even in Britain – to move with the times, to be relevant to the age and the society in which he lives, and to anticipate the future. It is a world in which people are challenging and questioning all the accepted values and conventions of the past because they have come to realize they are not serving our needs; a world filled with tensions and the strains of overcrowding; and a world where too much emphasis is placed on profit at the expense of the earth's resources. To give support to alternative methods, therefore, is simply pragmatic.

Take complementary medicine, for example. To explain his thinking he says:

> More working days are lost because of back pain than for any other reason. It is a chronic problem in Britain. Surely we should be investigating every method that might reduce that number, and there are two forms of alternative treatment, chiropractics and osteopathy, which have proved to be successful in a great many cases of back pain. Even doctors consult them. So what is there to lose by giving them a try?

He believes that racial and religious differences, and a lack of understanding of other people's cultures and traditions, are the most explosive issues of the day. They are the cause of tension, bloodshed and misery not just on the streets of Britain but all over the world; and have been for centuries. In opening the Tenth International Council Meeting of UWC in 1985 he said, 'It is a great pity that there aren't enough students from the Middle Eastern countries. There aren't enough Moslem students. One of the great problems, it seems to me, is the increasing degree of misunderstanding between the Islamic approach to life and the Western Christian approach to life and indeed the misunderstanding between different branches of the Islamic faith.' To try and improve understanding in Britain, where large numbers of Moslems live, the Prince suggested to Sir Richard Attenborough that he should produce a series for Channel 4 television to explain a variety of different religious beliefs. The Prince contributed a foreword.

Charles is naturally tolerant of other people's views, and it would be wholly inconsistent if this did not stretch to other men's religious convictions. It was no surprise, therefore, that he should have wanted to attend a private Mass with the Pope during his visit to the Vatican in 1985 – not because of any weakness in his own Anglican faith, but because he believes that by demonstrating religious tolerance himself he might in some way be able to ease the tension between Anglicans and Catholics, especially in Northern Ireland. He was prevented, not by the Queen, as was reported at the time, but by politicians and the church hierarchy.

According to the Act of Settlement of 1701, which was drawn up to prevent descendants of the Catholic King James II from returning to the throne, those who inherit the crown are forbidden 'to be reconciled to or hold communion with the See or Church of Rome'. As a student of history he should have anticipated the reaction, but the Prince was nevertheless bitterly upset and angry. A year later, while staying privately with some Catholic friends, Hugh and Emily van Cutsem and their family, he accompanied them to a little country church and heard Mass. Someone reported his presence and the church traditionalists were once more up in arms. 'In attending Mass he compromises the position of the crown,' raged the Director of the Church Society, Dr David Samuel. 'The coronation oath is very clear. The monarch promises that he or she will uphold the Protestant reformed religion.' The Prince, he said, could 'never act in a private capacity with regard to this religious question'. The Prince is unlikely to abandon his ecumenical lead. He sees it not as a failure to uphold the Protestant reformed religion, but as another pragmatic step to meet the needs of modern society.

Listening is another. He believes that if you give people a chance to talk, to air their grievances and express their fears and anxieties about personal as well as cosmic problems, you have a far happier, healthier person and thus a happier, healthier society. His staff are endlessly fidgeting because the Prince is behind schedule; the reason is that he gives people time to talk, and about matters of real concern. During a visit to the Lozells Road area of Handsworth in Birmingham, ripped apart during the 1985 riots, he spoke to locals about the problems of getting compensation for the damage to their shops and property. After ten months they had only been paid £300,000 of over £7 million owed, which meant that plans to build a new shopping centre had had to be shelved. 'It was the Prince, not us, who raised the issue of compensation,' said Basil Clarke, chairman of the local traders' association. 'It's marvellous – I can't get ten minutes of the councils' leader's time, but our future King gives me fifteen.'

After the Manchester air crash in 1985, when dozens of holidaymakers were burned to death aboard a charter plane that crashed on take-off, the Prince, on holiday himself at the time, made immediate arrangements to go to see the survivors, many of whom had lost relatives, in hospital. There was no need, and no one advised it – in fact they were all taken by surprise – but the fact that the Prince of Wales cared about their loss was a tremendous help to the victims.

It is this demonstration to people who feel that no one gives a damn about them – the black community, the unemployed, the no-hopers festering in the decaying inner cities – that has perhaps been his most valuable contribution to society so far. He is seen to be championing the underdog, the most oppressed and dangerous section of society, and by opening lines of communication to them has provided a vital escape valve for their anger and frustrations. It is not just pragmatism; it is genuine concern, and having come thus far out of the royal cocoon it is inconceivable that, even as King, Charles would give up this close contact with people.

There is equally little chance that he would give up the ceremonial side of monarchy. Pomp and circumstance are entirely to his taste and he enjoys the opportunity to dress in the full kit for Trooping the Colour, or the State Opening of Parliament. He is no radical, and anyone who thinks that his visionary outlook on life indicates a desire for fundamental change is mistaken – his devotion to history is too intense. He will learn history's lessons and apply them to our own age, but is no more likely to dismantle the traditions on which the continuity of centuries has rested than fly to the moon. Neither will he alter his privileged lifestyle, save possibly for the financing of it. Lord Mountbatten was always worried about the cost to the nation. 'Unless you can get an informed reply published making just one point,' he told Prince Philip in 1971, 'the image of the monarchy will be gravely damaged. It is true there is a fortune, which is very big, but the overwhelming proportion (85 per cent?) is in pictures, "objets d'art", furniture etc. in the three State-owned palaces. The Queen can't sell any of them, they bring in no income.' He wanted an authoritative article in *The Times* for the rest of the world's press to pick up – otherwise people would resent being asked to pay more and more while the Queen economized on her '£100 million fortune'. 'So will you both please believe a loving old uncle and *not* your constitutional advisers and do it.'

There is no doubt that the influence behind many of the Prince's ideas and beliefs came from his great-uncle, although Mountbatten is far from being the only source. Charles is a compendium of ideas and philosophies taken from a wide range of people. He is easily influenced, even today, and whoever has his ear therefore wields considerable power. The man who enjoys that position in 1987 is no sinister influence, but in the past the Prince has been used by people for their own ends; there must therefore be a very real fear for the future that, unless Charles manages to conquer his own lack of self-confidence, to come to terms with his position in life, to see that he is playing a very positive and worthwhile role and to have the strength to be his own best counsel, he could be led astray.

In the course of my interview with the Prince I suggested I might usefully talk to Sir Laurens van der Post. Yes, agreed the Prince, he would indeed be a good person to meet, but I would have to make the approach myself. The Prince also agreed to a second interview, and seemed quite pleased at the idea of showing me his garden at Highgrove. I duly contacted Sir Laurens, who, although charming on the telephone, would not talk about the

Prince. He does not, I discovered later, believe in biographies of people still living. Not long afterwards I had a letter from the Prince's office. He was sorry, but he had had a change of mind. There would be no further meeting. It appeared that, on reflection, he did not think biographies of living people were appropriate.

People have come and gone; they have been important in helping to shape his thinking for a time, then they have faded from centre stage as the Prince's direction has changed, to be replaced by someone more expert in his latest field of interest. He keeps in touch with all his old friends, however, mostly by handwritten letter, and is constantly concerned for their welfare. When George Thomas retired as Speaker of the House of Commons, the Prince's first thought was 'Where are you going to live now you will no longer have Speaker's House?' and he insisted on providing his Welsh friend with a flat in Duchy property south of the river. When he heard that his old housemaster from Gordonstoun, Bob Whitby, was retiring prematurely as headmaster of Bembridge School because of ill health, the Prince organized a less arduous job for him with a BiC scheme called Young Enterprise, aimed at getting the enterprise culture going at school level, and helping fifteen- to nineteen-year-olds start their mini-businesses. He takes care of those people who have helped him along the way, and will frequently telephone them for advice if he is writing a speech, for example, in an area in which they are expert.

Rock star Pete Townshend, who became involved with the Prince through performing at pop concerts in aid of the Prince's Trust, is an unlikely admirer. He is not the only one in the pop world, as the number of stars that played in the Trust's tenth anniversary concert at Wembley proved. The arena literally shook the ground as people like Elton John, Paul Young, George Michael, Mark Knopfler, John Illsley, Paul McCartney, Mick Jagger and David Bowie took to the stage; many of them were once the sort of youngsters whom the Prince is trying to help with the Trust. Townshend compares Charles's position to that of a miner's son. 'The mine has closed down, but his father was a miner, his grandfather was a miner, and he's going to be one too.'

The only flaw in the comparison is that the miner's son could break the mould and go and be an actor or a singer, as any number of Welsh miners' sons have done. Prince Charles cannot. He has no choice in his destiny whatsoever. So long as the people of

Britain want our present constitution, the Prince of Wales must remain in the valleys. His task is to make sure there is a mine to work, because, as Frederick the Great of Prussia observed, monarchy is like virginity – once lost, gone for ever. An exception is Spain, where the monarchy was restored, after forty-four years of dictatorship, in the person of King Juan Carlos I in 1979. But, as the many deposed kings and queens of Europe who languish in exile bear witness, it was a rare exception.

Over the centuries the role of monarch has changed dramatically, and long gone is the divine right of kings. It was the Roman Emperors, who had believed they were deities, who gave us the 'royal we'. Whenever they spoke they began with the phrase, 'We the gods'; and until the seventeenth century English monarchs, as elsewhere, were all regarded as appointees of God. It was Charles I who shattered the illusion. For eleven years he attempted to govern without Parliament, and so abused his power that Civil War raged for seven years in England until he was finally beheaded in 1649. The Long Parliament, which had already abolished the Royal Prerogative, abolished the monarchy and the House of Lords and for a while, with Oliver Cromwell as Lord Protector of the Commonwealth, power was largely in the hands of the army. In 1660 the monarchy was restored in the person of Charles II, who reigned for twenty-five years and did much to stabilize the uneasy relationship between Crown and Parliament.

Britain is unique in that it has no written constitution. The basic liberties of Englishmen are enshrined in Magna Carta, sealed, under pressure from the barons, by King John at Runnymede in 1215. It confined the power of the monarch and established the fundamental political principle of no tax without representation and the right to trial. 'To no one will we sell,' he guaranteed, 'to no one will we refuse or delay, right and justice.' The sovereign's power was further curtailed and defined by the Bill of Rights in 1689, to prevent the abuses of James II who claimed he was above the law. Thereafter he and his descendants retained the right to reign but not to rule, but because so little was ever committed to paper the role of monarch has gradually changed over the years. During the reigns of George I and II in the first half of the eighteenth century Parliament's power increased while the monarch's diminished, partly because neither king was very interested in his role; when George III came to the throne and tried to reassert the power granted the monarch in the

Bill of Rights the House of Commons passed a resolution in 1780 'that the influence of the Crown has increased, is increasing, and ought to be diminished'.

By Queen Victoria's day its influence was so diminished that the Crown had detached itself from party politics entirely; thus began the gradual move towards the present situation, where the Queen in theory is all-powerful but in practice is little more than symbolic. Officially she is head of the Executive, head of the Judiciary, Commander-in-Chief of the Armed Forces and temporal head of the Church of England. As such she appoints the Prime Minister, and legally other ministers only assume office on receiving their seals of office from her. Similarly bills passed by the House of Commons and the House of Lords can only become Acts of Parliament upon the Queen's assent. In practice she has no freedom of choice in the selection of a Prime Minister, but appoints the leader of whichever party has been duly elected to form a government. Even if there were no clear winner, she would in all probability leave the politicians to decide between them who should be selected. Thus, although all government is carried out in her name, 'On Her Majesty's Service', and the Prime Minister and Cabinet are her servants who may only advise her and recommend a course of action, but never command, they are not recommendations she could ever actually refuse. To quote Dr Johnson's remark, 'I should throw you out of a two pair of stairs window and *recommend* you fall to the ground.' It is the Prime Minister, not the Queen, who is the pivot on which the whole constitutional machinery turns, but it is still only a matter of convention, and the success of the whole system is dependent upon there being a stable monarchy.

It is perhaps because of the total illogicality of this set-up that Britain has retained her monarchy, where so many other countries have despatched theirs, although even Britain has had her shaky moments. It is hard to imagine – or remember – in the present fever of popularity that things were ever different, but the antics of Edward VII as Prince of Wales did drag the monarchy through the mud, and although it was rescued by George V and his magnificent Queen Mary the institution was undoubtedly plunged to a perilous depth by Edward VIII's 'shabby dereliction of duty'. The public loves to idolize royalty, and in the partnership of George VI and the present Queen Elizabeth the Queen Mother they felt it was once more an institution of dignity and respectability. Queen Elizabeth II has continued in the same vein. She has been the symbol of Christian qualities which the people revere. In his book *Crown and People*, based on reports of a social studies group, Philip Ziegler said of the Silver Jubilee, 'It was striking in 1977 how many tributes were paid to her conscientiousness and dignity, to the way in which she embodied qualities such as decency, respectability, family loyalty, which were often represented as being out of fashion. . . .'

It was during those celebrations, just ten years ago, that the Queen first went on a walkabout, now the most natural and accepted part of any royal visit. Prince Charles has taken the concept one stage further; he does not just walk about but walks straight into awkward situations and meets people who are not necessarily going to be polite – all part of his determination to understand what makes them feel the way they do.

Such behaviour cannot help but reduce the mystique and magic that surround him, and any last vestige was surely destroyed by the two occasions recently on which he has allowed television cameras into his private life. The importance of maintaining the mystique of royalty has long been debated. One Spanish queen refused a gift of silk stockings because it was not thought wise for her people to know that she had legs. Edward VII's Queen, Alexandra, on the other hand, was once visiting a hospital when she noticed a man looking particularly downcast. He had been wounded in the leg, she was told, and had just been told that his knee would be permanently stiff and useless. The Queen went straight to his bedside. 'My dear, dear man,' she said, 'I hear you have a stiff leg; so have I. Now just watch what I can do with it', and lifting up her skirt she swept her lame leg over the top of his bedside table.

The Princess of Wales might have taken lessons from her predecessor. Visiting an office with her husband on one occasion, she spotted a poster on the wall that said: 'Save the Whales'.

'Hey, look darling,' she said, 'they're trying to save us.'

The Prince looked blank.

'Oh well,' she said, 'he never gets my jokes.'

Diana may not be much good at preserving the mystique, but she is astonishingly talented at putting people at their ease. On a visit to Skelmersdale in Lancashire Diana was escorted round an exhibition by the deputy chief executive, a normally rather relaxed and jolly man who was so frightened by the prospect of having to deal with the Princess of Wales that he could barely speak. As they set off together, two little fountains sprang into life.

'I really do wish they'd turn those fountains off,' said the Princess.

'Why, Your Royal Highness?' asked the chief executive anxiously.

'Because they make me want to go to the loo all the time.'

This is the side of monarchy that the man and woman in the street sees and judges it by, and the success with which Diana goes out to meet people and jokes with them cannot help but keep the institution safe.

'Your head's much bigger than it looks on telly,' said a small boy as she passed.

'Don't worry,' she replied, laughing. 'There's nothing in it.' She embodies everything the public want: she is pretty, and witty, she wears beautiful clothes, she has small children – she has something for everyone, whatever their age or gender – and her frothy, rather coltish nature, is the perfect foil for the Prince's often serious demeanour. It would be dangerous to underestimate the importance of that decorative role for the monarchy, but it is not the only one. The monarch may have little power these days, but the Queen is as well informed and as politically astute as any of her ministers. Her knowledge of the world, of world affairs and world leaders is infinitely greater. She has travelled many times more than any of them, and she has built up a unique trust and friendship with kings, presidents and emperors. Thus there is a continuity in relations with other nations that a country like the United States could not begin to hope for, with Presidents that come and go. The Queen is therefore able to give her Prime Ministers an insight into the affairs of other countries that they might never have been able to learn anywhere else, and which may be of immense practical value.

Prince Charles already has a considerable knowledge and understanding of foreign countries, largely as a result of acting as the Queen's ambassador abroad. So much harm is caused, he says, by people's lack of understanding. Television pictures of black shanty towns in South Africa, for example, shock people in Britain and provoke intense condemnation of the whites in the country. What they don't know is that this is the way black people live all over Africa, and that a pathetic shack at Cross Roads is probably considerably better, of its type, than many of the rooms in which people are living in Britain's inner cities. When Bob Geldof, who created Band Aid and Live Aid and raised millions of pounds to feed the starving in Africa, went to Australia to receive an award, the Prince and Princess of Wales attended the ceremony.

'Don't you find it odd, Bob,' said a reporter, apparently expecting Geldof to attack the royal couple, 'to be here trying to raise money for the starving at the same time that Prince Charles arrives? He must be one of the richest men in the world. How do you cope with the contrast between his life and those of the people you saw in Africa?'

'I do not draw comparisons like that,' said Geldof. 'The gap between the Third World and our world is so wide that it would be a nonsense to try to compare them. If I did, the discrepancy between your own lifestyle and that of the average Ethiopian would be pretty sickening. Compared to them, even the poorest person in the West is wealthy beyond imagining.'

Bob Geldof says that of all the people he has met since his fund-raising began – the list includes a great many of the world's philanthropists, leaders and politicians – there is no doubt that the one he has been most impressed by was Prince Charles. 'I find myself more in agreement with him than anybody else. He is concerned, compassionate, highly intelligent and I think nervous about expressing himself. He is a maverick, and not just within the narrow parameters of the Royal Family.'

The admiration was mutual. Prince Charles was extremely impressed by Geldof, both by his extraordinary achievements and, in a sneaking way, by his anarchic attitude to life. Not many people invited to Kensington Palace to meet the Prince of Wales turn up unshaven, in jeans and sneakers.

'Why do you have to talk to that man?' said Prince William, finding his father too busy to play.

'Because we have work to do,' said the Prince.

'He's all dirty,' said William.

'Shut up, you horrible boy,' said Geldof.

'He's got scruffy hair and wet shoes,' said William, undeterred.

'Don't be rude,' said his mortified father. 'Run along and play.'

'Your hair's scruffy too,' said Geldof as a parting shot.

'No, it's not,' said William. 'My mummy brushed it.'

No two men, on the face of it, could be at further extremes from one another: Geldof an unshaven, tousle-haired rock singer from the suburbs of Dublin, son of a travelling salesman; Prince Charles the pillar of respectability, son of the monarch, future King of England. And yet here from this unexpected quarter was support for all the things Charles had been saying about architecture, about medicine, about the quality of life – all things, agreed the Irishman, which millions of people believe intuitively. It was a tonic for his confidence. 'How ironic,' observed Geldof, 'that royalty should become Everyman.'

Yet for all his cosmic intuition, and all his access to leaders the world over, to great men and women and to politicians of every persuasion, Prince Charles is still curiously innocent at times. He sends through the public postal system long handwritten letters filled with indiscretions of a political nature which could be highly embarrassing for him if they were to fall into the wrong hands. His staff appear to be politically unaware too. Just one of the many invitations that was sent through to BiC for guidance was an invitation from a women's association in Brent in north London to open their conference. The Prince had written at the top: 'Do you think I should? Charles.' No one had apparently noticed the item on the agenda: 'Police brutality in Brent'.

One of the basic tenets of the constitution is that the sovereign, and likewise his or her heir, must remain above politics, and this is the single greatest advantage that a monarchy has over any other system of government. Personalities don't come and go with each election; the monarch is the one constant in an ever-changing world, and by virtue of the fact that he or she is not involved in the wrangles and plots of politics the monarchy provides the country with a reassuring sense of continuity.

The Queen is politically very astute, as is Princess Anne, and is often able to offer advice to her Prime Ministers in their weekly audience. These briefings, in addition to the state papers that arrive in battered red leather dispatch boxes, on which she has to work on most days, keep her very well informed about everything that is happening. Any such advice, however, is given in the complete privacy of her office at Buckingham Palace and should never go any further, although how much is either proffered or accepted inevitably depends upon the relationship between them. The Queen and Mrs Thatcher do not naturally warm to one another; but even if she were to disagree violently with a course of action that her government had decided upon the Queen would have no other way, save by private discussion with her ministers, of making her feelings known. The sovereign cannot stand up and be counted to the extent that her eldest son does. It would be quite wrong, and dangerous for the stability of the system. Even the Prince's wisdom in doing so is questionable, and although he endeavours to stick to areas that are non-political, much of what he has said to date is borderline. This is why Edward Adeane was negative so much of the time: his only real fault was a desire for his boss to be constitutionally beyond reproach.

Speaking as frankly as he does means to some extent that the Prince has more power in his present role than he would ever have as monarch – although, if he continues to plunge into contentious and politically loaded areas such as housing without ensuring that he has heard or appreciated the full story, there is a danger that people will stop listening even when he speaks for millions of ordinary folk. He runs the risk that the establishment and the politicians, in whom rests the power for change, may simply ignore him.

When the Prince delivered a philosophical speech in Canada in 1986, in which he talked about 'the mirror of the soul', the press laughed at him: a load of mystic mumbo-jumbo delivered to a bemused bunch of lumberjacks. In fact he was addressing a well-educated audience with not a lumberjack in sight. A speech he delivered in Boston shortly afterwards, at the Harvard 350th Commemoration Ceremony, was treated with much the same scepticism. In fact it said as much about the Prince of Wales as any of his speeches ever have, and a great deal about the sort of kingdom he would hope to reign over.

> I like to think you have included me in your celebrations partly because of the enduring significance and value of the Anglo-American relationship and, more broadly, the Atlantic Alliance. Occasions such as this do help to re-emphasize the ties that bind us; the trials and tribulations we have been through together; the arguments and recriminations that from time to time have served to separate us. Well-worn clichés, I know, are inclined to abound when talking about the Anglo-American relationship – special or otherwise – but when all is said and done the mortar that holds all the bricks together is so often made up from warm personal relationships between individual human beings. Such friendships help to withstand the destructive nature of the appalling simple

generalizations by which nations tend to judge each other and through which so much harm can come to the fragile relationships between so many countries. . . . I am sure many people consider that the United Kingdom is in an ideal geographical and historical position to act as an interpreter and mediator between the United States and Europe, and I can foresee that having, as it were, a foot in both camps the United Kingdom will have an increasingly important role to play in this area. . . .

There is no doubt that we of the English-speaking nations, in particular, must obey the clarion call and remain constantly on our guard. 'We must be free or die, that speak the tongue that Shakespeare spake, the faith and morals hold that Milton held.' . . .

Perhaps, too, as parents you may be wondering, like I do on frequent occasions, whether the educational system you are confronted with is the right one to produce the kind of balanced, tolerant, civilized citizens we all hope our children can become? . . .

I cannot help feeling that one of the problems which is gradually dawning on the western, Christian world is that we have for too long, and too dangerously, ignored and rejected the best and most fundamental traditions of our Greek, Roman and Jewish inheritance. I would suggest that we have been gradually losing sight of the Greek philosophers' ideal, which was to produce a balance between the several subjects that catered for a boy's moral, intellectual, emotional and physical needs. While we have been right to demand the kind of technical education relevant to the needs of the twentieth century it would appear that we may have forgotten that when all is said and done a good man, as the Greeks would say, is a nobler worker than a good technologist. We should never lose sight of the fact that to avert disaster we have not only to teach men to make things, but also to produce people who have complete moral control over the things they make. Never has this been more essential and urgent than at this moment in man's development. Never has it been more important to recognize the imbalance that has seeped into our lives and deprived us of a sense of meaning because the emphasis has been too one-sided and has concentrated on the development of the intellect to the detriment of the spirit. . . .

It is the recognition of that broad world – certainly

consisting of more than the physical dimension – which it seems to me is so vital. All the best thought in Greece, Rome and Judea emphasized the interdependence of moral and intellectual training if we are to escape from the leadership of clever and unscrupulous men. There is no doubt in my mind that the education of the whole man needs to be based on a sure foundation – in other words the values of our own Christian, western traditions, which in turn are the product of Hellenism and Judaism. That of course does not mean we have to deny the validity of other men's traditions. We should indeed look for those elements that unite us rather than concentrate on the things which make us different. What I am trying to say is that if during the course of a person's education he is introduced to the principles of a religious attitude to life, as the Greek philosophers and Hebrew teachers would have seen it, then it is perhaps possible to learn to equate human rights with human obligations. It is possible then to see a relationship between moral values and the uses of science and for those who affect our lives in some way or other through planning and administrative committees to appreciate that at the end of the process there is always a man or a woman, or a family. Surely it is important that in the headlong rush of mankind to conquer space, to compete with Nature to harness the fragile environment, we do not let our children slip away into a world dominated entirely by sophisticated technology, but rather teach them that to live in this world is not an easy matter without standards to live by.

And yet, at the same time, how do we guard against bigotry; against the insufferable prejudice and suspicion of other men's religions and beliefs which have so often led to unspeakable horrors throughout human history and which still do? How do we teach people to recognize that there is a dark side too to man's psyche and that its destructive power is immense if we are not aware of it? This, of course, is the universal dilemma, but I would venture to suggest that an instrument has been lying within our reach for nearly a hundred years and is still not used enough. There is in existence a proved and tested natural science dedicated to the study of the soul of man and the meaning of his creation. As in the past religious teaching was an essential part of the curriculum, perhaps there is now a need in universities for some introductions

> to the natural science of psychology? We are, to all intents and purposes, embarked on a perilous journey. The potential destruction of our natural earth; the despoliation of the great rain forests (with all the untold consequences of such a disaster); the exploration of space; greater power than we have ever had or our nature can perhaps handle – all confronts us for what could be a final settlement. But if we could start again to re-educate ourselves the result need not be so frightening. Over Apollo's great temple was the sign 'Man know thyself'. This natural science of psychology could perhaps help to lead us to a greater knowledge of ourselves; knowledge enough to teach us the dangers of the power we have acquired and the responsibilities as well as the opportunities it gives us. Could man, at last, begin to learn to know himself?

Prince Charles gave up part of his holiday at Balmoral to deliver the speech, and wrote it while flying the Atlantic. No one had provided him with notes or research: this was the real Prince of Wales, stripped bare. At least one American newspaper had been critical of Harvard for inviting someone 'as appallingly undemocratic as the Prince of Wales'. It just showed, it went on, how out of touch Harvard was with the United States.

'Have no fear, ladies and gentlemen,' said the Prince. 'I am used to being regarded as an anachronism. In fact, I am coming round to think it is rather grand.'

INDEX